CURRENT RESEARCH IN ETHNOMUSICOLOGY

Edited by

Jennifer C. Post
Middlebury College

A ROUTLEDGE SERIES

CURRENT RESEARCH IN ETHNOMUSICOLOGY

JENNIFER C. POST, *General Editor*

BAAKISIMBA

Gender in the Music and Dance
of the Baganda People of Uganda

Sylvia A. Nannyonga-Tamusuza

Routledge
New York & London

Published in 2005 by
Routledge
Taylor & Francis Group
270 Madison Avenue
New York, NY 10016

Published in Great Britain by
Routledge
Taylor & Francis Group
2 Park Square
Milton Park, Abingdon
Oxon OX14 4RN

© 2005 by Taylor & Francis Group, LLC
Routledge is an imprint of Taylor & Francis Group.

Printed in the United States of America on acid-free paper
10 9 8 7 6 5 4 3 2 1

International Standard Book Number-10: 0-415-96776-7 (Hardcover)
International Standard Book Number-13: 978-0-415-96776-1 (Hardcover)
Library of Congress Card Number: 2005013539

Library of Congress Cataloging-In-Publication Data

Nannyonga-Tamusuza, Sylvia A.
    Baakisimba : Gender in the Music and Dance of the Baganda People of Uganda / by Sylvia A. Nannyonga-Tamusuza.
        p. cm. -- (Current research in ethnomusicology)
    Includes bibliographical references (p.   ), discography (p.   ), and index.
    ISBN 0-415-96776-7 (alk. paper)
    1. Music--Uganda--Social aspects. 2. Ganda (African people)--Music--Social aspects. 3. Dance--Social aspects--Uganda. 4. Sex role--Uganda. I. Title. II. Series: Current research in ethnomusicology (Unnumbered)

ML3917.U33N36 2005
780'.89'963957--dc22   2005013539

T&F informa

Taylor & Francis Group
is the Academic Division of T&F Informa plc.

Visit the Taylor & Francis Web site at
http://www.taylorandfrancis.com

and the Routledge Web site at
http://www.routledge-ny.com

*To My Mothers: Agatha Nabukeera Kizito
and Rev. Sr. Dr. Miriam Duggan*

Contents

List of Figures and Plates

FIGURES

PLATES

Note on Orthography

Luganda is the language spoken by the Baganda people of Uganda. The general understanding of the structure of Luganda will not only enhance the reading of indigenous terms the Baganda use in reference to gender, music, and dance, but it will also facilitate my discussion of the interrelationship between Kiganda music and Luganda, issues that I deal with in chapters 3 and 4. However, I do not claim to offer a detailed language study of Luganda; I provide only the basics. For detailed explanations, please consult A. R. Snoxall (1967). Apart from the personal names and quotations, the spelling of the Luganda words cited in this book follow the orthographic style recommended by the all-Baganda conference of March 1947 as adapted in Luganda-English Dictionary edited by A. R. Snoxall (1967). Unless indicated, the translations into English from Luganda are my own. I indicate the closest pronunciation of the Luganda sounds in English, first the vowels. The italicized syllables or letters correspond to the pronunciation of letters of the Luganda alphabet.

a	ant	o	orange
e	egg	u	wool
i	yeast		

The consonants of Luganda are pronounced approximately as follows:

b	*ba*r	d	*da*ddy
c	*cha*t	f	*fa*n

g	*gua*rd
j	*jac*ket
k	*ca*r
l	*la*mb
m	*ma*n
n	*nu*n
p	*pu*mp
r	*la*mb
s	*sa*t
t	*te*rm
v	*va*n
w	*wa*nt
y	*ya*m
z	de*si*gn

Luganda, like many African languages, is a tonal language in which variations in the relative duration and pitch of syllables often determine the lexical meaning of a word. There are two syllabic units, "short" and "long," but only relative to specific words, phrases, sentences, and in relation to the intended meaning. A syllable with double vowels has a long duration, while one with a single vowel is short. I use the sixteenth note as the shortest durational note. For example the word *muzaana* (female servant in the king's palace) has the following durational value:

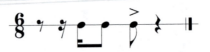

mu - zaa - na

On the other hand, if a syllable has double consonants, it is stressed. For example the word *kutta* (to kill) has the following durational value:

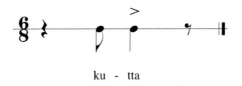

ku - tta

When consonants *n* and *m* combine with other consonants, they are pronounced as nasal sounds. For example, the word *mbuutu* (large conical double-membrane hand drum) has the following rhythmic pattern:

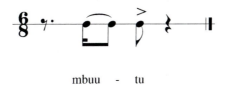

mbuu - tu

If these nasal syllables are preceded by a vowel, the vowel is pronounced long (even if it is not doubled). The words "Baganda" and "baakisimba" have vowels preceding nasal syllables and are pronounced using the following rhythmic pattern:

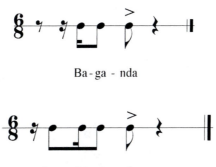

Ba - ga - nda

baa - ki - si - mba

Further, consonants that are followed by *w* and *y* create semi-vowel com-pounds. When vowels come after semi-vowel compounds, they are pro-nounced long.

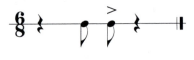

mwa - mi

However, if vowels that follow semi-vowel compounds precede double con-sonants, they are pronounced short. For example:

Kya - ddo   ndo

Further, single vowels and single consonants are usually pronounced short. For example, the word *Kabaka* (king) has the following rhythmic pattern:

Ka - ba - ka

Moreover, the position of the syllable either at the beginning or at the end of word affects its duration. For instance, a single-consonant-and-single-vowel syllable appearing at the end of a word tends to have a long duration, espe-cially if this word is the last in a sentence or a phrase. Further, it is common to have a long syllable at the beginning of the word with a single vowel.

In most cases, vowels at beginnings of words are usually short, while vowels at ends of words tend to be long if the vowel is the last one in a sen-tence. Further, the fusion of a final vowel with the initial vowel of the follow-ing word—as for example, in *nnyenya endagala* (shake the banana leaves)—is pronounced *nnyeny'endagala*.

The other important characteristic of Luganda is pitch level. Luganda has three relative pitch levels: low (L), medium (M), and high (H). I represent these pitches on a three-line staff. These pitch levels can be approached directly or through slides (*okuwugulira*). The pitch rises or falls depending on the syllabic organization of the word, as well as its contextual meaning. For example, when a single vowel follows double consonants, the pitch falls on the double consonants, making a descending contour, as in *kutta* (to kill):

ku - tta

Words with double vowels followed by a single syllable tend to slide up or down depending on whether this word appears in a statement or a question or an exclamation. For example the word *muzaana* will slide down if it is a statement and slide up if it is a question, as in the following

mu - zaa - na?

mu - zaa - na!

If a syllable with double vowels is followed by more than one syllable, the same pitch is maintained in the next syllable, as in *baakisimba:*

baa - ki - si - mba

Preface and Acknowledgments

The study of music and gender is not a new topic in music scholarship. However, since the majority of the studies, until recently, have been done by (historical) musicologists, the study of gender and Western art music has been the primary focus. As such, there is inadequate scholarship on music and gender of the African cultures in general. Moreover, by over-emphasizing sound structure, scholars have defined music of the African people in Western terms and yet, music and dance are inseparable. Although a number of ethnomusicologists have acknowledged this integration of music and dance, little attention has been given to the interaction of music and dance and the resulting implications for understanding social processes, structure and meaning. And yet, while some research has been published on the Baganda's court music, reference to dances, which are also part of the court repertoire, has been only in general surveys or on cassette and CD jackets. This book is just a minimal contribution to this immense gap.

Based on both my personal experience as a performer and teacher of baakisimba dance music and informal and formal research since 1983, the major issues this book addresses include: How does performance practice in baakisimba, dance choreography, drum symbolism, interaction of performers and audience participate in defining gender, and how does gender shape ideas and structures of baakisimba of the Baganda people (of southern Uganda)? Employing primarily interviews, participant observation, video and audio recordings and performance as methods of research, this book reveals that there is a reciprocal relationship between the Baganda's gender and baakisimba music and dance. One of the challenges I faced during this study was the limitation of conventional language in presenting the nuances of a culture quite unique from that one whose language I must use. Particularly, in order to access the unique construction of gender among the Baganda, there is need to deconceptualize your understanding of gender of the Western world.

Nonetheless, I hope that the discussions in here will broaden the appreciation of the diversity of culture and how performed arts can open doors to a better understanding of other peoples.

This book has resulted from the contributions of many people. I apologize if I am not able to fully acknowledge all of them. I am grateful to all whom in many ways helped in the preparation of this book, which began as a doctoral dissertation. Special thanks go to the University of Pittsburgh for the Andrew Mellon Fellowship that made it possible to carry out the formal research. I am greatly indebted to Andrew N. Weintraub for his great academic and moral support since the proposal of this study. Thank you for reading through the drafts of this work and the critical and constructive comments you made. To Deane Root, Mary Lewis, and David Brodbeck, thank you for your immense support. Anne LeBaron, thank you for offering spiritual and moral support, and for always sharing in my success. I am also grateful to Patricia Cochran and David Kanis, without whom important communications necessary for the production of this book would not have been possible. I acknowledge the support of friends and family in Pittsburgh, especially the members of the Episcopal Church of Ascension. Special thanks go to Mark and Karen Stevenson, Stacey and Kelsey Reagan, Jack Gabig, Gregg Podnar and the Love and Care Family Support Group.

I am greatly indebted to Jean-Jacques Nattiez for his continued support and encouragement since the time I decided to undertake this study. Thank you for granting permission to use your research photographs. Waalabyeki Magoba, thank you for permitting the use of one of your photographs. Denise Cox, Leonora Kivuva, Linda Lucas, Suzan Perkins, and Caroline Thomas, I appreciate the time and the perspectives you shared when you read through the drafts of this book. I am grateful to Jill Pribyl for the extraordinary interest in my research and the important reviews you contributed. Adelaida Reyes, thank you for allowing me to benefit from your expertise in cultural analysis; I am especially grateful to your incites about the conceptual framework. I wish to acknowledge Max Novick the associate editor of Routledge for his commitment to the completion of this project. I am also grateful to Jennifer C. Post for her great interest in and for providing useful comments for this book.

I thank Bukalasa Catholic Seminary for providing me with accommodation, food, and lodging during my research trips to Buddu County. I am especially grateful to Rev. Fr. Dr. Joseph Namukangula, Rev. Fr. Selverus Jjumba, and Rev. Fr. Alpio Kyambadde. I am grateful to my former baakisimba teachers, Katambula Busuulwa and James Makubuya for explaining many things that culture would not allow them to do when I was their student. I acknowledge Violah Naluwooza, a lecturer at Makerere University for the discussion we had on language and gender. Special thanks go to Mohammed Kiggundu, also a lecturer at Makerere University. Thanks to all my African drumming and dance students at the University of Pittsburgh. Special thanks go to my undergraduate and graduate students in ethnomusicology at Makerere University, Uganda. Thank you for being the laboratory where I have tested a number of views.

My research would not have been possible if the Baganda were not willing to share their knowledge with me. Special thanks go to the following people: Mzee Sulaiti Kalungi, Mzee Paulo Kabwama, Tereza Kisolo (RIP), Peter Ggayira, Janat Nakitto, Augustino Kisitu, Consitantino Lwewunzika, Kizza Ssaalongo (RIP), David Mukasa (RIP), John Baptist Kabuye, John Chrizestom Musisi and Peter Ssenkubuge. I am grateful to Rehema Nnabanoba for the time and courage to share your experience as a "manly-female" drummer. I acknowledge the contribution of the Catholic sisters, brothers, and priests whom I cannot mention here because they requested anonymity. And all the anonymous informants thank you very much. I would like to thank my research assistants Lawrence Ssekalegga and John Bosco Mwase for their patience, hard work, and the extraordinary interest they expressed in everything we did together.

To my family, I extend my heartfelt appreciation. I owe special gratitude to my mother, Mrs. Agatha Nabukeera Kizito. I thank her for nurturing me and although she was not able to reach the level of my academic accomplishment, she has always been the silent voice behind all my struggles. Special thanks go to Rev. Sr. Dr. Miriam Duggan for nurturing me and participating in all my success. I am grateful to my sisters Nnaalongo Nakazibwe and Goretti Birabwa for their care and support. My great support, Geoffrey Kizito, thank you very much. I am grateful to my dear children, Joseph Kiwanuka Buuzaabalyawo, Oliva Kwagala, Wasswa Kirabo Buwembo, Kato Ttendo Ggyingo, Fransis Kalule-Kasujja and Miriam Kkula Nakitto for your understanding. Although you quietly questioned why mummy could not play with you during the time of this project, your smiles and acceptance were great incentive towards the completion of this book. My greatest appreciation is reserved for Ssaalongo Dr. Justinian Tamusuza, my dear husband, friend, and colleague. Thank you for the love, support, and encouragement that have made me realize my potential. As a colleague, thank you for being my partner in the field whenever it was possible. Thank you for your constructive perspectives, and for editing the Luganda text in this book. I thank God to whom all the Glory belongs.

About the Author

Sylvia Nannyonga-Tamusuza is a senior lecturer in music (ethnomusicology) at Makerere University in Uganda. She recieved her Ph.D (ethnomusicology) from the University of Pittsburgh, PA (USA) under the supervision of Andrew Weintraub. Her research includes children's music, school music, popular music and identity, Church music, music in the diaspora, and dance.

Chapter One

Introduction

GENDERED BAAKISIMBA DRUMMING AND DANCING

Whenever my music teachers at Makerere College School (1981–1987) announced that baakisimba was the next item on the rehearsal list, the boys ran for the drums, while the girls struggled for the best dance skirts and skins. Roles in performance of baakisimba—a set of drums, a music genre, and dance type accompanied by this music—were clearly distinguished; boys were restricted to drumming and the girls controlled the dancing arena. Whenever I tried to "beat" the drums, my teachers outwardly told me "women do not beat the drums, they are the dancers."[1] This distinction of roles was not only in baakisimba performed in schools, but also in Catholic churches, at wedding ceremonies, and other village festivities.

In this book, I examine how baakisimba connects with gender of the Baganda people of southern Uganda. I stress that there is a historically recip-rocal relationship between baakisimba and gender of the Baganda. The shapes of the drums, drum sounds, dance movements, costumes, and the interaction of drummers, dancers, and the audience during baakisimba per-formances participate in the construction, crystallization, and challenge of constructed gender identities, roles, and relations among the Baganda.[2] And yet, the constructed gender is a basis for assigning roles of beating drums and dancing in baakisimba performance, as well as defining, to some extent, the baakisimba dance and music structure. While drum sounds and dance motifs cannot in themselves produce gender, the meanings the Baganda assign them construct views about gender. However, baakisimba perform-ance practice is historically contingent on cultural, social, and political struc-tures that have shaped Buganda, a context in which gender has been continually resignified.

1

The historical construction of gender in Buganda presents a concurrent dual definition dependent on the existence of two domains: the *lubiri* (palace), the "private" domain, reserved only for the royalty; and the *bweru w'olubiri* (outside the palace), the village, "public" domain, for the *bakopi* (commoners). The established myth among the Baganda defines one's belonging to either domain as supernaturally prescribed. Outside the palace, gender refers to the differences and values assigned to males and females and, the man and woman genders are assigned, respectively. However, failure in any of the prescribed roles as a man or a woman, one is branded *kikazikazi,* womanly-male (diminutive of a woman) and *nakawanga* (a she-cock), manly-female, respectively. With the introduction of Catholic celibacy in the early twentieth century, the *faaza* (reverend father) gender, *bulaaza* (reverend brother) gender, and *siisita* (reverend sister) genders were added to the Baganda's construction of gender. Within the palace context, the Baganda construct gender based on one's social class, which is determined by whether one belongs to the royal or commoner's class. The biological differentiation is only important in hierarchical structuring. Gender socialization within the palace assigns both the *balangira* (princes) and *bambejja* (princesses) a man gender, and the *bakopi* (both male and female) a woman gender. However, the woman gender assigned to the male *bakopi* is only situational; they may acquire a man, father, brother, and womanly-male gender outside the palace contexts. The female *bakopi* may maintain a woman or acquire manly-female or sister genders. The construction of gender among the Baganda's crystallizes the view that: "social identities are themselves complex fields of multiple and even contradictory struggles; they are the product of the articulations of particular social positions into chains of equivalences, between experiences, interests, political struggles and cultural forms, and between different social positions" (Hall as quoted in Grossberg 1996a: 156–157). It should be noted, therefore, that the gender definitions are not stable and absolute; they are in continuous contradictory struggles.

Baakisimba is an on-going sociocultural process through which Buganda's gender constructions are continually structured and negotiated. I explore how the performance practice of baakisimba, designs of the drums and their sounds, dance choreography[3] and costumes, and the interaction of drummers, trainers, adjudicators, dance students, dancers, and the audience during baakisimba performance crystallize the ongoing process of gender construction. In Buganda, like in many African cultures, roles in music and dance performance have long been assigned based on the performers' being "men" or "women." Until the mid-nineteenth century, the female-women within the palace and women outside the palace, in most cases, were the dancers. However, during the mid-nineteenth century, the male-women also began to dance within the palace. Yet, until the 1940s, it was unheard-of for a man to dance formalized baakisimba outside the palace (Lwewunzika, interview).[4] On the other hand, until the 1960s the males—male-women in the palace and men outside the palace—were assigned to beat the drums in baakisimba performances. However, female-women beat the drums only during rituals that empowered the king and the kingdom. Although the *ngoma* (drum),[5] the basic instrument in baakisimba, is also central to the self-identification of the Baganda—every clan has a specific drum rhythm that identifies it—women outside the palace were not allowed to beat it or even touch it. However, women occupied the dancing space until the mid-twentieth century when they started encroaching on the "forbidden fruit," the drum.[6] Since the 1960s, men lost control over women's access to the drum when manly-women and sisters began beating the drum outside the palace, especially in churches and schools. While baakisimba has evolved through time and location, change was especially noteworthy in 1967 after the Buganda kingdom was abolished, because of the radical social upheaval of the time. Drastic changes in the music, dance choreography, costumes, and the context of performance became especially evident. Baakisimba began to be performed in theatrical contexts, schools, and churches. Further, more womanly-males joined the dancing arena, while manly-females, although still with limitations, began to beat the drums. With changed political, cultural, social, and economic structures of the Baganda, baakisimba took on new meanings and helped to negotiate new gender identities, roles, and relations in significant ways.

Why have male-women and men traditionally been the drummers and female-women and women the dancers in baakisimba performance? What accounts for the shifts in these gendered performance roles and how do they articulate with the shifts in gender construction among the Baganda? The book reveals that baakisimba is a site for struggles over power. In Buganda, the drum is symbolic of power and, therefore men must control; and yet, women's dancing is associated with their sexual objectification. However, men dance either for economic reasons or as a way to negotiate their homosexual identities. Baakisimba is a "stage" where gendered relations, identities, and roles are performed. As such, baakisimba is a space where this fluid complex of ideas, associations, attitudes, and beliefs about the nature of man, woman, womanly-male, manly-female, father, brother, and sister genders are formed and transformed. Since baakisimba, the culturally constructed sequence of body movements is highly integrated with its accompanying music; I emphasize the integration of dance and music in my pursuit to examine baakisimba as a site for constructing gender in Buganda.

Since the Baganda created and have continually recreated baakisimba within a specific social and historical setting, it is to these settings that we must turn in order to understand the ways in which baakisimba and gender are connected. Buganda is one of the oldest and most dominant kingdoms in Uganda whose origin is still subject to speculation among scholars. For instance, M. S. M. Ssemakula Kiwanuka suggested that the waves of clans that constitute Buganda settled in the region between the thirteenth and sixteenth centuries (1972: 31). However, four broad historical periods are important in Buganda's gender construction: 1) the pre-Kintu era (from time immemorial until ca. 1300); 2) the period before the abolition of the Buganda kingdom (pre-abolition period), which is subdivided into pre-colonial (ca. 1300 to 1894), colonial times (1894–1962), and transition to abolition (1962–1967); 3) post-abolition (1967 to 1993); and 4) post-restoration (1993 to the present).

Buganda's kingship has strongly defined gender in Buganda. From Kintu the first king, to Muwenda Mutebi II, the present king, there have been thirty-six kings (see appendix 2 for list of Buganda Kings). Until 1966, Buganda was under the rule of the Kabaka (king) whose power established a royal family of *balangira* and *bambejja* as rulers of the *bakopi*. The coming of Christianity and British colonialism in the late nineteenth century and its accompanying European education and culture redefined social relations in Buganda. Moreover, after independence in 1962, Buganda lost its autonomy as a kingdom and became a region of the Republic of Uganda, which further redefined the Baganda's gender. And yet, the political changes after 1966 that led to the abolition of kingship in 1967 produced new gender constructions. Although President Yoweri Museveni restored the Buganda kingdom in 1993, he "agreed only to reinstate the kabaka in ceremonial roles. The kabakas are prohibited from holding political office" (Africa Report 1993: 11). Because of the existing conditions, gender constructions, in the Buganda of the twenty-first century, are less dependent on inherited tradition. As such, the restoration did not recapture gender constructions of the pre-abolition period. Instead, the struggles to define gender, which have roots from the European education and Christianity, were promoted.

Although changes in gender construction in Buganda can be traced earlier, it is after 1986—when Yoweri Museveni became president of Uganda—that the changed position of women in Buganda and Uganda in general began to be vividly noted. Anne Marie Goetz, for instance, records that "Uganda . . . ranks above many developing countries in terms of women's numerical representation in the national legislature" (1998: 241).[7]

Moreover, it is now possible, although with some constraints, for women to negotiate for "equality and justice in marriage—and divorce—after ironing out differences over the issue of polygamy" (Fiedler 1999: 21), a position Baganda women have long struggled to achieve (Obbo 1974). While I do not mean to say that the women's position in relation to men is not contested, some changes are evident as will be discussed in this book.

THE BAGANDA PEOPLE

The Baganda people (*sing.* Muganda), who belong to the Bantu family, constitute the largest group among more than forty different ethnic groups in Uganda.[8] About five million Baganda are located in Buganda region, in the south-central region of Uganda, north of Lake Victoria and south of Lake Kyoga. Buganda lies on the equator and thus enjoys a tropical climate, which enables the growth of food, especially *matooke* (bananas) throughout the year (see figure 1).[9] Buganda is hilly with a mixture of grassy lands and with forests, are slowly disappearing because of the increased populations. The trees are not only used for building houses, firewood, and furniture, but also for making musical instruments, especially the drums. Informants told me that it was a taboo for a Muganda not to have a drum in his house.[10]

Buganda has seventeen counties, but this study was focused in Kyaddondo (1), Busiro (2), Mawokota (3), Butambala (4), Buddu (5), Kyaggwe (6), and Busujju (7) counties. However, a great part of this research was concentrated in Kyaddondo, Busiro, and Mawokota counties. Since Kyaddondo, Busiro, and Mawokota were among the initial counties of Buganda (Richards 1960:43), these counties are symbolic to the Buganda kingdom. For example, Kyaddondo County houses the headquarters of the Buganda kingdom and the *kabaka's* main palace at Mengo and "for many years, too, the capitals of the kings have been established in [the county]" (Roscoe 1911: 248). On the other hand, most of the *masiro* ("burial grounds for the kings") are found in Busiro County. Further, more than any other areas in Buganda, these counties have a number of important cultural sites that provide contexts for baakisimba performance. Kyaddondo, which includes Kampala, the national capital of Uganda, houses a number of educational centers and churches, which provide numerous contexts for performing baakisimba. These areas are accessible in terms of transport, contacts, and because they are famous for talented musicians, dancers, and performing groups, I knew a number of them, prior to the study.

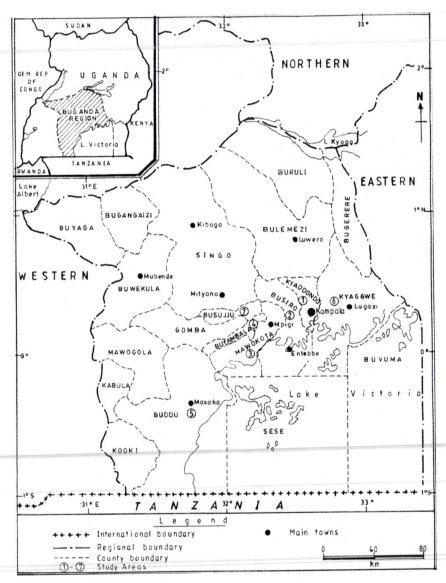

Figure 1. Buganda and its location on the map of Uganda.

The Baganda speak a language referred to as Luganda and the term "Kiganda" denotes what belongs to the Baganda. Therefore, one can speak of Kiganda music, Kiganda culture, Kiganda gender, and so on. Sometimes the generic term "Ganda" is used to refer to the region, the people, their language, culture, music, and so on. However, scholars and people who are not Baganda mainly use the term Ganda; the Baganda never refer to themselves as the Ganda or refer to their language as Ganda. One is considered to be a Muganda if his or her father belongs to a Kiganda clan. In fact, the Baganda have a proverb that: "Nnyoko abanga omunyolo: n'akuzaala mu kika." Your mother may be a Munyoro: as long as you are born in the clan (of the father). [Meaning that] the child follows the clan of the fathers. It is better that you are born of a non-Muganda mother and a Muganda father than vice versa" (Walser 1982: 298, no.3316). As such, the Baganda consider the man to be the core of the Baganda's identity. In the next section, I discuss the contradictory struggles of whether the man, from time immemorial, has been the center of Baganda's identity.

GENDERED-MYTHOLOGICAL ORIGIN OF BUGANDA

Since Buganda kingdom and its changing nature form the basis for gender construction, there is need to examine the origins of the Buganda kingdom and how its changing nature has shaped ideologies about gender roles, identities, and relations of the Baganda, Contexts which have defined baakisimba. Many scholars have constructed different histories relating to the origin of Buganda.[11] Nonetheless, based on the analysis of oral tradition, these scholars have argued that Kintu is the founder of the Buganda kingdom. For instance, M. B. Nsimbi, a Muganda linguist, has noted, "Kintu was the first [person] to bring together the people he found in Buganda and to rule them as one nation" (1996: 149). However, Kiwanuka argues that all the histories "contain much that is myth and legend" (1972: 95). Two kinds of narratives constitute the oral traditions about Kintu: *lugero* (*pl. ngero*), story or legend and *byafaayo* (both *pl.* and *sing.*), history. The Baganda use Kintu's story or legend to tell how Kintu "became the progenitor of the Baganda and the guarantor of their life on earth . . . how [Kintu] entered Buganda, established the kingship and organized the clans" [12] (Ray 1991: 54). In my discussion, I use both the *ngero* and the *byafaayo* to analyze the origins of Buganda as a basis for gender structuring among the Baganda. I note, however, as other authors have pointed out, that the *byafaayo* and the *ngero* do not provide historical facts about Buganda. Similarly, Lois Pirouet has noted that Oral traditions are "concerned with explaining and legitimizing the present, not with providing precise chronologies . . ." (1995: 7). Moreover, these narratives are recounted in various versions and most of them are full of contradictions. Nonetheless, my study considers them as important sources of information to understand gender structuring in Buganda, since these narratives participate in shaping the Baganda's worldview about gender. Analyzing the discourse of myths in Central Africa, V. Y.

Mudimbe contended that legendary and historical narratives are "embued with the sacred mission of cultural representation and being" (1991: 99). Likewise, in her discussion of gender in Buganda, Hellen Nabasuta Mugambi emphasized that these mythical legends "are embued with *unquestionable* [her emphasis] power in the construction of collective cultural, political and gender identities" (1994: 108). My research revealed that the Baganda use both *byafaayo* and *ngero* to establish opinions and authority for their beliefs and attitudes about gender identities, roles, and relations. In this case, I am not establishing historical facts; instead, these narratives are sites through which the Baganda explain who they were, who they are, and who they will become.

In order to situate my discussion, I present a summary of Kintu's legend as my late grandmother Vikitoria Nannyonga narrated it to me when I was a child. She said:

> Once upon a time, there was a man called Kintu. He lived alone with his cow and fed on its blood, dung, and urine. One day, a woman called Nnambi came from the Sky and found Kintu very lonely, only with his cow. When Nnambi saw Kintu, she admired him and proposed marriage to him. However, Nnambi had to first introduce Kintu to her father, Ggulu. After Kintu had gone through a number of tests, Nnambi was given to him, but the two were warned never to return to the sky because Nnambi's brother Walumbe (Mr. Death) would follow them and kill all their children. Unfortunately, Nnambi forgot the millet of her chickens and despite Kintu's refusal for Nnambi's return to the sky, Nnambi adamantly returned to the sky. When Walumbe saw her, he said 'oh my sister, you wanted to run away from me?' Nnambi could not refuse his request to follow her. For some time, Walumbe lived happily with Nnambi and Kintu, until when he started killing their children. This is how death came to the earth. [13]

As Nancy Bonvillian has argued, "Myths of creation and the identity and actions of creators reveal and reinforce a people's accepted notions of the proper place of women and men in society" (1998: 246). Similarly, based on the Kintu and Nambi myth, men have constructed, justified, and viewed women as weak beings that need the supervision of men. This construction relates to the perception that women are emotional and physically weak. From childhood, Baganda women are socialized to be weak while the men are trained to be strong and protective of the women. In fact, Apollo Kaggwa[14] attributes the Baganda women's historical suffering and subordinate position to this myth (1934:161). The constructed weakness of women explains a number of superstitions about Baganda women. For instance, a "traditional" [15]Muganda man, and ironically a woman too, "setting out for a journey would return if he or [she] met a woman first; as it is believed to be a bad omen" (ibid.). In addition, Kaggwa has mentioned that when men were leaving for war, their friends would say to them, "kill them like women" (1934:104). This myth about women's weakness forms one of the justifications for assigning drumming roles to men and dancing roles to women.

Similar to many myths of creation, people have reinvented and reconstructed the meaning of Kintu's *lugero* as the narrative passed on from one person to another and from one generation to another. They have recreated this narrative to produce meanings relevant to particular situations and times. For example, after the introduction of Christianity in the late nineteenth-century, prominent Baganda, including Apollo Kaggwa, began reinterpreting the *lugero* of Kintu to suit the Christian ideology. For instance, Kaggwa noted that Kintu's story "is very similar to the works of the Holy Bible of God where we read about Adam and Eve" (1951: 115 as translated and quoted in Ray 1991: 60). Explaining the connection between the two stories of Kintu and the Bible, Kaggwa noted that: "We see how Eve, the wife of Adam, brought death, and in the same way Nnambi, the wife of Kintu brought death. As the words of Adam begin with the creation of the earth, so the story of Kintu also begins with the creation of the country of Buganda" (ibid.). Kaggwa appropriates the myth to reaffirm that the women's subordinate position, as inherited from her disobedience, is a given position since it existed even in Biblical times, a context that was outside Buganda.

On the other hand, according to the Baganda's *byafaayo* (history), Kintu allegedly founded the Buganda kingdom.[16] As in the case of Kintu's legends, people have reconstructed the narratives of Kintu's history. My own research presents, in some cases, versions of already published histories of Kintu, while in other cases, informants gave me just fragments of these published stories. On the one hand, some stories, especially those told by Sulaiti Kalungi and David Mukasa, relate to Kintu as a foreigner who came from eastern Uganda in search of greener pastures for his cow (interview). These stories revealed that when he reached Muwawa (which later became the core of Buganda), he heard about a powerful King Bemba who mistreated his people. With the help of his immigrant army, Kintu fought Bemba and defeated him.[17] On the other hand, the story narrated to me by Blazio Kalyango only differs in details with that of Charles Kabuga (1963). Like Kabuga, Kalyango emphasized that Kabaka Kintu was born in Buganda and was not a "foreigner" as most sources claim. Kalyango argued that Kintu only left Buganda because of the disagreements he had with his brother King Bemba who was ruling at the time. Kalyango narrated that Kintu first went to Bunyoro (western Uganda) before moving to the east (Masaba mountain in Bugisu) in search of "power" and armies that would enable him to overthrow Bemba. Kalyango's narration proposes an explanation to the claim made about Kintu's origin before founding Buganda; some claims say he came from Bunyoro, while others say he came from Elgon mountains, east of Uganda. Kalyango proposes that although Kintu is known in Bunyoro and Bugishu, his origin is in Buganda.

Despite the various stories, almost all of them point to Kintu as the first king who established the Buganda kingdom, although some writers claimed that Kimera, who came from Bunyoro, was the founder of Buganda (Speke 1863: 252; Cox 1950: 1). Nonetheless, what is common about these histories is that the present clans of the Buganda, although sharing a culture and language, have diverse origins (Gray 1935: 264; Kiwanuka 1972: 31). Further, most oral sources contend that the Buganda kingdom resulted from struggle and shedding of blood.[18] Unfortunately, there is scant information about the pre-Kintu period and even the oral narratives provide inadequate information. Majority of the informants I interviewed claimed that by the time Kintu founded Buganda, there were either five or six indigenous clans. Although there is no consistent list of the original clans, most writers also suggested that there were five or six clans that Kintu found in Muwawa.[19] The people who inhabited this area were called Balasangeye ("those who shoot black and white colobus monkey") and most often hunted animals for food. It is alleged that the heads of these "clans" were only males, which posits that patriarchy is as old as Kintu. Other sources claim that the Balasangeye were not organized in a formalized sense, as the Baganda later became united under Kintu and his descendants (Wrigley 1996: 71) and reveal that these people were organized on the basis of kinship *maka* (household) (Musisi 1991a: 53). For instance, Tobi Kizito noted "Before it was even imagined that Kintu would ever come here, this country [Buganda], had people scattered everywhere; they were all on their own" (1915a: 6). [20]

Based on the assumption that Kintu found five or six clans headed by men, most Baganda that I interviewed were convinced that since time immemorial, men have always been the leaders of women in Buganda. When I asked Sulaiti Kalungi, a seventy-three-year-old man, whether there had ever been a woman king in Buganda's history, he said, "no, never," with strong conviction. He said "the kingship of this place [Buganda] has always been in the hands of men since our origin and that is a ruling from God." Similarly,

Nuludin Ssekitto, in his thirties, stressed that: "Kingship is from God and that He did not create Kingship or royal seats of power only for the Baganda; the Basoga [Eastern Uganda], Banyankole, and Banyoro [all ethnic groups from Western Uganda] also have their kings."

However, further research reveals that Kintu's story is not the only story.[21] To understand this kingship calls for an examination of Buganda state formation. As B. Nakanyike Musisi also suggested, we need to examine the legends and histories of the pre-Kintu/pre-Buganda period (1991a: 52). There is a need to critically examine the way of life of the Balasangeye before and just after Kintu created Buganda. Roscoe testifies to the existence of chiefs or clan leaders before Kintu: "Prior to Kintu, there were a few aborigines who dwelt in isolated communities or clans; each was governed by its chief, who owned allegiance to no other chief" (1911: 186). Musisi's analysis, which focuses on the division of labor, and land ownership and distribution in the pre-Kintu period, presents a starting point to reexamine the basis for gender construction in Baganda. I adapt Musisi's argument that "the processes resulting in hierarchical stratification and state formation altered kinship relations based on claims made on land and women's productive and reproductive labour" (Musisi 1991a: 50–51). According to Musisi, the "social organization during the pre-Kintu/Nambi *[sic]* era was based on subsistence hunting and hoe cultivation as well as gathering" (1991a: 53).

Further, Tobi Kizito reports that before Kintu, the Balasangeye "never had villages that were well cultivated; they used to grow a few annual crops and a majority of them concentrated on hunting and fishing [in Lake Victoria]" (1915a: 6). Unfortunately, Kizito does not provide information on any shared roles, whether women worked on the farms and men were the hunters or did the fishing. However, Musisi reported from *Lugave* (pangolin, scaly ant-eater) clan history "men leaned more towards hunting and women more towards cultivating" (1991a: 54). She rightly pointed out that "leaning more towards" does not mean that men never cultivated and women never hunted; it simply means that men and women were more inclined towards certain activities, hunting and cultivating, respectively. Although men and women may have been more inclined to certain activities, the evidence available suggests that there were no restrictions prescribed based on one's sex. As Musisi noted, "The division of labour at the subsistence level was not sufficient to warrant male dominance and female subordination . . ." (1991a: 54–55). Similarly, Katambula Busuulwa, who is an elder of the *kkobe* (yam) clan and has conducted extensive research on Kiganda customs, informed me that before Kintu, social roles among females and males were not distinct (interview). Musisi and Busuulwa's arguments suggest that the concept of "men," which alludes to dominance, and that of "women," which relates to subordination, in the twentieth-first-century Buganda, may not have existed among the Balasangeye of the pre-Baganda period. Musisi's research suggests that women and men may have beaten drums and danced together since there were no restrictions on division of labor based on one's sex or class. In Chapter Four, this line of reasoning, namely, that in the pre-Kintu period women may have beaten drums for their own entertainment and pleasure as men did, is explored in greater detail.

While there are many stories and legends about Buganda's past, few relate to the point in time when there seems to have been no gender differentiation. One would ask: why is so little known about a period when it is possible that women were empowered? Anyhow, Buganda is not the only culture were women's power in pre-history is concealed. For instance, inadequate information is available about women's leadership in Celtic society (Miller 1987), in early Japan (Wheatley and See 1978), and in the Silla state of Korea (Nelson 1993) to mention a few. Explaining why the history before Kintu is not well known, Kizito Tobi said: "After Kintu had arrived in the country Buganda, then, every Muganda stopped referring to [his or her] paternal ancestry. But they always talked about Kintu alone. Even when swearing, they used to swear that 'we, the children of Kintu; even if we die, we can never get wiped out completely'" (1915a: 7). Kizito argued further that the five male clan heads remembered are those who were best known and those whose lineage survived Kintu's wars (Ibid.). The questions are: 1) How did Kintu manage to make these people forget about their ancestry? 2) Who are those forgotten ancestors? 3) Why was it possible that only the five men could be remembered? Could it have been the women clan heads that did not survive Kintu's wars, and they are the forgotten ancestors?

If we assume that before Kintu females and males may have engaged in any activity with no restriction, one can envisage the possibility that females could have been clan leaders. Busuulwa affirmed that females shared the role of leadership before the coming of Kintu and stressed that:

> Before Kintu came, there were many female kings. In fact, history recounts that Nnaggalabi was the last female king. As a matter of fact, in order to overthrow this kingship a lot of blood was shed during the war. Men fought hard in order to rule after the overthrow of Nnaggalabi. Until now, Nnaggalabi is remembered and the hill from which she ruled still stands at Buddo [Busiro County].

Kintu nga tanajja, abakazi baabeera nnyo bakabaka. Era ebyafaayo
bigamba nti Nnaggalabi ye Kabaka omukazi eyasembayo. Era okujjako
obwakabaka buno nti waaliwo okuyiwa omusaayi mungi nnyo nnyo.
Abasajja baalwana nnyo okulaba nga bafuga okuva ku Nnaggalabi. Era
Nnaggalabi ajjukirwa nnyo, n'olusozi we luli e Buddo kweyafugiranga
okwo (interview).

It is true that Nnaggalabi is the name of a hill in Buddo, Busiro County and it
is still an important hill where coronation ceremonies of kings are performed.
There are a number of points that support the possibility that Nnaggalabi
may have existed as a person. First, according to Kiganda nomenclature,
Nnaggalabi could be a feminine name. Nsimbi, a Luganda linguist, has noted
that, "the syllable *Sse* denotes a name for a male or an activity performed by a
male, while on the other hand, the syllable *Nna* denotes a name for a female
or an activity performed by a female" (1996: 3–4). However, he also noted
that sometimes there are masculine names that may start with *Nna,* although
these are not as common as those for females (1996: 4). He ascertained that
the Baganda had specific names for females and males, although there were
also some names, especially from proverbs, that were neutral (1996: 9). There
is a distinction between feminine and masculine names. For instance, "Nannyonga" is a feminine name, while "Ssennyonga" is a masculine name, both
from *nnakisinge* (brown grass-finch) clan. Second, Nsimbi explained that
choices of names are not random; places, animals, rivers, lakes, and people
were named for particular reasons. At times, one could be named after a certain saying or proverb or even after a good or bad event (1996: xiii, 1). It is
also true that places were, and still are, named after events, powerful or bad
people that lived there at one time. The fact that Nnaggalabi hill exists suggests a likelihood that a powerful woman called Nnaggalabi could have lived
on this hill. Third, the rituals and ceremonies, which are vital to Buganda's
kingship, which are performed at this hill, suggest that Nnaggalabi was probably a king. Kaggwa reported that in the mid-eighteenth century, Ssekabaka
Namugala[22] instituted new coronation rituals; the prospective king had to go
to Nnaggalabi to reenact Kintu's conquest before being declared the Kabaka.
Explaining why Kabaka Namugala introduced the new coronation ritual,
Kaggwa wrote that:

> After Namugala had eaten the kingship[23] as the heir to his elder brother
> Mwanga I . . . he went to a medium [called] Buddo who made him
> climb over his charm. . . . But that medium clearly told Kabaka Namu-
> gala that ['] at this hill Nnaggalabi your ancestor Kintu won Bemba,

who was the king of Buganda who was called a snake. After killing
[Bemba], he ate Buganda. Therefore, I impress upon you that whenever
your son and descendants eat the kingship, they must first come here
and climb over this charm in remembrance of Kintu when he won
Bemba and he took over his [her?] country. Therefore, whoever shall
come to this hill shall become the king (1952: 7–8).

Is the Nnaggalabi war, mentioned by Katambula Busuulwa, the same as that
one which Kintu fought with Bemba? Busuulwa told me that for women to
lose power as kings or clan leaders, men had to fight a big war. It is striking
that both wars happened at Nnaggalabi and were both fought and won by
Kintu, a man. Then, does the commemoration of the Nnaggalabi war during
the kabaka's coronation emphasize the memory of that great day when
women, the forgotten ancestors, lost their power? Could Bemba be a woman
king since the name sounds feminine? Many informants described Bemba as
partly human and partly a snake. They said Bemba had only the upper torso
as human and the bottom part as a snake, with no lower limbs. However,
Bemba's sex could not be explained, which makes it difficult to determine
whether Bemba was a female (as suggested by a feminine name, Nnaggalabi)
or a male. Nonetheless, it is possible that Bemba's true name was concealed.
Bemba could have been Nnaggalabi, but to maintain a history that concealed the presence of powerful women, Bemba had to be presented as a
monster. If, as the evidence suggests, women had power during the pre-
Kintu era, the only way to suppress them was to erase them from history.
And since the past informs the future, an unknown past yields no future.
Maybe some of the forgotten ancestors were women, the powerful Nnaggal-
abis. In order to establish the men's dominance over the women, Kintu had
to disempower them.

More suggestive evidence for women's leadership and power during the
pre-Kintu period can be drawn from the legend of Kintu and Nnambi. In his
narration, Kaggwa mentioned that "Nnambi took an immediate liking to
Kintu . . . and she told Kintu that she wished to marry him. . . . Then
Nnambi invited Kintu to come to the sky. . . ." (1951: 1, as quoted and
translated by Ray 1991: 55). In Buganda, a woman's proposal for marriage or
even, a casual relationship to men is taboo. In fact, one is regarded as a prostitute, which negatively affects her identity. The fact that Nnambi proposed
to Kintu and Kintu accepted—indeed he went with Nnambi to the sky—
suggests that Nnambi had certain powers, which later women do not have.
Further, according to the legend, Kintu had to prove his power before
Ggulu, the father of Nnambi, before being allowed to marry her. Winning

over Nnambi after performing Ggulu's tricky tasks can be viewed as a parallel to Kintu's conquest of Bemba in order to take over Buganda. Kintu could only conquer women's power by shedding blood. Pursuing the view that women were as powerful as men in the pre-Kintu era, I interrogate the reasons why the Kiganda culture constructs women as being weak and, therefore, not able to beat drums in entertainment contexts. Yet, when it comes to rituals where the king is empowered, they are allowed to beat the drums. In Chapter Four, I argue that because of this historical power of women, the king depends on women for empowerment, one reason why they must beat the drums during the king's annual twin rituals. However, in other aspects and contexts, women's power must be concealed to cover this dependence.

CONCEPTUAL FRAMEWORK

The theories presented in this book resulted from the nature of data I collected, although I have borrowed ideas from gender studies, anthropology, political science, cultural studies, and ethnomusicology. In my conceptualization of the dialectical relationship between baakisimba and gender among the Baganda, I present three broad theories: Kiganda gender concept, baakisimba theory, and the articulation of gender and baakisimba theory.

KIGANDA GENDER CONCEPT

As a Ugandan gender theorist Sylvia Tamale has also observed, it is important not to force the Western conceptual framework of gender onto other societies. Most important, she notes that gender should not be isolated from other concepts including social class, politics, religion, age, and sexuality (1999: 3). It should be noted, however, that these variables do not impact gender at the same level; some are stronger than others. Moreover, their impact is time and context specific. I add that gender is cultural and time specific; therefore, its definitions vary from culture to culture and from one period to another. I strongly contend that gender is not static or absolute; it is continuously being reconstructed and renegotiated dependent on social, cultural, and political structures, which have changed in Buganda over time. For example, Christianity and European education—which introduced new social relations and in some cases legitimized already existing ones—need to be critically evaluated when dealing with gender in colonial and post-colonial periods of Buganda. Specifically, I argue that gender is strongly defined by the establishment and strength of the Buganda kingdom, the chief custodian of the Baganda's beliefs and code of conduct that sets up guidelines for social relations of the Baganda, both within and outside the palace. It should be noted, however, that only data necessary for understanding the connection of gender and baakisimba are presented in this gender analysis.

In Buganda, gender definition is contingent on whether one belongs to the palace or outside the palace. On the one hand, biological and cultural factors shape gender identities, roles, and relations; I refer to this process as biocultural construction. On the other hand, social class, as structured by the Baganda, defines one's gender identity, role, relations; and I refer to this process as sociocultural construction. The biocultural conceptualization of gender outside the palace is based partly on biological characteristics and arbitrarily assigned traits. The arbitrary basis for gender structuring is human cultural creations and one's sex, which is determined when a child is born, is a natural phenomenon. Male and female are the recognized sexes among the Baganda and, form the basis for assigning gender outside the palace. When analyzing the biocultural construction of gender among the Baganda, age plays an important role, because the assignment of roles is an ongoing process; roles assigned at an earlier age, in a number of cases, are preparations for roles at a later age.[24] On the basis of one's sex and age, the Baganda prescribe specific roles and life expectations for women and men that define relations between them. These roles include drumming for men and dancing for women; I will explore these issues throughout the proceeding chapters.

On the other hand, any female outside the palace contexts who gets involved in activities that were culturally designated for men automatically loses her woman gender. This person becomes *nnakawanga* ("she-cock"), *nnalukalala* (intrepid person), *kyakulassajja* (manly-female) or *nnabyewanga*, a proverb that states: "nnabyewanga: ng'akaliga akaliira mu nte [meaning] a pretentious person: like a lamb that grazes amongst the cows. [It claims] I want to be among the great" (Walser 1982: 285). A woman is equated with a lamb, while a man is related to a cow. To do what is meant for men is a lie, because a female outside the palace can never become as "great" as a man. In addition to the biocultural distinctions between men and women, the Baganda use body appearance to assign manly-female and womanly-male genders. In this case, a female may be assigned *kyakulassajja* ("manly-female) gender, if that person has physical features that according to the judgment of the Baganda are masculine. Likewise, one is assigned womanly-male gender if that person physical body has features considered to be feminine. The body appearance may be biological or artificially recreated through makeup and costume, both permanent and temporary. Generally, a round body, full breasts, big buttocks, big legs, and long hair (braided or straight) are associated with femininity. Jewelry and makeup enhance one's femininity. However one is considered a man if that person is muscular, "tough," with short hair, but with a beard, whether shaved or not. Jewelry and makeup are not acceptable for Baganda men. Those who do not fit the Baganda model for men or women belong to a third gender.[25] Although a third gender existed among the Baganda, even before the "discovery" of Buganda (as discussed in Chapter Eight), the Baganda do not outwardly recognize an individual as a third-gendered person. The categories of *kikazikazi* and *kyakulassajja* do not necessarily refer to one's sexual orientation, although it may be true with some third-gendered people. These two categories are most used in reference to one's physical appearance and the societal roles that person undertakes. With the influence of celibacy as introduced by the Catholic Church in the early twentieth century, new genders emerged namely, *faaza* (reverend father), *siisita* (reverend sister), and *bulaaza* (reverend brother).

The Baganda's sociocultural construction of gender within the palace challenges the biological basis for gender assignment in many cultures, especially in the West. Presenting a Western differentiation of gender and sex, Paula S. Rothenberg explains that sex is "a biologically based category, and 'gender' refers to the particular set of socially constructed meanings that are associated with each sex" (1995: 8). Rothenberg suggests that there is a link between one's sex and socially constructed gender. She rightly notes that "While it is true that most . . . of us are born unambiguously 'male' or 'female' as defined by our chromosomes or genitalia, the *meaning* [her emphasis] of being a man or a woman differs from culture to culture and within each society" (ibid.). The Baganda's definition of gender within the palace strongly legitimizes Rothenberg's view. The sociocultural construction of gender is based on a two-class stratification: 1) the *balangira* (princes) and *bambejja* (princesses) and 2) the *bakopi* (commoners), both males and females. While the *balangira* and *bambejja* constitute the man gender, the *kabaka* (king) as its head is the *ssaabasajja*, "the Man among men." He is "One who dominated and subdued all men" (Musisi 1991a: 66). On the other hand, all the *bakopi*, whether male or female, are assigned a woman-gender, to emphasize their submissiveness and total accountability to the royal family. This categorization of men and women based on social status strongly emphasizes the notion that gender is constructed rather than given. If females can be men in one context and women in another, the categorization of men and women are, therefore, categories of dominant and subordinate relations. Likewise, Omulangira (Prince) Sam Kimbuggwe explained, "A prince and a commoner may be compared with a man and a woman. The man remains as a man. Likewise, a prince is a prince. A prince is very powerful! A prince is that one who heads the commoner" (interview).

The Baganda present an example of the ambiguous and fluid nature of gender. Because of its ambiguity and unstable character, Western concepts of gender cannot adequately fit the Kiganda conceptualization of gender. In the West, while male, female, and the "other" are the concepts used to identify the different genders, the Baganda's conceptualization of gender would be related to concepts like man, woman, manly-female, womanly-male, father, brother, and sister. This conceptualization is based on the view that every male is not necessarily a man and, not every female is a woman. In the Baganda's conceptualization, man and woman genders relate to power relations, who holds power and who does not. For example, because princesses hold power, although females, they are considered men. Consequently, it becomes quite difficult to explain a concept, which is conceived differently in one culture, through the language of a society that understands the same concept differently. Moreover, since gender studies have been more developed in the Western world, no adequate cross-cultural concepts have yet been developed. For instance, what pronouns would one use to differentiate between a male who is a man and one who is a male-woman? What pronouns do I assign a manly-female, a womanly-male, or even a father, sister, and brother? How can I present a discussion that illustrates this gender complexity when the language to be used does not facilitate me? Christy Adair has also been confronted with a similar language problem. She notes, "There are no easy solutions to the problems of creating viewpoints which are appropriate to women's experience when the language which we use reflects a vision constructed from the point of view of men" (1992: 2). In order to understand the Baganda's conceptualization of gender, the reader ought to deconceptualize the Western view of gender.

In this book, I maintain the Baganda's construction of gender: the kabaka is assigned the man gender, the "female-men" category is given to the *bambejja,* the females of the royal class, and "male-men" to the *balangira,* males of the royal class. The male *bakopi* belong to male-women gender, while the female *bakopi* are of the female-woman gender. Outside the palace, I maintain the man, womanly-male, woman, manly-female, father, brother, and sister genders.

Gender as a social relation involves both hierarchical and lateral structure, relation of dominance and subordination. In Buganda, power relations are in hegemonic struggles. The dominant men have to continuously construct strategies for sustaining power; yet, the subordinates are always challenging these strategies. Hierarchical strata exist within and between the constructed genders within and outside the palace. In figure 2, I present gender hierarchical structuring among the Baganda in a diagram form.

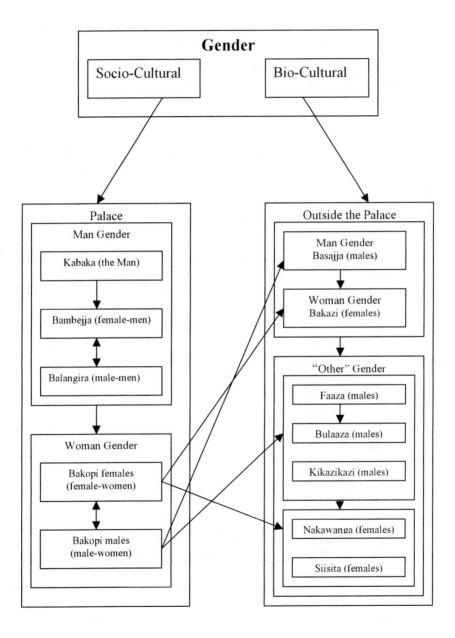

Figure 2. Gender construction of the Baganda.

According to the figure, there are two domains; palace and outside the palace on which gender assignments are based. As shown by the arrows, the *bakopi* (commoners) shift genders depending on the context; outside the palace, a female-woman may become, either *omukazi,* woman; *nnakawanga,* a manly-female; or siisita, a sister. And yet, outside the palace, a male-woman may become, *musajja;* a man; *faaza,* father; *bulaaza,* a brother; or *kikazikazi,* a womanly-male.

Within the palace, the man gender, headed by the kabaka dominates the woman gender. The reciprocal arrows between the female-men and the male-men relates to the fact that not all the female-men dominate the male-men and vice versa. From the *bambejja,* the king chooses his *nnaalinnya* (queen sister). *Nnaalinnya* surpasses in power all the other *bambejja* and *balangira,* and is actually referred to as a "king" in his (conventionally) own right (see detailed discussion in Chapter Four). Besides the nnaalinnya, being males, the balangira surpass the rest of the female-men folk. Further, the *nnamasole* (wife to a former king), the queen mother, who is always chosen from among the female-women (commoners), becomes powerful when her son becomes the king. As such, the *nnamasole* is the most dominant among the women, male and female, of the palace. And yet, the *kabaka* also chooses his *katikkiro* (Prime Minister) among the male *bakopi,* who held the highest position among the male-women and second only to the nnamasole among the entire women folk within the palace. The dialectical arrow shows this nature of relationship within the woman gender. In Chapter Four, I give a detailed discussion of how palace gender connects with baakisimba.

Outside the palace, the general position of these genders has been the basis for assignment and justification of roles in baakisimba performance. Although these positions have not been stable, men have tended to dominate all genders. Women are said to have more power only when they surpass fellow women in productivity and reproductivity. However, the women gender heads all the other genders, father, brother, sister, womanly-male and manly-female. As far as the relations within the "other" genders are concerned, the Catholic values play a role in determining the hierarchical positioning of the genders, but only among the Catholics who value celibacy. Among the Catholics the father gender is positioned higher than the brother and the sister genders, as will be explained in Chapter Six. To some conservative Baganda, and mainly among the non-Catholics, father, sister, and brother genders may be considered subversive genders and as such, may hold no hierarchical positioning. However, the physical appearance of fathers and brothers, being masculine, may offer them a temporal position over the manly-woman and womanly-male gendered persons.

It is important, however, to note that the construction of gender of the Baganda has not been static; different sociocultural gender constructions have existed in Buganda at different times. While changes may have existed, it was not until after Christianity was introduced in the late 1880s that drastic changes in sociocultural gender construction began to emerge. With the crumbling of the kingdom, which happened drastically after Buganda became a British Protectorate in 1894 and finally collapsed after the abolition of the kingdom in 1967, the sociocultural construction of gender became less predictable and more open to new definitions. While similar sociocultural categories for the different genders may still be used even today, they carry different meanings. After all, the kingdom now exists as a cultural institution and not a political entity. Nonetheless, the monarchy underpins the every existence of present-day social relations.

BAAKISIMBA THEORY

In this study, I examine baakisimba as an integrated music and dance genre. James Kika Makubuya has rightly stated: "Whereas in the Western sense, singing, instrumental music playing, dancing, drama and miming may be considered as separate disciplines, among the Baganda, the distinction between them is almost nonexistent; they form an inseparable bond during performance" (1995: 41). Therefore, understanding baakisimba calls for the examination of how baakisimba dance and music co-create each other in a given performance context, since different performance contexts produce different musical and dance structures. As Anthony Seeger has argued in his work on the Suyá of Brazil:

> Music is much more than just the sounds captured on a tape recorder. It is the use of the body to produce and accompany the sounds. Music is an emotion that accompanies the production of, the appreciation of, and the participation in a performance. Music is also, of course, the sounds themselves after they are produced. Yet it is intention as well as realization; it is emotion and value as well as structure and form (1987: xiv).

Baakisimba, being both a dance and music genre, fits well in Seeger's definition of music.[26] Like Seeger, I contend that looking at the sound structure, while ignoring the process that created it, provides an incomplete study of music. Moreover, the process of music making is never completed until the created sound is given meaning by the audience. However, meaning is constantly in flux and performance is a site for the creation of multiple meanings.

During the performance of baakisimba, when performers and the audience interact, the audience creates new sounds beyond what the performers produce. The audience shouts, ululates, and claps; adding to the structure of the sound heard when the composition is recorded.

If dance is part of music, as Seeger also rightly suggests, then some "sounds" are not heard, but seen. In all the performances I attended, I observed that the audience had little reaction at the beginning of the performance when the music introduced the mood of the dance. However, as soon as the dancers came on stage, the audience clapped to the beat of the dancers' body movements. Moreover, audiences reacted less to baakisimba music performed without dancing, even when drums were beaten. It was evident that the body movement accentuated the rhythmic and melodic qualities of the music. Similarly, Judith Lynne Hanna has observed that "dance contributes yet another rhythm to the distinct rhythm of each instrument in the musical ensemble accompanying the dancers" (1983: 48–49). Since the contexts of my study involved performing baakisimba as a dance and music genre, studying baakisimba music and neglecting the dance "is like studying Greece without its architecture" (Warren 1972: i). Similarly, in his efforts to understand Ghanaian Dagomba drum music, John Chernoff was told to mind the dancers. Among the Dagomba: "a musician orders or extends his rhythmic variations to suit the movement of . . . [the] dancers. . . . [The] drummer must make his music in reference to how tired or disaffected the dancers are becoming, giving them time to rest as well as inspiration. . . . The drum beaters should be following the dancer" (1979: 66). Like the Dagomba musicians, I argue that in baakisimba, music and dance co-create each other. Music and dance are highly integrated to create a unified genre called baakisimba. The Baganda create specific drum rhythms that induce particular body movements and any changes in the music propose changes in the body movement. As a result of this integration, any innovations in the dance movements result into recreations in the drum music and vice versa. Moreover, there is a constant interaction between musicians, dancers, and the audience. And yet, this interaction does not only contribute to the fluid meaning in baakisimba, but also participates in the structuring of music and dance. For instance, energetic drumming induces vigorous dancing, and yet, when the audience applauds the interaction is intensified more. However, the vigor of the dance is dependent on the performance contexts; a performance in the church will require a reserved behavior than one in a village context at a wedding party.

ARTICULATION OF BAAKISIMBA WITH GENDER

The relationship between music sound, dance, and social relations has been an important one for music scholarship during the 1990s. For instance, Thomas Turino has examined music as a strategy that the Andean immigrants in Lima (Peru) use to recapture their sense of cultural identity in new urban settings (1993). Jane C. Sugarman has looked at wedding songs among the Prespa Albanians as a space for performing gender (1997). And yet, Jane Cowan focuses on dance as a site for the contestation of gender identities. My study reveals that both music and dance are spaces for gender construction and contestation. Informed by the data I have collected, Stuart Hall's theory of articulation (1977; 1980; 1996a) facilitates my conceptualization of the relationship between baakisimba and gender in Buganda. The articulation theory, which was developed in the 1970s was a reaction against reductionism, essentialism, and reflectionism, and is mainly attributed to Ernesto Laclau and Stuart Hall.[27] The theory is a result of critical questioning of 'classical' or 'orthodox' Marxism and its dependence on reductionism. It is important to examine how baakisimba and gender, like other aspects of society are linked to form units in a non-reductionist way.

While many cultural theorists have contributed to the development of this theory, Hall's conceptualization resonates with the analysis of my data in fruitful ways. In an interview conducted by Lawrence Grossberg, Hall noted that:

> I always use the word 'articulation,' though I do not know whether the meaning I attribute to it is perfectly understood. In England, the term has a nice double meaning because [to] 'articulate' means to utter, to speak forth, to be articulate. . . . But we also speak of an articulated lorry (truck): a lorry where the front (cab) and the back (trailer) can, but need not necessarily, be connected to one another [.] . . . An articulation is thus the form of connection that can make a unity of two different elements, under certain conditions. It is a linkage which is not necessary, determined, absolute and essential for all time (Grossberg 1996b: 141).

Similarly, in this book, I argue that although there is a relationship between baakisimba and gender of the Baganda, the connection they have is "not that of an identity, where one structure perfectly recapitulates or reproduces or even 'expresses' another; or where each is reducible to the other. The

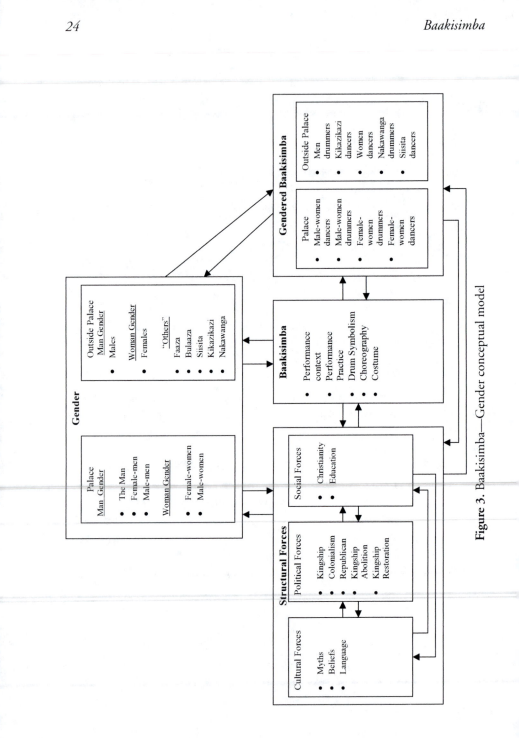

Figure 3. Baakisimba—Gender conceptual model

unity formed by this combination or articulation, is always, necessarily, a 'complex structure': a structure in which things are related, as much through their differences as through their similarities" (Hall 1980: 325). The differences exist because baakisimba is an art form, while gender is a social relation. On the other hand, the two are similar because both are cultural constructions. Further, Hall's theory affords us to view culture as a complex unity always having multiple and contradictory determinations, always a historically specific phenomenon.

Moreover, Hall's view of culture resonates with my conceptualization of baakisimba as a discursive site through which the Baganda struggle to define their social relations. The articulation of baakisimba and gender is dialectic; baakisimba constructs and defines gender, yet gender in return shapes baakisimba. And yet, this articulation is "a process never completed—always 'in process'" (Hall 1996b: 2). The articulation of baakisimba and gender is ongoing and over determined; it exists historically in a particular formulation, anchored directly in relation to changing cultural, social, and political forces.[28] Baakisimba and gender are dialectically connected through a historical "web of connotation and codes" (Grossberg 1996a: 157). I summarize this web in a graphical representation in figure 3.

There are four major actors in the baakisimba-gender web: 1) baakisimba dance and music; 2) gender, within and outside the palace; 3) gendered baakisimba; and 4) structural forces, mainly the cultural, political, and social forces. The actors in this web dialectically interact in an inherently historical process; they have a reciprocal relationship. While gender roles, identities, and relations shape baakisimba, baakisimba reciprocates and defines, and crystallizes gender roles, identities and relations. Baakisimba crystallizes and yet, contests gender. Gender and baakisimba are articulated through performance context, performance practice; drum symbolism, dance choreography, and costumes. The roles assigned to performers, the negotiated gender identities, and the involved relations of power make baakisimba an active stage for gendered performances.

Moreover, the structural forces have defined gender and baakisimba performance and vice versa. It is important to note that the structural forces are continuously structured by their relationships with each other. As part of a collective social and cultural process, they impact and define the Baganda's gender construction. I argue that the definition of gender and baakisimba are contingent on the stability of the kingship, the custodian of Kiganda culture (for example, myths, beliefs, and language). The Baganda use myths, beliefs, and customs to explain and legitimize gender constructions, and language crystallizes these constructions. The connection between baakisimba and social relations works in reciprocity while baakisimba reinforces the structural forces; they in return provide contexts of performance that define baakisimba. These actors form a site of struggle over defining gender roles, identities, and relations, which have shaped baakisimba. The dialectical relationships between and within the actors are made more apparent in the course of the book.

What, then, are the ways in which gendered meanings in baakisimba are constructed? The main participants in baakisimba performance including: performers, teachers, dance students, adjudicators, audience, and dance and music critics participate in the production of meanings in baakisimba. Stuart Hall has argued, "The meaning of a cultural symbol is given in part by the social field into which it is incorporated, the practices with which it articulates and is made to resonate" (quoted in Grossberg 1996a: 157). Therefore, meanings in baakisimba cannot be deduced solely from what happens in the structures of music and dance, because baakisimba is also historically constructed by cultural, political, and social forces. Meanings are contingent on structures outside baakisimba including, but not limited to myths, folk tales, proverbs, language and other forms of discourse as well as the contexts, which in this case, include, the palace, village, church, and schools. Indeed, "Cultural practices articulate the meanings of particular social practices and events; they define the ways we make sense of them, how they are experienced and lived" (Grossberg 1996a: 158). Following Lawrence Grossberg, I argue that, "the meaning is not [only] in the text itself but is the active product of the text's social articulation, of the web of connotations and codes into which it is inserted" (ibid.). Meaning in baakisimba is a product of an intense interaction between the musical and dance discourses, gender constructions, and cultural contexts within and outside the palace of the Baganda. While I attempt to analyze the multiple and conflicting meanings of baakisimba and their relationship to gender, what I present in this book are just some of the many meanings that can be constructed. Nonetheless, my analysis is authoritative because it is based on thorough research and draws on the meanings the Baganda, the creators of the genres, give to baakisimba. My discussions include the views of the people I interviewed as a way to represent the different interpretations of baakisimba in relation to gender.

BOOK OVERVIEW

The major questions this book addresses include: 1) How does baakisimba help to construct gender both within and outside the palace domains of the Buganda? 2) How do the cultural, political, and social forces impact on the articulation of baakisimba and gender? 3) Why is it that only women (male and female) dance for the king? 4) Why did female *bakopi* beat drums in the palace context and yet it was a taboo for them to beat the drums outside the palace? 5) Why did the Baganda prescribe men outside the palace, as the drummers and women outside the palace as the dancers? 6) In what ways does baakisimba performance support or contest the common attitude that women, outside the palace, cannot beat drums as men do because of women's biological construction? 7) Why are women said to be better dancers? 8) What are the social issues that distinguish men as "musicians" and women as "dancers" outside the palace? 9) What meanings do the historical shifts in dance and music roles—where women and schoolgirls began to beat the drums and men and schoolboys began to dance—construct within the larger Buganda society? 10) How do the different performance contexts, palace, village, church, and school shape baakisimba? 11) What does it mean for celibate sisters to perform baakisimba in church? 12) How does baakisimba act as a stage for performing alternative genders? In order to address these questions, this book is divided into nine chapters.

Based on the premise that the meaning of any art form can only be constructed within particular historical, cultural, political, and social contexts, I discuss the historically structured performance contexts of baakisimba at the beginning of every chapter. Although these broad contexts can be analyzed in terms of several "contexts," I examine baakisimba specifically in relation to gender constructions in the palace (Chapter Four); outside the palace, in the villages (Chapter Five); in the Catholic Church (Chapter Six), in schools (Chapter Seven) and the construction of the alternative genders (Chapter Eight). In these contexts, I examine the continuity and change of baakisimba in terms of performance practice, choreography, costume, musical repertoire, drum symbolism, recruitment of dancers and musicians, training process, and interaction of the musicians, dancers, trainers, adjudicators, and audience, all sites that help to define and contest gender roles, identities, and relations in Buganda. Because Baakisimba performance stresses the integration of music and dance, my discussion of the two is blended in all chapters.

In Chapter Two, I discuss the research methodology as well as share my field experience. I examine the challenges of being an indigenous researcher and explain how fieldwork is an issue of negotiating ethnic, gender, social, cultural, and religious identities. I advocate for a dialectical approach to analyzing data; both the researcher and the researched must participate in the interpretation of data for a balanced understanding of the researched culture.

In order to situate the conceptualization of baakisimba, in Chapter Three, I examine the origin of baakisimba. I examine the concepts used to explain the dance and the system I have used in the notation of music and dance excerpts in this book. My focus is only on the musical and dance aspects that form the bases for the analyses presented in this book. I discuss the basis of the Baganda's, gendering of the *mbuutu* and the *ngalabi* (the drums that provide the basic accompaniment) as woman and man drums, respectively as well as the genderization of baakisimba as a women dance.

In Chapter Four, I examine the symbolic power of the drum and its relationship to Buganda kingship. Although men control women's access to beating the drums in "entertainment" contexts outside the palace, female-women must beat the drums in contexts that empower men within the palace. I explain why and when female-women must beat the drums in the palace. My discussion reveals that because men need women to empower them, the rules that regulate the women's access to the drums are relaxed in empowering rituals.

In Chapter Five, I discuss the ways in which men control women's access to the drums. I explore the subverted gender space, where women "eat the forbidden fruit" and beat the drums. A focus on the personal experience of Rehema Nnabanoba, one of the most musically fluent manly-women drummers, helps to elucidate on the view that females outside the palace context are redefining themselves through drumming. Since the main instrument in dance is the body and the body is the object of sexuality, in this chapter, I tread on culturally forbidden ground among the Baganda, namely, the reference to sexuality. To be a proper Muganda woman, one must procreate. Baakisimba performance forms one of the training grounds for marriage roles, including "successful" sexual life thought to determine one's procreative ability. I also examine how baakisimba defines women as food producers and procreators. I analyze how, on the one hand, baakisimba projects Baganda women as sexual objects, constructing them as the subordinate sex, and on the other hand, how women appropriate baakisimba to empower themselves and subvert the control of men over their bodies.

In Chapter Six, I examine the impact of Christianity, particularly Catholicity, on baakisimba performance. To become a religious sister is to subvert the gender assignment of women as sexual objects since sisters vow to celibacy. What then are the implications when celibate sisters perform a dance that defines them as sexual objects? Does the sisters' performance of baakisimba during mass create a liturgical crisis? This chapter examines how sisters redefine their "vowed" gender when they perform baakisimba in the church contexts.

In Chapter Seven, I explore how competitions at schools' music and dance festivals are basic agents for innovation in school baakisimba. On the one hand, baakisimba affirms the Kiganda gender construction and yet, on the other hand, it challenges and restructures it. The school contexts define the structure of baakisimba especially in terms of the musical accompaniment, dance motifs and levels, as well as costuming.

In Chapter Eight, I interrogate the generalized allegation that the Arabs[29] introduced homosexuality in Buganda. I examine the implication of womanly-males performing a woman's dance and what this performance practice points to in the overall redefinition of gender identities among the Baganda. My field research revealed that baakisimba avails space for male homosexuals to assert their identities. In the last section of this chapter, I report on my encounter with a male homosexual dancer. Finally, Chapter Nine recapitulates the most salient issues of the study and summarizes the overall implications of the study to the understanding of the integration of music, dance, and social relations. I point out the major contributions of the study to the scholarships of ethnomusicology, gender studies, cultural studies, and other related fields that resonate with the articulation of Gender with baakisimba of the Baganda. I also suggest possible areas of further research.

Chapter Two
Ethnography of Baakisimba

INDIGENOUS SCHOLARSHIP: FORMAL AND INFORMAL RESEARCH

A researcher's narration of the process of learning and understanding a culture of his or her study is not only important to the reader to understand the environment of data collection and its analysis, but also offers a forum for the researcher to share experiences from which other researchers can learn. However, as Chou Chiener, an indigenous scholar of Taiwanese music, has rightly noted, "Perspectives on fieldwork from those who study their own culture are still comparatively rare in ethnomusicology (2002: 456). While Chiener's presentation focuses on a comparative analysis of experiences of indigenous scholars and non-indigenous scholars, my discussion is not an intended comparison, but probably a reflection on a number of issues we indigenous scholars take for granted as we research and write about our own cultures.

This study presents my understanding of baakisimba that resulted from both informal and formal research since 1983, when I began performing baakisimba. The informal part of this research consists of my personal experience as a student, dancer, drummer, teacher, and a member of the audience for baakisimba. The formal part of my research began in 1993–1995, when I researched on selected Kiganda traditional secular and sacred music for my master's thesis (1995). Although I did not focus on baakisimba, or even address gender issues, my study considered baakisimba as entertainment dance and music. Later, in the summers of 1995, 1996, and 1997, I was a research assistant to Jean-Jacques Nattiez during his research in Uganda, first as a general survey of Ugandan cultural music and later, focusing on *mbaga* wedding music and dance. During these field experiences, I was able to meet a number of musicians, who subsequently provided most

contacts for the present study. The fieldwork specific to the study of baakisimba as an integration of music and dance and how it relates to the gender
of the Buganda was conducted between October 1999 and August 2000 and
2002.

As Kofi Agawu has rightly pointed out, there exists biases in conventional scholarship "that encourage us to privilege fieldwork . . . and knowledge acquired during relatively short periods of intentional search for
knowledge over knowledge and experience gained as part of an informal and
extended music education" (1995: xiii). While my formal fieldwork was
more focused to specific issues, my experience prior to formal research
framed not only a number of questions of this study, but also the analysis of
the collected data. In fact, my prior experience of baakisimba performance
informed the very decision to undertake this study. As in Chiener's case, my
pre-formal research offered more than mere background to field research; "it
led to understandings that were in some cases distinct from, rather than inferior to, those gained through fieldwork" (2002: 457).

Indeed, different cultural backgrounds offer different experiences to
scholars; indigenous scholars experience the cultures they study differently from scholars whose experience of the same cultures is mainly
through formal research. For instance, by over-emphasizing sound structure, Western scholars have defined Kiganda "music" in Western terms[1]
and yet, as in other African cultures music and dance are inseparable
among the Baganda. I also posit that there is a connection between
Baganda's conceptualization of what music and dance are and their cultural worldview about social relations.

Despite the personal experiences that indigenous scholars bring to
the study of their music and dance, the historical scholarship in ethnomusicology has tended to privilege mainly the non-indigenous scholarship; a
view deeply rooted from the historical nature of ethnomusicology. Ethnomusicology has for a long time operated as a discipline in which Western-
trained scholars study the music of non-Western cultures or the "Other."
While the discipline is evolving, some ethnomusicologists somewhat still
hold similar views as those formerly held by one of their founding father
Bruno Nettl:

> The studies of West African tribal music by African scholars, such as J.
> H. Kwabena Nketia, [have] become perfectly acceptable to Western eth-
> nomusicologists, [even though] many would surely deny that investiga-
> tion of one's own culture is ethnomusicology at all, since the idea of
> comparing other cultures and styles with one's own, and the principle

that one can be more objective about other cultures than about one's
own, are important fundamentals of [ethnomusicology] (1964: 70).

Like Agawu, I contend that indigenous scholars' experience is knowledge
worth including in scholarly studies since it is knowledge acquired over a
longer period (ibid.). Moreover, if I qualify to be an informant, then my
experience is indeed valued research data. Why should my experience and
knowledge as an informant qualify to be valid data only if someone else collects it from me? Why is it that other people's experiences contribute to
"objective" knowledge and yet mine only becomes objective knowledge if
someone else collects it from me?[2] However, I am not advocating for privileging indigenous scholarship, I am only stressing that both scholarships
have a rich contribution to offer to ethnomusicology.

In order to study baakisimba of the Baganda, a culture to which I
belong, I had to redefine the established meaning of "the field" and my role
as a "researcher," since the predominantly Western definition has a tendency
not to accommodate indigenous researchers studying their own cultures.
According to Timothy Rice, the definition of the "field" has roots in the theoretical framework of ethnomusicology, namely the study of "music as part
of culture" (1997: 102). Although "culture" has a multiplicity of definitions,
it is specific to a group of people and bounded by space and time. As such, "a
member" of "a culture" and those outside it are designated as "insider" and
"outsider," respectively. As a result, "the field" came to be a "place where we
outsiders must go to encounter these insiders and their culture, and explain
to other outsiders the relationship between music and culture posited by our
theories" (Rice 1997: 105). The field is further circumscribed by the very
definitions of the discipline. Klaus Wachsmann defined ethnomusicology as
one "concerned with the music of the *other people*" [my emphasis] and that
"the observer does not share directly the musical tradition he [or she] studies" (1969: 165). Although the discipline has evolved, the initial terminologies and their definitions are still held in ethnomusicology and, therefore,
tend to exclude indigenous scholars from the discipline. These are deep-
seated formative concepts in the West and, as such, must continually be critically examined and challenged.

As an indigenous scholar, I asked myself "where am I and who am I in
relation to this ethnomusicological theoretical understanding of "the field"
and the "researcher?" Do what I am doing really count as ethnomusicology
at all? How do I change from the "traditional role" of being an informant or
even from a higher position as a research assistant, "a pawn in that international division of labor in which natives provide data and Westerners analyze

it" (Obbo 1990a: 297)? While I would be considered an "insider" by blood and by the fact that I have participated in Baganda's music making and dance since childhood, the training in ethnomusicology exposed me to new ways of thinking; I am "neither insider nor outsider, neither fully emic nor fully etic" (Herndon 1993: 77). Moreover, as a performer, teacher, and a member of the audience for baakisimba, I had never considered the possible associations between baakisimba and gender in Buganda. My participation in baakisimba in no way went beyond the pleasure of performing on stage, to show my dancing skills, and how well I had replicated my teachers when instructing my own students.

I began interrogating the nature of baakisimba during a cultural theory and musical practice seminar at the University of Pittsburgh. During my first year at the University, I performed baakisimba and after the performance one of my colleagues asked me whether the dance had any sexual connotations. I was so embarrassed! How can he ask me such a question? And yet, in Buganda, sexual matters are not supposed to be discussed in public except in sacred contexts like twin rituals and worship ceremonies and sex discussions are limited to specific people. Moreover, being a Christian, I could not imagine myself performing a "sexual" dance on a public stage. How can baakisimba be a sexual dance and yet it is also performed in the Catholic Church and even religious sisters perform the dance in church? Further, how could my dance teacher at Makerere College School, a respectable man, and a Muganda elder teach me a sexual dance? As a matter of fact, one of the first cultural shocks I had when I first went to the United States of America was to see people kissing on the streets, a taboo in my culture. My response to the colleague's question was an outright denial; I stressed how baakisimba was a mere entertainment dance. After all, my teachers always emphasized that I had to be entertaining on stage.

Another experience that gave background to the interpretation of baakisimba occurred when I introduced baakisimba to my African Drumming Ensemble course that I taught at the University of Pittsburgh. For the first two years of my teaching, I could not make the students perform the dance. They would all sit back and watch me dance claiming "the dance was very difficult." One day, one brave student confronted me and told me that "I am sorry, I do not intend to offend you, but in our culture, such movements are only made in sexual contexts." While I respected my students' opinion, I still held the view that baakisimba had nothing to do with sexuality.

However, I did not stop thinking about this issue. It was, rather, by distancing myself from my culture and using a different lens to understand baakisimba that I could think critically about this dance music in relation to issues of gender and sexuality. I had to "undergo a productive distantiation necessary for the explanation and critical understanding of [my own culture]" (Rice 1997: 117). I had to bridge the process of "knowing" with that of "understanding" culture in order to present a richer account of my own culture. It is by "not knowing" that I was able to learn more about my culture. Therefore, there is need for indigenous scholars to move beyond knowledge to understanding their culture so as to transform personal experience into academic knowledge. They must be open to new knowledge and different approaches to understanding.

While the informal experience of an indigenous scholar is worth knowledge, care must be taken in the use of prior knowledge so as not to hinder in-depth field research. Although my prior experience provided important data, I took care to ensure that voices of the Baganda are fully represented for a more inclusive and nuanced study of baakisimba and gender in Buganda. Indigenous scholars have to guard against the view that as people studying their own culture, they know and understand that culture. For instance, in 2001, Jean-Jacques Nattiez received a stiff resistance from a Ugandan dance scholar who did not believe that the Baganda gender their drums as man and woman. Nattiez was researching on *mbaga* wedding dance of the Baganda and as methodological approach he gave a lecture to Makerere University music students and lecturers. According to the Ugandan dance scholar, the definition of drums as man and woman was a mere construction, "a problem typical of foreign scholars." He said, "I have done great research on *mbaga* dance, but I have never found such a thing [the concept of man and woman drums]." Nattiez was challenged mainly because he was a 'foreign' scholar; the Ugandan scholar could not provide empirical evidence for his argument against the gendering of the Kiganda drums. And yet, my own research had already revealed the concept of man and woman drums existed among the Baganda, especially in the palace quarters (In Chapter Four and Five, I gives the detailed discussion). Although it is true that the Ugandan dance scholar had done some research on the wedding dance, it was mainly informal experience and not documented. Moreover, he claimed that he did the research in the 1960s, a period when issues about gender were not considered as important. [3] And yet, the nature of questions we ask in the field greatly affect the research outcomes.

Further, at an SEM (Society for Ethnomusicology) conference in 2000, some scholars criticized me for making a joint paper presentation on *mbaga* wedding music and dance with Jean-Jacques Nattiez, a supposedly "foreign" scholar. These scholars, who happened to be researchers of their own music cultures, argued that Nattiez had no right to make the claims he presented. That, I was better placed to make the same arguments, since it was my culture that Nattiez was discussing and after all, I had also done the research. Some of these critics interpreted it as a colonial legacy, while others understood it as a man-dominance syndrome. In my opinion, our collaborative research and thus this paper presentation enhanced a better understanding of the Kiganda wedding music and dance. Nattiez's semiotic analysis and my cultural analysis of the wedding music and dance contributed to a better access of meaning in mbaga dance, as a result of which is a joint publication (Nannyonga-Tamusuza and Nattiez 2003).

These dialogic exchanges transformed my thinking about the field, and what baakisimba actually means in Buganda society. From this stance, I propose to redefine the "field" as a dialogic space for research where people interact with the aim of understanding themselves and others better and then to communicate this knowledge to a wider audience. My definition deconstructs the notion of outsiders and insiders and circumscribes a more embracing and interactive space, one where there is collaborative interaction between so-called outsiders and insiders. I believe there is information that I gathered just because I am a Muganda and there is also information that I may have not accessed because I am a Muganda.

FIELDWORK: NEGOTIATING IDENTITIES IN THE FIELD

The ethnography of baakisimba revealed to me that fieldwork is a process of negotiating identities, some of which I went with in the field, while others were acquired as I interacted with the people whose lives I studied. I had always to deal with issues of ethnic, gender, class, social and racial identities. The ways in which I negotiated these identities affected not only the kind of questions I asked and analyses of the data I collected, but also the relations that I built with the people I studied during the field and thereafter. A full awareness of my identities and a quick adaptation to new ones, especially those that were both ethical and necessary to bridging the gap between my informants and me, were very important for the success of my fieldwork. As a female student, teacher, performer and observer of baakisimba, and occupying a position of power over my informants as a woman of higher university education and belonging to the Baganda ethnicity, I was aware of the possible bias in my data collection as well as its analysis. I cannot deny the fact that my own participation in dance and teaching experiences shaped some of the questions that I asked; however, I was greatly aware of the limitation of my experience. In order to collect representative data, I had to map out a strategy before and during the fieldwork. I had always to be aware of my own views and how they could influence my data. Philip V. Bohlman constantly reminded me that fieldwork "requires that we be prepared at all times for the unexpected and for the fluidity of experience" (1997: 141). My training in drama (during my first degree at Makerere University) enabled me to switch to new characters or recreate new identities whenever the need arose.

The most challenge I had was to become a researcher. One can never realize how hard it is to research a culture that one thought he or she knew because he or she belonged to it, and to research a dance that one had performed for sixteen years and taught for ten years. I had to learn to be a student, one who had never performed baakisimba, in order to be open to the training and information that was available to me. I had to behave as if I did not know how to dance in order to understand the training and learning process and to experience a new approach to learning the dance. I had to make my teachers believe that although I may have seen the dance before, and probably admired some good dancers; I had never performed the dance myself. The whole process of being a researcher was a challenge and I needed to remain "in character" throughout the training and performance sessions. The impersonation of a dance student may raise ethical questions, since researchers are supposed to be open to their informants about their intentions in the field. However, my intent was clear; I wanted to relearn baakisimba in order to come to a better understanding of the dance and its connection with the Baganda's gender conceptualization. Although I was a baakisimba dancer before I went to the field, learning is an ongoing process. Moreover, I had never had the opportunity to question why I was taught to move in a particular way in baakisimba performance. For example, I had never questioned why movement in baakisimba is concentrated in the waist rather than in any other parts of the body; and why women were the assigned dancers and men the drummers. In order to address the questions this book set out to discuss, I had to impersonate a student in order to relearn baakisimba.

And yet, it was difficult for the informants who had seen me perform baakisimba on stage to accept me as a student, a researcher. They knew me as a dancer and on a number of occasions, I was handed a dance skirt during the research sessions with a suggestion for me to join the dancing (see plate 1).

Plate 1. The researcher performing (right) with the informants. Courtesy of Jean-Jacques Nattiez.

However much I tried to reject the identity of a baakisimba dancer, I was reminded that I was one of them. While keeping faithful to my student identity and research role, I performed with them not only as an entertainer, one of the apparent roles of these dancers, but as a researcher with the aim of getting more information. Since my performance was to enhance my understanding of baakisimba, I had to perform with a "researcher's observational-eye."

Moreover, being a woman was not only an advantage to accessing gendered information from fellow women, especially relating to men's dominant position, but also a challenge. It was not always safe for me to go to the field alone, especially since a number of performances were at night. Having

Ssaalongo Tamusuza, my husband, with me at the overnight wedding sessions was not only for "protection," but offered me credibility as a woman of respect. How can a woman move at night alone, without a man, her "protector"? Moreover, my two research assistants were all men, partly for the related reason, but also because of their abilities. And yet, some men could not give certain information, because I was a woman; I had to go through some male informants to get such information. And yet, holding a video camera or an audio recorder was a recreation of my gender identity. At one of the wedding ceremonies, I was the only woman with a video camera among about five cameramen. I saw some of the members of the audience pointing at, and commenting about me. One woman said, "My dear, she is holding a camera like a man. A woman should sit down and not move around like a man" ("maama akutte kamera yenna alinga omusajja. Omukazi yeetaaga naatuula si kwe wuubawuuba atyo ng'omusajja"). To this person, to hold a camera is to be a man.

While my privileged position as an indigenous scholar enabled access to some emotional and intimate perspectives of my culture, some social and cultural constraints hampered the ability to transform some of my observations into ethnomusicological knowledge of how baakisimba is connected with the gender constructions of the Baganda. Some situations were very challenging and I had to make quick decisions. Sometimes, I had to take a break for some days and later resume the research. It was most striking when I went to the palaces (*mbiri*) and the kings' tombs (*masiro*). The first constraint was my Christian faith. In a number of cases, the environment in which I worked contradicted my faith as a Christian. For instance, one attendant to the sacred twin-house (*ennyumba ya balongo*) of the Ssekabaka Wamala was refusing to give me information and accused me of being a "Christian spying the pagans." When I was baptized in the Catholic Church, I denounced all cultural rituals and indeed those associated with twins, those related to the veneration of any other gods, besides the God of the Catholic Church. By introducing my self as "Sylvia Nannyonga," the informant could certainly determine that I was a Christian because "Sylvia" is considered as one of the Christian names among the Buganda. It was only after I told him that I was a *nnaalongo* (mother of twins) that he became relaxed with me, but accused me of not have mentioned that I was a *nnaalongo* immediately.[4] In order to get information from him, I had to denounce that I was a Christian, an act that made me very uncomfortable until I reconciled with my God.

On another occasion, while at King Kyabaggu's tombs, my informant talked to people (probably ancestral spirits) I could not see whenever I asked him questions. He would look up to the sky and then his eyes become wide and begin to roll. I became afraid when he asked me "Do you know why you are researching the drum? You may not know now, but you will know later" ("*omanyi lwaki onoonyereza ku ngoma? Toyinza kukitegeera kati, naye olikimanya edda*") (anonymous, interview). Was I going to be involved with Kiganda spiritualism, which I denounced since as a child when I was baptized in the Catholic Church? What if I get possessed with the spirits? And yet, before this research session, an informant had informed me that all the Baganda are connected with their ancestral spirits and can get possessed if they get involved in rituals or activities that involve evoking these spirits. She had narrated how a student who was performing a Kiganda worship song at a schools' festival got possessed while on stage. This time, the challenge was to get possessed and loose my role as a researcher because I was not ready to denounce my God again. For sure, once possessed, I would not have understood what was going on, which meant I would have needed someone else to research on me, instead.

During one of our field trips, Nattiez challenged me whether as a Christian I would participate in the promotion of traditional worship music since one of the roles of an ethnomusicologist is to promote all music as being good (Merriam 1964: 8). My stand was clear, I only wanted to be a researcher, but not an activist for traditional worship music. By being a researcher, I could escape confronting this worship music since researchers can set boundaries of their research. As a matter of fact, Nattiez had wanted us to examine how baakisimba music and dance functions in worship music, since my scope did not include sacred contexts of baakisimba performance. I could not do the field research with him, but I will collaborate in the analysis of data for a joint project. It is important to note, therefore, that much as one has to take on a character of a researcher, one cannot denounce completely her or his original identities. Although, I continuously tried to convince myself that my research was separate from my faith, I was always confronted with whom actually I am, a Catholic. It was a challenge to come to terms with these conflicting identities. I could not pretend, because while I was a researcher, I still remained a Christian.

Further, being a researcher was a challenge because, in a number of cases, I took the field experiences personally; my field tended to extend in the day-to-day of my life. It was somewhat difficult to determine where and when the field began and when and where my private life began since all experiences were important to my research. The field experiences were similar to my day-to-day experiences as a Muganda woman. However, as a researcher, I had to look at my culture with a more critical "lens," than before I became a researcher. The issues that affected me most were related with gender constructions. For instance, how would I classify the experience when I observed the dominance of a male relative during a graduation party of my niece? On another occasion, one young man (about seventeen years old) said, "all women are stupid. My mother is stupid too. That is my reason why I support that men should control the women." It was even harder since I could not impose my views. It was more stressing when I shared these views with relatives, both men and women outside the field context, who somewhat seemed to endorse these views. One of them said "nnaalongo, much as I agree with you, you cannot change our society; that is what has been in place since time immemorial." Of course, when I shared my frustrations, I was not intending to change the Ganda society; I was only seeking some consolation. In another instance, while attending a graduation party with Ssaalongo Tamusuza, my husband, I was introduced as his "minister for home affairs." It was most disappointing that much as I was Tamusuza's wife, I had been invited at this party as one of the lecturers of the graduand. In this case, the non-indigenous researcher may be better off than me. He or she would probably not take the field experiences as personally as I did, since these experiences are only data materials and may not be translated in personal life. Besides, he or she does not directly confront these experiences once he or she goes back home after research. Yet, non-indigenous researchers enter the field with no attachment or less attachment to what is happening in the field. As such, they may not take the field experiences personally.

The other challenge I faced was my identity as a Muganda. One would imagine that being a Muganda, I would have access to information about the palace and other cultural sites. Although I had made all the necessary arrangements to visit Mengo Palace, for the first four months of my research, I could not enter the palace. However, when Gerhard Kubik, a German/Austrian anthropologist and renowned scholar of Kiganda music, requested to visit the palace when he came to Uganda in February 2000, he was openly accepted. Ironically, I was allowed into the palace as Kubik's interpreter. I kept asking myself whether the people we talked to in the palace were not aware that I was hearing what they were saying. Was my presence ignored because they took me to be an "interpreting machine" that did not understand anything? I had to accept this identity. Meddie Musisi and Angel Lubowa have reported the *Bazzukulu ba Buganda* ("grand children of Buganda," the core of Baganda conservatives) as saying "we want the palace to have secrets, but not anybody to visit it, which may take away its honor" ("olubiri lwetaaga okubaamu ebyama sso ssi buli muntu kukyalayo, ekiyinza okulumalako ekitiibwa") (2000:2). While I respect that secrets must be kept in the palace, I felt there were double standards. Why is it that such secrets are open to other people and not me, a fellow Muganda? I wondered if this behavior was part of the colonial legacy. Do the Baganda still consider the "white" man as the master, one they have to please, as was the case in colonial times? One should not misunderstand me as someone complaining about Kubik's access to the palace; rather, I aim to illustrate that being an indigenous scholar does not necessarily guarantee access to knowledge of one's culture.

In a similar situation, Alphonse Tierou, a choreographer and researcher from Cote d'Ivoire, relates to this colonial legacy as follows:

> Africans do not trust Africans. Whites enjoy more consideration and are given more resources than blacks. . . . In 1987, during a lecture tour in black Africa, I was arrested in one country and brought before the ministry of youth, sports, culture and scientific research, which considered my speech on African culture suspicious. At the end of the prolonged interrogation, a white man walked into the office. He spoke out on my behalf. The minister immediately changed his tone. After a few phone calls, he opened doors for me to all the media while the most beautiful conference hall in the city, the place used by the country's sole political party, was placed at my disposal (quoted in Sopova 2000:43).

In my situation, Kubik had to "introduce" me to the palace before the palace gates could be opened for me. And when the gates were opened, I was then able to interview a number of *bambowa* (royal guards) and *bazaana* (female servants of the palace). Moreover, I had the honor of formally being invited to the Kabaka Mutebi II's seventh coronation anniversary (see appendix 3). Further, the first time I visited the Kasubi tombs, I was never allowed to take any pictures. However, when I visited the tombs again with David Wylie, a friend from Ireland, I was even allowed to make a video recording. I was only forbidden from taking pictures of the drums because I was a woman. My gender conflicted with the rules of the culture, yet Wylie, although foreign to the Kiganda culture, was allowed to take the pictures on my behalf because he was a man[5] (in Chapter Four, I discuss the taboos associated with women and drums).

On the one hand, being a *nnaalongo,* a mother of twins, my prescribed cultural immunity that enables mothers of twins to surpass cultural taboos (in this case, taboos related to discussing sex and gender relations), empowered me to discuss issues that may be sensitive to any Muganda who does not have this immunity. On a number of occasions, informants only opened up when I told them that I was a mother of twins. For instance, when I asked one informant why men enjoy women dancing, he was too shy to answer me. However, when I told him that I was a mother of twins and that he needed not to be shy, he was able to open up. He said, "you should have told me immediately that you are Nnaalongo! You see, I can never be vulgar to a Nnaalongo; parents of twins are free to speak and hear any obscenity." On the other hand, the nnaalongo identity was a challenge not only as I did research, but also as I translated my field experience on paper for a wider audience. First of all, the language in which some informants spoke to me, at times, was very vulgar. Listening to replays of recordings of these interviews was somehow embarrassing. I could not even give these recordings to my research assistant to transcribe. Much as I am a nnaalongo, I had never experience such vulgar. As I write, I wrestle with how to present these experiences, important as they are, without making my readers, some of whom are my relatives and fellow Christians, doubt my identity as a moralist. However, I have to recall my recreated identity as a researcher, who must report ethically my field experiences.

Doing fieldwork within one's own culture and, in some cases, among one's friends and relatives is particularly sensitive. Through the clan structure, I was related in one way or another to a number of the people I interacted with in the field. Anybody from *nakisinge* (a brown grass-finch) clan was either my brother, paternal uncle, sister, niece, nephew, or a paternal aunt. Any one from the *ngabi* (antelope) clan (my mother's clan) was either a cousin, a maternal uncle, or aunt and anyone from the *ngeye* clan (my husband and children's clan), was my son, daughter, or an in-law. For instance, Sulaiti Kalungi, a celebrated drummer, could not hold my hand or accept anything handed to him by me. He shares the same clan as my husband, and at his age, he considered himself a father-in-law to me. Among the Baganda, a father-in-law is not supposed to touch or look into the eyes of his son's wife. And yet, these relations carried benefits as well as responsibilities, which went beyond the fieldwork expedition. Because I belong to the *nakinsige* clan, Peter Ggayira, one of my informants, considered me his mother, since his mother belonged to my clan. To Ggayira, I was not a researcher, but his mother. This relationship enabled me to access as much information as possible from him and he introduced me to many other musicians. However, when Ggayira introduced me to his children as their grandmother, they took it formally. Even to date, they expect me to perform roles of a grandmother. In this case, fieldwork was not a mere academic adventure, but also an experience of rediscovering lost extended family members.

DATA COLLECTION

The need to critically understand a dance and music culture that I thought I knew, but did not understand, called for specific methodological tools. The methodological tools used in the collection of this data included: 1) participant-observation; 2) music and dance performance 3) formal and conversational interviews; 4) photography, video, and audio recordings; and 5) documentary research. While the tools that I chose are to a greater extent the standard tools for most ethnomusicological expedition, as an indigenous scholar, I had to redefine some of them to suit my situation.

As Paul Atkinson and Martyn Hammersley have argued, "in a sense *all* [their emphasis] social research is a form of participant observation, because we can not study the social world without being part of it" (1998: 111). More emphatically, Gerard Béhague has contended that, "a possible hierarchy of levels of meaning and of structure cannot be elucidated through observation alone but through various degrees of participation" (1984: 9). As such, I attended training and rehearsal sessions and performances of baakisimba in the various contexts. My research involved attending schools' music and dance competitions as an adjudicator as well as an observer. The schools I was invited to included Mengo Senior Secondary School (Kyaddondo county), a Protestant-founded school; Ndejje Senior Secondary School (Bulemeezi county), also a Protestant-founded school; and Kawempe Muslim Senior Secondary School; I also attended music and dance competitions at Makerere College School; St Lawrence high School and Mukono District Music and Dance Competitions, where a number of schools were featured (Kyaddondo county). It was important for this study to share views with the other adjudicators on the criteria used to judge baakisimba performance at school competitions. Further, I attended a performance at St. Kizito Senior Secondary School Bethany (in Busujju county), a school run by religious sisters. In this case, I was a full-time observer. In all these contexts, baakisimba was one of the dances among a variety of representative dances from other ethnic groups of Uganda.

I also attended a number of church functions, especially the Catholic masses and carol services, where baakisimba performance predominate the music repertoire. Notable of these functions was the commissioning ceremonies for two religious sister's congregations, and two carol services performed by the Catholic Centenary Memorial Choir (CACEMCHO), Rubaga Cathedral Choir, and three church weddings. Most important was the celebration of the Uganda Catholic Martyrs' Day on 3 June 2000. Baakisimba music and dance performance featured significantly at this celebration, which drew Catholics from all over the world. Further, on 5 August 2000, the Baganda celebrated the seventh coronation anniversary of Kabaka Ronald Muwenda Mutebi II. I had the opportunity to study the preparations and celebratory performances involved in royal settings. In all these performance contexts, which were in Mawokota County, baakisimba music and dance were part of the repertoire. I attended seven wedding ceremonies with representation of both rural and urban settings (in Kyaddondo, Mawokota, and Butambala counties). I also attended four graduation parties, one in Busujju County and the others in Kyaddondo County (see appendix 4 for events attended).

In addition to attending formal performances during ceremonial celebrations, school functions and church contexts, I organized "out-of-context" performances. I commissioned musicians and dancers to perform baakisimba outside the usual performance contexts. These performances were useful "for bringing forth and clarifying certain aspects of musical performance practices, generally not as readily obtainable in the natural context" (Béhague 1984:9). It was possible to interrupt the performances and ask questions that where important to the understanding of many concepts of baakisimba.

Emphasizing the importance of the performance as an approach to understanding music (as well as dance), Charles Keil and Steven Feld have noted, "In order to understand what any musician [and dancer are] doing, you have to have done some of it yourself" (1994:29). Moreover, just listening to the music or watching the dance alone, "won't let you connect to the music or the other people" (ibid.). Therefore, I involved myself in baakisimba music and dance training sessions as well as stage performances in schools and village contexts. I met with my dance teacher Hajati Madina Nakintu of Bazannya n'Engo Cultural Group of Kasangati in Kyaddondo County twice a week for two months and each training session lasted for three hours. I chose Hajati Nakintu not only because of her expertise, and the fact that she was recognized as a good dancer in the area, but also because she had other students with whom I could train. Moreover, she was willing to take me as a dance student, an opportunity not offered by many dancers. Further, she had been trained by an aunt, a former court dancer, who introduced her to the dance styles of the palace. Equally important was the fact that the ensemble that Hajati Nakintu directed was actively involved in performances at wedding contexts. As such, I had the opportunity to perform once with her group. Since she had a full-fledged ensemble, her drummers also became my drum teachers, most notably, Peter Lubwama. I also had further training in drumming by Augustino Kisitu, a former court drummer of Kitenga (Buddu county), whom I met three times for three hours each session.

It is important to explain the difference between performance as a research tool and performance as an artistic skill. The aim of my performance was not to show how experienced a dancer or a musician I had become, but to experience how it feels to be a dancer and a musician in a particular performance context. At the same time, as a performing researcher, I had to watch out for the audience's interpretations of my performance and that of my fellow performers. When dancing and making music for the purpose of understanding baakisimba, I had to perform with a "researcher's eye" during the training and performance sessions. I had to be a student; my prior experience as dancer did not count; I performed only what I was instructed to do. I was no longer a teacher to any students, not even one who had ever choreographed a dance, but a learner and a faithful one too. I had to "behave" as a learner in order to understand the teaching and learning process and to see how the "village" musicians teach, since I had learned baakisimba mainly in a school setting. To become a student was to accept the benefits (of learning) as well as the responsibilities; I had to accept all my teacher's reprimand. For instance, she would hit my feet when she became impatient with my incorrect footwork. Moreover, in all my training sessions, I had to dress in full costume. My teacher had to make sure I knew the proper way of dressing for the dance and insisted that I had to buy the full costume before we could begin the training. Although I did not like to dress up in a petticoat (slip), I had to put it on for learning purposes. When I suggested to use a T-shirt, she refused and said, "T-shirts are for school dance, but if you want to learn the 'real' dancing, you have to dress like the real dancers." These training sessions reminded me of another teacher, who during a research trip in 1995 hit my ankles because I was lifting my feet; yet I was dancing the palace baakisimba where I was only supposed to shuffle. However, as an indigenous performing researcher, I had to be careful not to impose my views about baakisimba dance and music onto the people I was researching, least I researched and reported only my own views about the baakisimba. The informants who knew that I was a university lecturer expected me to share the information I knew about baakisimba. For each question I asked them, they also wanted to hear my opinion. Although the notion of approaching a culture with distance is being criticized by ethnomusicologists and "is not available at all to the native researcher who is him- or herself a product and member of that culture in question" (Chiener 2002:481), it was always important for me to remember that I was out there to learn more about what the informants had to offer, but not to "preach" what I knew about baakisimba. It was only during the data analysis that I shared my opinion, not so much to show how much I knew about baakisimba, but to check my interpretations of what I had gathered.

Further, I had to be careful not to have a strong attachment to a particular performing group because the politics between groups would have affected accessibility to important data. Indeed, researchers should avoid getting entangled with the conflicts between rivalry groups. I made a mistake and mentioned to one performing group that I was going to meet its rivalry, which I did not know. The members of the group become very cold to me and did not want to give me any more information. At first, I could not understand why they all over sudden became cold until I was later informed that they were rivaling with the group I had mentioned I was to meet. In fact, each group accused the other of witchcraft. Their rivalry was so great that the two groups can never perform together at the same function. When I went to the other group, I made sure that I did not tell the group that I had met with their rivalry group before.

The performance tool was not only important during data collection, but also during analysis. I found the performance tool particularly important during the analysis and transcription of the dance motifs. It was easier for me to transcribe a motif that I could perform. At this point, my video recordings became my teachers; I would learn a motif from video replays before I began transcribing them. Similarly, I first performed all the music excerpts before I put them on paper.

In addition to performance, I conducted interviews with performers and patrons of baakisimba, as well as with scholars in related fields including gender studies, linguistics, and sociology at Makerere University in Uganda. I was careful not to be trapped into limiting my research to only the "formally-resourceful informants." Many researchers have tended to concentrate on interviewing people who are supposed to possess specialized cultural knowledge, often disregarding the ordinary people's views. In addition to focus on male-oriented music, men have been the core groups of informants that many scholars of Kiganda music have interviewed. While it is true that women have greatly contributed to the richness of Kiganda music culture, in many of their writings, Gerhard Kubik (1960, 1968, 1969), Lois Anderson (1968, 1984), Catherine Gray (1993, 1995), and James Makubuya (1995) never quoted any female informant. When I asked Gerhard Kubik why he never included female informants in all his publications, he told me that during his fieldwork visits in Uganda, women concerned themselves mainly with issues of hospitality. However, he agrees that he never paid particular attention to dance music where women performed as dancers.[6] In my case, I took everyone as potentially resourceful, so I considered as resourceful whomever I was able to communicate with; I interviewed and conversed with them freely (see appendix 5).[7] However, this is not to suggest that all informants' contributions had the same weight. Depending on the age and experience of the informants, some were more knowledgeable and their contributions were very valuable.

As a member of the Buganda society with good knowledge of the language and the culture of the Baganda, I was in a privileged position to communicate with the people. While some researchers have found closed-ended and structured interviews useful in the collection of data, I used open-ended and non-structured interviews. A trial with closed-ended and structured interviews at the beginning of the research proved unsuccessful. Such interviews limited the informants' answers. I resorted to open-ended questions, but focusing on specific themes of the study. I had initially planned to conduct some questionnaires particularly important when seeking views of the elite audience, but it turned out to be unsuccessful; instead, I intensified my interviews. Further, Informal conversations (which I call "conversational-interviews") in taxis, market places, and on the street provided important information, especially when people were suspicious of formal interviews. In most cases, these were people whose views were important for my generalization about gender, yet the environment, which they were in was not conducive to formal interviews. Related to interviews was field note writing. I had to be careful not to take any data for granted. Being an indigenous researcher, one may tend to write only those observation that he or she thinks are important and those he or she does not know or ideas one thinks he or she might forget. These researchers tend to forget that after the research they have to report not only the new things they have discovered, but also those things that are important to the research, that they might have known before they went to the field.

In addition, I gave a paper presentation on gender and baakisimba for students and faculty members of Makerere University's departments of political science, gender and women studies, sociology, and music, dance, and drama. The discussion after the presentation gave me insights into some important questions I had not originally focused on. One important issue that was raised was the interpretation of homosexuality when males perform baakisimba, presumably a women's dance.

The other tool I used was video and audio recording sessions in and out of performance contexts as well as still photography. I did the recording mostly during sessions when I was attending performances; in other instances, especially when I was performing or conducting interviews, I had to engage the services of Lawrence Ssekalegga and Bosco Mwase, my research assistants. I had to train them, but each had advantages because of their prior training. Ssekalegga was a second year bachelor-of-music degree (BMus) student at Makerere University in Uganda. Since he was a music student and himself a performer of baakisimba (drummer), Ssekalegga was an ideal research assistant. Mwase was a first year bachelor-of-technology (mechanical engineering) student also at Makerere University, and had a good knowledge of the recording equipment, which enabled us to work together easily.

Mass-mediated programs—radio, pre-recorded tapes and TV programs (especially "Omubala" on Wavamunno Broadcasting Services [WBS])—formed part of my data collection. These programs aim at reviving the "traditional" forum in which the Baganda used to discuss issues that concerned them. The themes that were discussed included gender relations, clan systems and the upbringing of children, among others.

Since my study involved examining how baakisimba is a central part of the social, historical, political and cultural environments of Buganda, the other tool was library documentation. My knowledge of Luganda enabled me to read historical documents by indigenous writers. Most important of these out-of-print writings include Apollo Kaggwa (1912a, 1912b, 1952); J. M. T. Ggomotoka (1934); Ham Mukasa (1938); B. M. Zimbe (1939), Kizito Tobi (1915a; 1915b). Although none of these studies focus specifically on gender in Buganda, they provided important historical evidence for this study.

DATA ANALYSIS

Throughout the analysis of data and writing of this book, I struggled over which aspects to be deleted and which ones to retain since some aspects of my study may not be favorable to some people. One of the most challenging discussions in this book that I had to negotiate whether to include it or not, was the section on homosexuality. Like many other African cultures, there is an outright denial of the existence homosexuality in Buganda. In fact, even asking about the subject is equally a social deviance. A number of informants could not believe that I was asking them about homosexuality. As a matter of fact, some Baganda friends and colleagues asked me to skip the homosexual section because they thought it was not politically correct. Should I delete those portions that draw unfavorable comments or conclusions about gender and sex in Buganda and yet, are important to this study? Would I be able to give the final versions of the study to my informants to read and make comments before the publication of this book? Would I still publish a study that is relevant to the field and yet not compromise myself or my informants, my actual relatives, especially where gender is a very sensitive subject in

Buganda? These are some of the questions I struggled with as I did the research, analyzed the data, and I write this book. However, Kay Kaufman Shelemay is always reminding me that as a researcher, I have to "honor confidence and protect it when necessary, but be equally ready to acknowledge and celebrate individual expertise and artistry when they are freely and openly given" (1997:201). My informants had divided opinions about whether I should or should not quote them in my writing. In some instances, some informants did not allow me to record certain information; they would ask me to turn off my tape recorder. However, some people did not mind me recording them and did not care if I wrote about everything they said as long as I did not mention their names. Others trusted that I would find a better way of presenting the information without implicating them. In deciding whom to quote directly, I was guided by the particular informant's consent, while for others I used my personal judgment. As a result, there is data presented in this book where the source is anonymous. All the priests and religious sisters and brothers that I interviewed requested anonymity.

In order to present the variety of Baganda's perspectives on how baakisimba dance music articulates with gender, I used a dialectical approach, as an art of debate and discussion to analyze my data. As John Blacking has argued, "The analysis of meaning can be achieved only by a dialectic between 'informants' and 'analysts,' in which there is a confrontation of two kinds of technical knowledge and experience, and 'informants' share in the intellectual process of analysis" (1995:233). The relationship between informants—musicians, dancers, patrons, scholars, and the Baganda, in general—and the researcher or "analyst" is crucial to bringing meaning to the baakisimba "text." Being a Muganda and a performer, my voice joins with those of other Baganda people, while at the same time, as a researcher or "the outsider" (my performative identity); I contribute an intellectual analysis to baakisimba discourse. As a result, I did both in-field analysis and after-field analysis. With the in-field analysis, the on-going analysis as I collected the data, I tested my own analysis of the data through formal and conversational interviews. I gathered views about my own interpretation of the data, which has contributed to a more balanced analysis of the data. My academic knowledge worked "in a dialectical tension with the popular knowledge of the [Baganda] people to produce a more profound understanding of [baakisimba and gender relations in Buganda]" (Reason 1998:270). After-field analysis involved critical evaluation of the in-field analysis as well as consulting other scholars, for more evidence and comparison, on related subjects of the study. This book presents an analysis, which includes my own interpretations as well as those gathered through a dialectical interaction with my informants, teachers, and relatives, the Baganda people. Further, the presentation of this data is based on an inductive analysis, whereby the categories, themes and patterns of this study emerged from the data. Throughout this book, I clearly show my own interpretations, presenting the discussions about my views, and those of fellow Baganda. As a result, in a number of cases, I let my informants speak to readers with their voices in Luganda. I make more or less direct translations in order to capture the tone of the informants. As such, while the intended meaning is evident, some translations have English grammatical errors.

Chapter Three

Conceptualization of Baakisimba Music and Dance

ORIGINS OF BAAKISIMBA

The origin of baakisimba is important to my discussion because it fore-grounds the historical contexts in which baakisimba was performed, provid-ing a point of departure for the analysis of change in baakisimba. Likewise, Hanna has emphasized, "dance is 'read' in light of knowledge of the histori-cal development of the dance genre and other expectations and experiences that color a participant's perception and interpretation" (1983: 17). Like the origin of Buganda, the origin of baakisimba is speculative. Some informants suggested that baakisimba performance began outside the palace before being introduced into the palace while others are convinced that baakisimba began in the palace before being introduced outside the palace by the *badongo ba kabaka* (the king's musicians and dancers). Moreover, no specific periodization can be attached to the origin of baakisimba.

Those who believed that baakisimba began outside the palace asserted that it developed at a beer party after the attendants had eaten *matooke* (cooked bananas) and drunk *mwenge bigere* (local beer, made out of bananas). They contended that baakisimba was created as a symbol of appre-ciation to the person who planted the bananas from which food and beer were prepared. In this case, dancing and celebration are linked to the origin and discourse of baakisimba. In Buganda, provision of food and beer is a very important gesture of hospitality. Roscoe reported that "Beer drinking was common, and many chiefs and peasants spent a large portion of their time, when not at war or actively engaged upon business, in talking and drinking from morning until night" (1911: 24). The Baganda's saying that "one who goes away hungry will never come back" *("olugenda enjala terudda"*) is actually taken literally. Moreover, the idea that baakisimba may have developed at a feast is accentuated by one of the onomatopoeic phrasing for the basic rhythm of baakisimba music as beaten on the *mbuutu*, the basic drum. The term "baakisimba" which may be translated as "they planted it," is a short form of the phrase "abaakisimba ekitooke" ("those who planted the banana plantation"). "Abaakisimba ekitooke" is one of the onomatopoeic phrase or words on which sound of the *mbuutu* is based and many of the other *bisoko* (*sing. kisoko*), motifs of baakisimba are variations derived from this basic sound.

Like other African music (see, for instance, Nketia 1974:177–188), Kiganda music is deeply rooted in the language of its practitioners. Although genres of purely Kiganda instrumental music exist, no genre is independent of text; in any music, there is some text in play. As Peter Cooke has also agreed, "no musicologist can study Ganda instrumental music and practice for long—if he [or she] lives in that region—before discovering that all the instrumental pieces he [or she] hears are, in fact, renderings of vocal compositions or are, in the case of drumming, inseparably bound up with song and other forms of speech communication" (1970:62). Luganda is a tonal language with three pitch levels, low, medium, and high and is rhythmic. In the case of baakisimba music, the *mbuutu* simulates different sounds of Luganda pitch levels if the drummer beats the corresponding rhythms, adapts the appropriate hand postures, and beats the drum in the proper position. Moreover, the timbre of the drum sounds depends on the parts of the hand used to beat the drum. When the whole palm hits the drum, a vibrating sound is heard, while hitting with only the fingers produces a sharp slap-like-percussive sound. Other sounds can be produced including a "scratchy" sound and "crackling" sounds, by scratching and slapping the drumhead, respectively. The combination of distinct pitches, timbres, and rhythmic patterns produces a non-verbal imitation of the set text. Similarly, any music set to a Kiganda text must relate rhythmically and melodically to the intonation of the text or words when spoken, if the intended meaning is to be achieved (Nanyonga 1995:16–17).

While the Western staff notation is inadequate for transcribing non-Western music (see Seeger 1958; Nettl 1964; and Hood 1971), I adopt it to illustrate the deep-seated relationship between Luganda language and Kiganda music. However, through out this book, the aim of these transcriptions is to provide a relative, but not a precise, representation of baakisimba drum music and dance. This visual representation of sound only facilitates my discussion. Different sounds are produced depending on how and where the drum is beaten. The tones of the drum gradually become higher as one beats the drum away from the center. Further, different hand gestures on the drum produce specific tone qualities. I have isolated four basic hand gestures: 1) "muting," dropping the palm heavily and pressing hard in the center; 2) "banging," dropping the whole palm heavily on the drum without pressing, so that the drum head vibrates; 3) "scratching," dropping heavily the fingers while scratching either in the center or on the side of the drum; and 4) "slapping," lightly hitting the drum on the sides. The slapping gesture is most predominant when beating the *ngalabi*. Figure 4, shows the symbols I use in the graphic representation of the sound produced on the drum with these hand gestures.

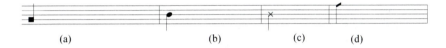

(a)   (b)   (c)   (d)

Figure 4. Drum notational symbols: a) muted sound; b) banged sound; c) scratched sound; and d) slapped sound.

The placement of these symbols on the staff is not fixed; it varies depending on the relative pitch of different drums. When notating more than one drum with varying pitches the positions of the muted (low) and banged, scratched, slapped sounds (high pitches) change. However, if one beats in the center of the same drum, a muted sound has the lowest pitch, the banged and scratched sounds are relatively at the same pitch level, and the slapped and scratched drum on the sides sounds higher.

In figure 5, I illustrate the speech intonation of the phrase, "abaakisimba ekitooke" as verbalized and the relative sound when beaten on the *mbuutu*.

Figure 5. Speech and mbuutu drum sound of "abaakisimba ekitooke".

The top staff is for the speech intonation, while the lower staff indicates the *mbuutu* drum rhythm. I use a three-line staff to indicate the three levels of speech intonation in Luganda. In this notation and throughout this book, I use 6/8 meter. Listening to baakisimba music one immediately hears a unit of six beats with a strong accent on every first beat and a slight emphasis on every fourth beat. However, the audience (or the chorus, in the case of the school context) claps on every first and fourth beats of this six-beat unit, which may suggest a 3/8 meter. Although both are compound meters, I am inclined to 6/8 because the baakisimba basic drum motif is completed within six beats. Although meters of 6/4 and 6/16 are also possible, I use 6/8 because it is easier to read. The use of the meter for the speech intonation should not imply that the Baganda speak in strict meter; I use it for the purpose of illustration to align the speech with the metered sound of the drum.

As shown in figure 5, in addition to replicating the rhythms of the text, the pitch contour of the drum follows closely that of the text. The drummer achieves a similar contour by alternating between muting, banging, and scratching the center or the side of the *mbuutu*. The muted sound of the drum tends to produce sounds that are relatively lower than the banged or scratched sounds. Without this timbre differentiation, the different tones would not be produced on the drum. The combination of the rhythm, pitch, and timbre of the *mbuutu* simulates the intonation of "abaakisimba ekitooke" and hence, the drum, like music is called baakisimba. In addition, the *kubiibya,* the basic dance motif for baakisimba, imitates the symbolic planting, maintenance, and harvest of the banana plant as well as the cooking of *matooke* (bananas) and preparation of *mwenge bigere* (local beer). I discuss this dance motif and its relation to food production in Chapter Five.

Further evidence to support the claim that baakisimba may have originated at a beer party includes numerous Kiganda proverbs that contextualize dancing in general. Most well known among these proverbs is "akajenjegule akazinya atanywa mwenge [meaning that] lack of reserve that makes one who does not drink to dance" (Walser 1982: 17, no. 0171). In this case, dancing and drinking beer are inseparable. Specific to baakisimba, a Kiganda proverb that states "ekiwumbya engalabi: guba mwenge kubula [meaning that] what makes the ngalabi drum rot, is scarcity of beer [;] no beer, no dance" (Walser, 1982: 129–130, no. 1422), reaffirms associations of drinking beer, drumming, and dancing in Buganda.[1] Considering that baakisimba may have started at a festival of *mwenge bigere* and the eating of *matooke,* it stands to reason that baakisimba can only be as old as the *kitooke* (banana plant) in Buganda. One of the theories about the origin of bananas proposes that Ssekabaka Kintu brought the fruit seven hundred years ago (Wainwright

1952: 146–147; Cooke 1996: 1). The other theory is that Kintu found the bananas already existing in Buganda and that it was only during his reign that the bananas were discovered. For instance, Blazio Kalyango, one of the elders I met at Ssekabaka Kintu's tombs, said that Nnambi, the legendary Kintu's wife, discovered the banana fruit in the forest one day. When she roasted it and gave it to her husband, Kintu liked it very much and it quickly became a staple of the Baganda's regular menu. Kalyango claims that more kinds of bananas were discovered in the forest and that they were put to different uses depending on their taste. Some bananas were chosen for making beer, others to be eaten while ripe, and others cooked while still green. He asserted, "When they tried to eat the *mbidde* [a kind of banana], it was bitter, so they started making beer out of it. In fact, the *mbidde* is the male banana, while the [bananas] for food, are the female bananas" (interview). Kalyango's view suggests that although the bananas were discovered during Kintu's reign, they actually existed in Buganda before. The story implies that Nnambi, a woman, "discovered" the bananas as opposed to Kintu, the king. However, irrespective of how the bananas came to Buganda, both theories point to the fact that bananas became part of the Baganda's menu after the coming of Kintu. Therefore, one can envisage that baakisimba is as old as Kabaka Kintu.

The other theory about the origin of baakisimba claims that baakisimba began in the palace. In fact, within schools and colleges, baakisimba is usually branded as "mazina go mu lubiri" ("the dance of the palace").[2] Muhamood Kasujja, a former court drummer, said, "As far as we know, baakisimba seems to have come from the palace because of its musical sounds *'kabaka ali nkuluze'* [the king is our treasury]."[3] He based his argument on the fact that the drum that accompanies palace baakisimba imitates the onomatopoeic sounds of "kabaka ali nkuluze." "Nkuluze" ("treasury of the Baganda"), relates to the belief that the king is the source of everything, including wealth and life.[4] Figure 6, shows the speech intonation of "kabaka ali nkuluze" and the relative sounds as heard on the *mbuutu*.

Figure 6. Speech and mbuutu sound of "Kabaka ali nkuluze"

Comparing the drum music of *abaakisimba ekitooke* in figure 5 and *kabaka ali nkuluze* in figure 6, one notices that although the two have different rhythmic and sound patterns, they share similar motivic figures of sixteenth and eighth notes which are characteristic of baakisimba musical style. The rhythmic and pitch patterns are different because of the different speech intonation of the two onomatopoetic phrases. Although both motifs are in the same meter, namely 6/8, *abaakisimba ekitooke* motif begins on the first beat of the measure, while *kabaka ali nkuluze* motif begins on an anacrusis beat.

It is well known, among the Baganda, that the Baganda always offered their best to the king. Because they had to perform in order to win the kabaka's favor, the Baganda were always compelled to present to the king only what they considered culturally valuable. In this sense, James C. Scott's concept of "public transcript," defined as "the open interaction between subordinates and those who dominate" (1990: 2), is useful. For instance, the Baganda presented beautiful girls as gifts to the king and chiefs. These gifts of girls were important because when the king or a chief took a girl to be his wife, "the clan from which she came profited by receiving presents and other favors from the king or the chief as the case might be" (Roscoe 1911: 9). Like the gift of girls, baakisimba may have found its way to the palace as a form of deference and respect for the dominant king in order to get favors. Scott has also noted that, "the public performance of the subordinate will, out of prudence, fear and the desire to curry favor, be shaped to appeal to the expectations of the powerful" (1990: 2). While baakisimba functioned to entertain the kabaka, it was a transcript of deference "intended in some sense to convey the outward impression of conformity with standards sustained by superiors" (Scott 1990: 24). Lois Anderson too has noted that, "music provided by the musicians at the court not only entertains the king but also recognizes him in the position as the head of the kingdom" (1968: 48). It is, therefore, reasonable to assume that baakisimba could have found its way into the palace as an offering to the king.

Moreover, the fact that the drum and its music are not called *kabaka* or *nkuluze* (words from the phrase of the palace drum rhythm), but instead "baakisimba" (a word from the phrase of the drum rhythm outside the palace), it is more convincing to believe that "kabaka ali nkuluze" was only a motif that developed when baakisimba was taken to the palace. It is likely that when baakisimba was introduced in the palace, the performers modified the rhythm to suit the status of the kabaka. As a matter of fact, my dance teacher, Hajati Madina Nakintu, clarified that there are two types of baakisimba: *baakisimba ey'omukyalo* (baakisimba of the village, outside the

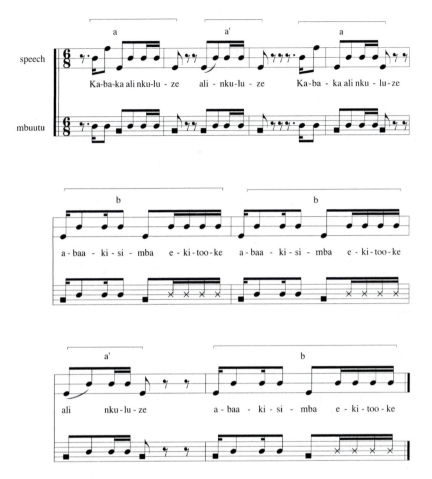

Figure 7. Baakisimba drum music performed by Omulangira Kaggwa.

palace), which she called *amazina amaganda* (Kiganda dance), and *baak-isimba ey'omulubiri* (baakisimba of the palace).

In fact, both motifs *abaakisimba ekitooke* and *kabaka ali nkuluze*, were beaten in the baakisimba performances that I attended. In most of my field recordings, the drummers beat the "kabaka" motif as preparatory *kisoko* (motif) before beating "baakisimba," which they said was the main *kisoko*. These motifs are played both within and outside the palace contexts. The only distinction is the difference in speed; the palace baakisimba is slower than the village baak-isimba. Figure 7, presents an excerpt of sixteen seconds of baakisimba per-formed by Omulangira Kaggwa during an interview session. The speech line above that of the drum rhythm helps to elucidate the use of these two motifs.

From the above musical excerpt, both the *abaakisimba ekitooke* (indicated "b," as in measures 5, 6, and 8) and *kabaka ali nkuluze* motifs (indicated "a," as in measures 1, 2, 3, 4, and 7) are included in what Kaggwa called baakisimba of the palace. As Kaggwa explained and also illustrated in his excerpt, the drummers use *abaakisimba ekitooke* and *kabaka ali nkuluze* motifs as their raw material from which they construct baakisimba music. When drawing on these two motifs, they do not necessarily repeat the whole motivic phrase; they fragment it as in measures 2 and 7 (indicated a'). From this excerpt, one can conclude that *abaakisimba ekitooke* and *kabaka ali nkuluze* are some of the motifs available to the drummer as raw materials that constitute the basic baakisimba drum music. Based on this evidence, it is tempting to agree with Peter Ggayira, a former palace drummer and a drum maker who said to me that "baakisimba started among the *bakopi* then it went to the palace and now it is back among the *bakopi*." Based on the assumption that baakisimba originated outside the palace before becoming a genre of music and dance of the palace, we can speculate that baakisimba was appropriated by the palace to enhance the power of the king and his monarch.

CHOREOGRAPHY OF BAAKISIMBA

As Judith Lynne Hanna has noted, there are indeed many definitions of dance (1979). For instance, Joann Kealiinohomoku's cross-cultural definition of dance states that "a transient mode of expression, performed in a given form and style by the human body moving in space" (1983: 541). She rightly notes that "dance occurs through purposely selected and controlled rhythmic movements: the resulting phenomenon is recognized as dance both by the performer and the observing members of a given group" (ibid.). Therefore, dance is "culturally patterned sequences of nonverbal body movements other than ordinary motor activities, [in which] the motion has inherent and aesthetic value" (Hanna 1988: 46). Dance scholars have used different terms to delineate the elements that constitute a dance. However, most dance terminologies are borrowed from music scholarship. Scholars in the field of ethnochoreology (study of non-Western dance) have not yet invented their own terms as opposed to those used in Western dance scholarship. Given this situation, I borrow terms from Western music and dance scholarship, which I redefine to suit my context.

The dance elements that constitute baakisimba include movement, level, and motifs. The transition from one position to another is through a series of movements. Movement is directional and forms designs or shapes. I use the term formation to denote the direction (left, right, forward, backwards) of a movement. The design of a movement may be circular, linear, diagonal, vertical, or horizontal. Formations may also be designed from letters of the alphabet or any other shapes. There are three levels in baakisimba: 1) low level, whereby the dancer stands with feet flat on the ground, on the balls of either both feet or one foot touching the ground, and bent knees; 2) medium level, standing position; and 3) high level, with stretched knees and on the balls of the feet touching the ground. I use the term motif to refer to a division of dance movements that correspond with a specific music structure. The footwork, hand gestures, and waist movements define the different dance motifs in baakisimba. Moreover, since baakisimba music and dance are so clearly connected, dance motifs are also defined by the tempo and drum music figures.

Since baakisimba is an ongoing creative art, there are as many motifs as there are teachers and dancers. Therefore, I cannot claim to present all the different choreographic features of baakisimba. I present the most salient features that I have gathered through my research and experience as a dancer and specifically those features that strongly resonate with the topic of discussion. In order to facilitate my discussion, I employ two means of representing baakisimba dance. In a number of cases, I have included photographs and in some instances, especially when illustrating the integration of music and dance, I use graphic representation. I have borrowed some aspects from Benesh dance notation, especially the staff and the footwork symbols, but I have recreated new symbols to suit my discussion.[5] Since the main aim of this graphic representation is to show the integration between baakisimba music and dance motifs, Benesh notation is most useful; it can neatly be combined with music notation. Like the music notation, Benesh notation is written on a five-line staff, each line representing five major parts of the body: head, shoulders/arms, waist, knees, and feet (see figure 8). However, I only concentrate on the footwork and the waist/hip movement because the basic movement in baakisimba is centered on these two areas of the body. Although the hand gestures and facial expressions contribute to the definition of the dance, the footwork directs the waist/hip movement, the basic movement in baakisimba.

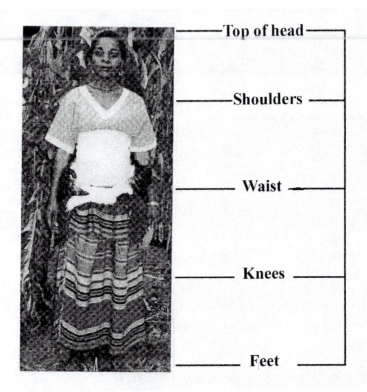

Figure 8. Baakisimba dance staff notation.

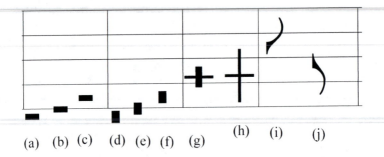

(a) (b) (c) (d) (e) (f) (g)   (h) (i)   (j)

Figure 9. Notation of footwork and waist/hip movements: a) flat feet on the ground (body level); b) balls of the feet touching the ground (body level); c) feet in the air (body level); d) flat feet in front of the body; e) ball of the feet touching the ground in front of the body; f) leg in the air in front of the body; g) flexed joint (in this case, the joint of the knee) at body level; h) flexed knee in front of the body; i) upward thrust of the hip and waist movement; and j) downward thrust of hip and waist movement.

In figure 9, the symbol written below the bottom line in (a), means the feet are flat on the ground and at body level. When the symbol is written through the bottom line as in (b), it means the balls of the feet are touching the ground at body level. The symbol written in the first space from the bottom as in (c) refers to the feet are in the air at body level. The symbol in (d) means that the dancer's feet are flat in front of the body. When this symbol cuts through the bottom line as in (e), the dance is on the ball of the feet in front of the body. In (f), the dancer's leg is high in the air, in front of the body. The vertical cross as in (g) represents a flexed joint at body level, while the horizontal cross as in (h) is flexed joint in front of the body. Since Benesh notation was initially created to transcribe ballet dance, symbols of movement that are not part of ballet were not developed. For baakisimba dance, I had to create symbols in (i) and (j). The symbol in (i) denotes the upward thrust of the hip and waist movement. On the other hand, (j) shows the downward thrust of the hip and the waist movement. In Benesh notation, a body midline is imagined as dividing the body into right and left sections. However, for clarity, I use letters r and l for right and left sections of the body, respectively.

THE NGALABI AND MBUUTU: MAN AND WOMAN DRUMS

The *ngoma* (drums) are the main accompaniment to baakisimba dance, and until the mid-twentieth century two drums, namely the *mbuutu* and the *ngalabi* accompanied the dance. The *mbuutu* is a large, conical double membrane drum, while the *ngalabi* is a long, single membrane hand drum with an open bottom end. Although the *ndongo* (bowl lyres), *ndingidi* (tube fiddles), *madinda* (xylophones), *nsaasi* (rattles), and *ndere* (flutes) may accompany village and palace baakisimba of the twenty-first century, the *ngoma* still surpass all of them in importance. The high status of drums in baakisimba is not only because drums provide the basic rhythm, which defines the dance motifs, but also because of their general significance to the Baganda. As Roscoe has noted, the drum announced both joy and sorrow; the birth of children mourning for the dead; signaling the call to war; and announcing the return of the triumphant warrior (1911: 25). Drums mediate between the worlds of the seen and the unseen. Further, drums symbolize family identity; each of the Baganda's clans is identified with the *mubala* (a clan drum-beat). As Roscoe has observed, "The drum was sacrosanct; for example, if a slave disliked his master, and escaped to the drum-shrine, he [or she] became a servant of the drum, and could not be removed. So, too, *[sic]* if any person had been condemned to death and was able to escape to the [drum] shrine, he might remain there in safety, he was a slave of the drum" (1911: 167). Elsewhere, I have defined the Kiganda drum as the "King" of instruments (Nanyonga 1995: 22). Drums are not only venerated among the Baganda, but also in many other cultures of the world. For instance, Jean Jenkins has explained the ways in which drums are associated with rituals and ceremonies in Argentina. She states:

> In Argentine [sic], the Mataco people use the drum to frighten away spirits associated with death and disease and spirits of hurricanes, tempests and drought. They also use it to animate the good spirits so as to ensure a good harvest. The same people beat it also at burial ceremonies and at girls' puberty rituals. It is a general magical instrument (1977: 41–42, quoted in Doubleday 1999: 103).

The drums of the Baganda have different symbolic values depending on their role and the context in which they are performed. The ritual drums play specific sacred roles and are only beaten for those designated purposes and by chosen people. They are specifically designed and their rhythms are named according to their functions (Ggayira, interview). Beyond the ritual roles, the Baganda assign symbols to these drums depending on their shapes and designs. When I visited Ssekabaka Suuna II's tomb at Wamala and Ssekabaka Mwanga, Ssekabaka Muteesa II and Ssekabaka Chwa II's tombs at Kasubi, I found the *ngalabi* kept together with three *mbuutu* drums used for ritual purposes, yet they are never performed together. Matiya Muyimbwa, one of the attendants at Ssekabaka Suuna's *masiro* (tombs), informed me that the *mbuutu* is the "woman" drum, while the *ngalabi* is the "man" drum.[6] Muyimbwa was reacting to the question relating to the keeping of the *ngalabi,* which is a festival drum with the ritual drums. When I asked Muyimbwa why they were kept together, he said that, "the *ngalabi* has to protect the woman drum. Even in our daily life, a man must protect the woman" *("engalabi erina okulabirira enkazi. Era ne mu bulamu obwa bulijjo, omusajja alina okuku-uma omukazi").* Plate 2, shows the *ngalabi* (tall drum), the man drum and two *mbuutu,* the woman drum.

Plate 2. Matiya Muyimbwa explaining the symbolism of the woman and man drums.

In the explanation of the gender of these drums, Muyimbwa referred to the shapes, pitches, and sound effects of each drum. To the *ngalabi,* he pointed out that "don't you see that its round big head on top with a long and slender bottom alludes to the sexual organs of a male!" *("Ggwe tolaba ng'ettama lyayo waggulu, n'obugogofu wansi, ate nga mpanvuyirivu, eraga busajja!").* He continued to say that the roundness of the *mbuutu* relates to the female sexual organs. Moreover, the women drums are, in most cases, more decorated than the men drums. However, the decoration of individual woman drum depends on the role the drum plays. The secular *mbuutu* is decorated with the neat lacing of the skin to the non-sonorous skin, in close "W-pattern" or "U-pattern." The sacred women drums are decorated with cowry shells and beads, as was the case with women drums at Ssekabaka Sunna's tombs. The *ngalabi,* a single-skinned drum, is decorated with wooden pegs that hold the skin to the wooden sound box, and sometimes may be given more decorations like markings. The *mbuutu's* head is made of a cow's skin (from a domesticated animal), and the *ngalabi's* head is made of either a monitor lizard skin or a python skin, both fierce and wild animals. Because of the fierceness of python, the Baganda created a proverb that goes: "Eby'omugagga bijja byokka: omusota tagukkiriza kujja gyali: [meaning that] the treasures of a rich man come in by themselves (so they say), but he does not let a snake come near him (Walser 1992: 113, no. 1233). And yet they relate the man's anger to a poisonous snake and say: "omusajja ow'obusungu: ng'omusta gw'enswera [meaning] An angry man: is as poisonous as a viper (Walser 1992: 385, no. 4298).

Further, Muyimbwa justified the gendering of the drums based on the kind of pitches and sound effects of each drum. He argued that the high pitch of the *ngalabi* in relation to the *mbuutu* makes the *ngalabi* outstanding and more dominant, hence attaining the man gender.[7] Moreover, "when the *ngalabi* sounds, even someone from a distance hears it" (ibid.). Because of its sound quality, the *ngalabi* tends to be louder, which enables it to overshadow the lower-pitched and softer *mbuutu.* Muyimbwa associated the penetrating timbre of the *ngalabi* to the domination of men, and therefore, strongly asserted that the *ngalabi* is a man drum. On the other hand, the low-pitched *mbuutu,* which Muyimbwa assigns a subordinate role, takes on a woman gender. However, Badru Ssebumpenje and Ibrahim Ggayi, both fluent drummers, argued that the *mbuutu* should be the man drum since it has a deeper pitch than the *ngalabi,* which sounds womanish. Their argument was based on the comparison of the drum sound to biological traits of males. Nonetheless, they agreed to the view that the high-pitched *ngalabi* tends to sound more dominant and takes a dominant role in the drum ensemble over the low-pitched *mbuutu* when they sound together. Their definition of these drums did not relate to the culturally assigned status of man and woman as dominant and subordinate, respectively. It is important to note that the assignment of genders to the drums is contingent on the context from which they are assigned. Muyimbwa of the palace context made his assignment based on gender construction within the palace, while Ssebumpenje and Ggayi, who constructed the gender of the drum from a context outside the palace, based their explanation on the biological traits of men and women outside the palace. Kwabena Nketia has observed that in Africa, "music that is frequently integrated with dance is bound to emphasize and develop those features that can be articulated in bodily movement, or to relate its form and content to the structural and dramatic requirements of the dance" (1974: 206). The analytical elaboration of the integration of baakisimba music and dance explains more on Muyimbwa's gendering of the *ngalabi* as the man and *mbuutu* as the woman. In an experiment with dancers and drummers of Agalyawamu Cultural Group at Mpigi in Mawokota County, I observed that although the *mbuutu* performer provided the basic motifs, the *ngalabi* performer controlled their dance movements. I asked the *mbuutu* and the *ngalabi* drummers (privately when the dancers were not hearing) to perform together at the beginning, but then, at a later stage, the *ngalabi* to pull out and then join in at a later stage. When the *mbuutu* and the *ngalabi* were beaten together, the dancing was very vigorous and lively. However, when the *ngalabi* pulled out, the dancers started complaining that the music was not good. They said the music was boring, and that it did not inspire dancing. One of the dancers said, "Oh no! What is that you are doing? Your drums do not motivate dancing! What has happened to the *ngalabi* drummer?" After the *ngalabi* performer rejoined, the dancing resumed. When I asked the *ngalabi* performer how he induced dancing, Peter Luyombya, a member of Agalyawamu Cultural Group said, "The *ngalabi* is thick, rich, full, and crackles like thunder! By being thick, rich, and full, it gives the dancers the pulsation of the dance and when it crackles it excites them". Rose Namusisi, one of the dancers, interrupted and said, "It is a good *ngalabi* beater that induces dancing. But that does not mean that we do not follow the *mbuutu*."

Since the dancers seemed to imply that the *ngalabi* is the leading drum in their dancing, I asked the *ngalabi* musician to beat alone while the dancers performed. The dancers told me that there was no rhythm to guide their footwork, and therefore, they did not know which dance motif to perform. Based on this experiment, it was clear that while the *mbuutu* must perform to outline the dance, the *ngalabi* must also perform to provide the driving force. Further, although the sound of the *ngalabi* is louder and higher than the *mbuutu*, it is only important to the dance as long as the *mbuutu* is performed. Therefore, the two drums are dependant on each other. When I asked Consitantino Lwewunzika, a male baakisimba teacher, which drum he follows when dancing, he said that after learning the dance, one takes the *mbuutu* for granted; it becomes basic and the *ngalabi* inspires vigorous dancing. He contended, however, that the *mbuutu* must perform the basic rhythm well so as to define the motifs and tempo of the dance.

An analysis of the musical structure of the *mbuutu* and the *ngalabi* elucidates Muyimbwa's view about the gendering of these drums. The woman drum introduces the basic motifs and the man drum follows with motifs based on the *mbuutu* patterns. Because of the dynamic level, high pitch, and the possibility for the *ngalabi* beater to improvise more than the *mbuutu* beater, the *ngalabi* is perceived as more dominant when it is beaten together with a less dynamic, less sonorous, and low-pitched *mbuutu*. The whole dance performance depends on the *ngalabi* beater, not because he introduces the motifs, but because he gives the driving force to dance. Moreover, the *ngalabi* performer provides signals for the dancers. The driving force is not only in the rhythm, but also in the kind of timbre that strongly contrasts with that of the *mbuutu*. The *ngalabi* sounds higher and louder, which may be interpreted as signifying dominance of men. Figure 10, presents only in relative terms a graphic representation of the basic rhythm of the *ngalabi* and the *mbuutu*. I do not focus on the exact intervals between the two drums, because the Baganda do not have a standard tuning for these drums. The tunings differ from performer to performer and from drum maker to drum maker. I provide a graphic representation of the prominence of the *ngalabi* in relation to the *mbuutu*.

The *mbuutu* begins with its muted and banged sounds; however, when the *ngalabi* comes in (measure 3), in addition to its muted sounds, it introduces the "slap" sound, a technique not performed on the *mbuutu* at all. The slapping technique of beating the *ngalabi,* coupled with its high pitch, as well as having an open-ended bottom (which facilitates resonance), allows the *ngalabi* to produce a very sharp and penetrating sound. Since the auditory system of humans, with time, tends to ignore continuous sounds and pays more attention to sporadic sounds, the *ngalabi* sounds predominate in relation to the *mbuutu*. The combination of high pitches, penetrating timbre, greater amplitude, and irregular rhythmic occurrences foregrounds the *ngalabi* relative to the *mbuutu*. Based on the combination of these musical features, the relationship between the *ngalabi* and the *mbuutu* has been

Figure 10. Mbuutu and ngalabi music.

coded by musicians as dominant-subordinate. This relationship between the drums is said to characterize man-woman social relations.

However, it was evident throughout my research that the gendering of these drums was mainly conceptualized within the palace quarters. Why is it that outside the palace these drums were not referred to by their genders? This practice is explained by the different customs that existed within and outside the palace. While it was acceptable to talk about gender and sexuality within the palace, it was a taboo outside the palace. The Baganda considered any reference to gender and sexuality, in "normal" discourse outside the palace, to be obscene. The only people that were allowed to speak "obsceni-ties" outside the palace were the parents of twins (*ssaalongo* and *nnaalongo*), the *basamize* (mediums), and the *balaguzi* (oracles), because the Baganda believed these people had sacred powers. However, people of the palace, especially those of the royal family, "were exempt[ed] from the general rules of behaviour and speech which governed commoner Baganda . . ." (Musisi 1991a: 79). Musisi explained further that "Like princes, the princesses were

free . . . to use obscene language *(okuwemula)* [her emphasis]" (ibid.).
Reporting from her own field experience, she said:

> In fact, I interviewed (recorded) a princess who was a great-great-grand-daughter of Sunna [sic] II, and granddaughter of Mbogo, brother of Mutesa [sic] I, who used obscene words in her discourse, even after I told her several times that I was taping our conversation. She said she could not help it (ibid.).

Although the concept of gendering the *mbuutu* and the *ngalabi* as woman and man drums was not in the people's discourse outside the palace, the majority of the informants outside the palace agreed that the categorization was relevant. For instance, one informant noted that "indeed the longness of the *ngalabi* and the big cheeks allude to the male organs" *("wamma obuwanvuyirivu bw'engalabi n'amatama amanene gafaananira ddala busajja!")* (anonymous, interview). The discussion thus far illustrates that the sound of the *mbuutu* and the *ngalabi* do not themselves produce gendered structures; instead, it is the meaning that people associate with these sounds that define their genders.

BAAKISIMBA: THE WOMEN'S DANCE

All informants agreed that baakisimba elaborates on the conceived Baganda women's beauty, prescribed roles and, therefore, it is a women's dance. Ezuliya Nannyonga, a former court dancer, informed me that if a man performed baakisimba, he was viewed as a woman. Nannyonga stressed, "baakisimba is a dance for women" ("baakisimba mazina ga bakyala") (interview). In defining baakisimba as a women's dance, the prescribed performance practice and context, choreography, and costume help to construct the womanliness of a Muganda woman. As such, when men dance baakisimba, a number of questions arise about their man gender, as discussed in Chapter Eight. Consitantino Lwewunzika, a former court male-woman dancer, confirmed that "this dance was for women; we, the men, only came into it, but it was never our job" (interview). He informed me that at the time he started dancing in 1945, it was most common for men to beat drums and women to dance. He recalled that the ratio of men to women dancers was about three to ten.[8] He mentioned further that it was not widely acceptable for men to dance outside the palace. Although men could dance among themselves at beer parties and among relatives during family gatherings, it was not "normal" for men to dance formal baakisimba, as is common at wedding ceremonies since the late twentieth-century. Juma Natyole was the first man to perform baakisimba at a wedding ceremony, outside the palace in the late 1940s (Ggayira, interview; Lwewunzika, Interview). Lwewunzika narrated further that it took time for men to be accepted as dancers. Moreover, there were not many contexts when men could perform the dance; they only performed at a wedding ceremony and at the request of the host. Whenever a host invited a performing group with no special request for men to perform, it meant that women were the dancers. I explore the roles of women's dancing at a wedding ceremony in Chapter Five.

Moreover, even in the 2000s, some people still do not accept men dancers; as such, compared to women, they are few men that perform the dance. For instance, during rehearsals of the Nandujja and the Planet (a semi-professional ensemble), I observed that while there were thirteen dancers that attended the training session, only one was a man. Further, a number of men who had danced before or were great dancers, resort to drumming at a later age. In a number of groups that I visited, some men learn both dancing and beating instruments, although, after a certain age (around thirty years), they usually stop dancing to concentrate on beating drums or other instruments. Ssekitto, a former dancer who is now a drummer, said that "time comes when it is no longer good for a man to dance. We do those things [dancing] when we are still young." He argued that the "the beating of instruments is better; it is more exciting than dancing. Moreover, men lose their dancing skills earlier; yet women take longer to lose their skills." The reality is not that men lose their dancing skills earlier than women; instead, as a number of the men informants commented, at a certain age, "a man must become 'serious' and behave like a 'man.'" According to these informants, to dance is to behave "womanish." However, by beating the drum, one affirms his manliness because the drum is symbolic power and a drummer is more respected than a dancer; drummers also have higher social status within the group (detailed discussion is in Chapter Five). As is the case with women beating drums, there are taboos to limit men's dancing. Julius Kyakuwa, a music student at Makerere University, asserted that men's dancing was controlled by the threat of becoming impotent if they performed baakisimba.[9] One becomes impotent, which means powerless, when he performs a role originally assigned for women who are regarded in society as powerless.

Some informants argued that baakisimba is a women's dance because it is graceful and slow. For example, Tereza Kisolo (RIP) explained that since women are supposed to be graceful, humble, submissive, and calm, a graceful and slow dance is definitely a women's dance (interview). However, the dance has changed; baakisimba of the 2000s is more vigorous compared to that of the 1950s, for instance. How does one then interpret the more vigorous dancing of the 2000s? The vigorous style seems to contradict the criteria used to define baakisimba as women's dance. Is it an indication that women are now louder and less graceful? Women of the 2000s are certainly outwardly more assertive than those of the 1950s. However, one cannot claim a direct correlation between the musical and dance style and the women's changed behavior. Instead, the change in the dance style only confirms that the definition of baakisimba, like any other cultural phenomenon, is dependent on social, cultural, and political forces; any change in the structuring of these forces leads to change in the shape of baakisimba.

As Patience Abenna Kwakwa has rightly pointed out, "in several African societies dance forms closely relate to the canons of beauty in the human body and the canons for dance appreciation tend to be linked with the appreciation of particular physical features of the masculine and feminine body" (1994: 10). Since the body is the major instrument in any dance genre, the Baganda's definition of the different body appearances of men and women forms the basis for the conceptualization of baakisimba as a women's dance. Generally, an idealized Muganda woman usually has a round body, full breasts, big buttocks, big legs, and long hair, braided or straight. Like most informants, Baaziriyo Nsubuga, a musician in Lwewunzika's group, argued that women's bodies are more attractive than bodies of men when they dance and, therefore, baakisimba should be a women's dance. Similarly, referring to dancing in Africa, Patience Abenna Kwakwa noted that, "for in spite of male chauvinism . . . even men appreciate the art of dancing most when it is performed by women" (ibid.). Nsubuga said "Usually women involve themselves in dancing and are more exciting in their way of dancing. Since the woman is our flower, when she gets on stage and she dances, we also feel good!" ("abakyala bebasinga okwettanira amazina, era basanyusa nnyo mu kuzina kwabwe. Nga omukazi bw'ali ekimuli kyaffe, bweyesimba mu ddiiro nazina, era naawe osanyuka!") The wriggling of the waist and the quivering of the buttocks, which is the basic movement in baakisimba is what excites men and confirms women as flowers, objects for pleasure. Likewise, baakisimba exploits "all the features of the female body in the total range of symbolism, natural functions and aesthetic values associated with them" (Kwakwa 1994:10). This view legitimizes Sally Banes' idea that "through dance, men's attitudes towards women . . . are literally given body on stage" (1998: 1). On the other hand, Nsubuga argued that a man dancer is not a flower, but an entertainer.[10] Peter Ggayira stressed that:

In fact, a woman was created to dance. The role a woman was created for is dancing. Although men forced themselves into dancing, it was a women's job. We forced ourselves on the job because of economic reasons, to get money.

Anti omukyala yatondebwa kuzina. Omulimu gwe ogwamutonderwa ogusinga gwa mazina. Abasajja lwa kugwekakaatikako, naye gwali mulimu gwa bakyala. Twagwekakaatikako lwa bya nfuna, kufuna ssente (interview).

Ggayira affirmed that although women are "weak" at beating the drums, when they dance, "you may also get tired to beat the drum and yet she says 'let us continue.'" In fact, Ggayira is just confirming that women are not weak, since they can go on to dance even when the drummers, supposedly "strong" men, are tired. Most of the informants, especially men held Ggayira's view that the women's role as dancers and the men's role as drummers were assigned by God. I discuss these mythical associations in greater detail in Chapter Four.

Chapter Four
Palace Baakisimba

SSAABASAJJA: THE MAN AMONG MEN

To understand the performance of baakisimba and its articulation with gender in the palace, calls for the examination of the structuring of the palace. There is need to explore how palace gender identities, roles, and relations are constructed; all of which participate in shaping baakisimba performance. However, I discuss only those aspects, which resonate with palace baakisimba.

Kintu, the first *kabaka,* established a kingdom that was based on hereditary rule. Although as it is alleged that he came with many clan leaders (Nsimbi 1996:150; Kaggwa 1912a:2), only descendants from his lineage could belong to the royal family and aspire to the Buganda kingship. Roscoe has reported, "From the earliest times in the history of [Buganda] there has been a king with despotic power" (1911: 186). The kings had control over the lives of the people as well as the animals in Buganda. For example, A. I. Richards has written: "Not only did the king [Muteesa1] condemn without trial wives and courtiers who displeased him, or send them to be tried in a court which did not dare to oppose his will, but evidently there were killings done simply as an expression of power" (1964a: 276). The kings' power was based partly on myths and fictions, "all designed to single out the uniqueness of the royal office" (Kiwanuka 1972: 93). Through myths, the *bakopi* (subordinates) were manipulated into believing that they were born to be ruled and that someone among the *balangira* (dominants) was to rule them (Roscoe 1911: 232). Ideologically, the kingship manipulated the *bakopi* to make its interests appear to be synonymous with the interests of the Ganda society at large.

The *kabakas'* power was distinguished further by titles given to him. First, he is the *ssaabasajja.* Explaining the title "ssaabasajja," Nsimbi wrote, "in Buganda, the king is surpasses all men in honor and power; that is why he is called Ssaabasajja" (1996:32). He is *ssemanda,* the charcoal of fire or the smith, "who can forge the kingdom as the smith forges iron." He is *ssegwanga,* "first in the nation"; and *ssaabataka,* "first among clan heads." The king is also the *ssaabalongo,* one who surpasses all fathers of twins (*ssaalongo*). He is *mpologoma,* "the lion" and *nnamunswa,* "the queen termite," who, Baganda say, feeds upon her subject termites (Richards 1964a: 268).

The titles of the king, like the Kiganda clan names, clearly designate the gender of the *kabaka.* As detailed in Chapter Five, names that begin with *nna* are for women and in most cases those that begin with *ssa* and *sse* are for men. Referring to the king as *ssegwanga* (first in the nation), for instance, emphasizes the position of the king as the descendant of Kintu, the believed founder of Buganda. As *ssaabasajja,* he is the man among men and dominates all men as well as women. When the king is called *nnamunswa,* he identifies with the feminine power of procreation, as the queen termite is responsible for the multiplication of the ants and termites. In this case, the king's power manifests in the metaphor of the queen termite feeding "upon her subject termites," one of the common sayings of the Baganda.

Plate 3. Kabaka Muwenda Mutebi II lifted high by the bakopi. Courtesy of Walabyeki Magoba.

As a way of showing the king's status, subjects lift him high. In plate 3, Kabaka Muwenda Mutebi II is lifted high by his subjects *(bakopi),* surrounded by the *balangira.* Although lifting the king is nowadays only done as a symbolic enactment to show the king's power, it was the practice to carry the king, especially before easy transport was introduced in the kingdom.

In order to crystallize the power of the *kabaka* as the *ssaabasajja,* the "man among men," the monarchy figuratively emasculated all the *male bakopi* and reconstructed them as women within the palace. By making them adapt a woman gender, the male *bakopi's access* to the throne was controlled because by being male, they were partially eligible for the throne. Roscoe mentioned that the "Kings had to be princes whose parentage was well known, and whose fathers were at least the sons of a monarch" (1911: 232) and "no woman could reign, nor any person not of the royal blood" (1911: 187)). Although the *bambejja* also belong to the royal family or clan, their femaleness placed them in the lowest strata of the hierarchy of men and, therefore, could not aspire to kingship. However, the Kiganda tradition assigns the queen sister a position claimed to be equal to that of the king. Roscoe reported that "Though there was a strong feeling against women reigning, custom permitted the Queen and the King's mother *(nnamasole)* to hold their courts, and conferred on them a certain measure of administrative power" (1911: 187).

As I have argued in the first chapter, gender construction was dependent on the stability of Buganda and its king. The *kabaka's* power is important for sustaining Buganda's gender structure since the king and his institution are the chief custodians of the Kiganda customs. Unfortunately, the king's power could not last forever as Apollo Kaggwa, claimed: "the Baganda as far back as can be remembered, have been an obedient and well governed people, respecting their kings, and [their] country" (1934: 172). While Kaggwa's view may suggest a "winning by spontaneous consent," the so-called consent, if it existed at all, was temporary; a "public transcript" enacted to conceal the true relationship between the dominant and subordinate groups (Scott 1990). James Scott warns us not to rely on this "public transcript" while analyzing power relations. When the hidden transcripts—those enacted "behind the backs" of the dominant—are given expression, they can explode into resistance and protest (1990: 4). The revolution that brought drastic changes in the Kabaka's power, which eventually impacted on gender, can be traced back to 1862 when the Europeans first came to Buganda. By the time John Hannington Speke and R. J. Grant, the first British came to

Uganda, Buganda—under the rule of a Kabaka—had a strong political and social base, which enabled the British to colonize the rest of Uganda with less resistance (Mutibwa 1992: 3). At the beginning, the Buganda kingdom had a close relationship with the Europeans and through them, especially in their provision of guns and skills, Buganda conquered many counties under its control (Mutibwa 1992: 2). However, this relationship did not last. It ended with King Mwanga's exile in the late nineteenth century and from that point, Buganda and its kingship began to decline.

Ssekabaka Chwa II, who became the new king, was too young to exert the traditional power and authority as the previous kings. For instance, T. V. Sathyamurthy has observed, "at the time the agreement [between the British and the Buganda monarchy] was signed, the *kabaka* was barely four years of age" (1986: 202). Although Ssekabaka Chwa II had strong regents, Kaggwa and Mugwanya, the British were able to manipulate them into signing the 1900 [B]uganda agreement that gave away the *kabaka's* power and the sovereignty of Buganda as a powerful kingdom.[1] The nature of the Agreement accounts for the numerous crises between the protectorate, and Ssekabaka Muteesa II. The agreement stipulated a number of issues that indicate the *kabaka's* loss of power. Phares Mitibwa has mentioned that "The Kabaka, at least in theory, was to rule; in fact he was to be the instrument through which the British would rule Buganda" (1992: 5). Article no. 6 of the agreement clearly explains the withdrawal of the king's traditional power and authority. It reads in part:

> So long as the Kabaka, chiefs and the people of Buganda shall conform to the laws and regulations instituted for their governance by Her Majesty's Government, and shall co-operate loyally with Her Majesty's protection in the organisation and administration of the said Kingdom of [B]uganda, Her Majesty's Government agrees to recognize the Kabaka of [B]uganda as the Native ruler of the province of [B]uganda under Her Majesty's protection and over-rule (Great Britain 1953: 14).

Although the article supports hereditary rule, it subjects the rule to election "by majority voice" whose nominees must first be "submitted to Her Majesty's government for approval." Moreover, the *kabaka's* absolute powers were retracted; he was to be accountable to "Her Majesty's government." In article 9, the *kabaka's* power to appoint and dismiss chiefs was reversed too (Great Britain 1953: 16). Because of the breach of the 1900 agreement, in 1953, Muteesa II lost the "protectorate's" recognition as the native ruler of Buganda, which climaxed in his deportation to Britain (Great Britain 1953: 13).

It should be noted, however, that there were other factors that led to the downfall of kingship in Buganda. Sathyamurthy has noted that in "the later years (from 1940s onwards), a new factor entered in the picture in form of more modern elements in society which were the products of secular education and adherents to such new socio-political ideologies as nationalism and representative democracy" (1986: 203–204). He notes that, "the continued communication, education and contact with the Europeans initiated challenges to both the indirect rule and the *kabaka's* powers" (1986: 207–208). Similarly, Richards observed that "When Buganda became literate, the writing of anonymous letters to the governor and to the Kabaka became frequent" (1964b: 305). This concealed form of aggression eventually became public when the Bataka federation that contested the king's rule was openly declared in 1918 (Wards and White 1971:199). In the 1940s, the Baganda elite, through the Bataka federation, began to demand that the Kabaka and his council govern Buganda in accordance with the wishes of the people (Wards and White ibid.). As a result, in 1946, riots broke out against the Kabaka, the Buganda government, and the colonial administration (Wards and White 1971: 200; Mutibwa 1992:11). In this case, the federation meant "common people standing up against the Kabaka and lukiiko" (Wards and White 1971: 200). Moreover, the increasingly changing money economy, through the introduction of cotton and coffee as cash crops, reduced the people's dependency on the *kabaka* as the *"nkuluze,"* the source of wealth and hence, his dominance.

Although Ssekabaka Muteesa II returned to Buganda in 1955 after two years of exile in Britain, his original power and authority could not be reinstated. Through struggle and instability the kingship only survived for four years after independence (from 1962 to 1966). The king was again exiled to Britain in 1966 where he met his death in 1971 (Pirouet 1995: xxvi). The Kabaka's second exile marked the end of kingship in Buganda. Although the monarchy was restored in 1993 with the installation of Kabaka Ronald Muwenda Mutebi II, the Baganda have described the act as "mere wings of the ants; an empty promise" *("ebyoya by'enswa"),* for the *kabaka* is "a king without political power" (African Weekly Review 1995: 27). The glory and the fame of the former kings do not exist any more.

Moreover, the reinstatement of the Buganda kingdom was received with mixed feelings in a socially, politically, and culturally changed Buganda (Lovgren 1996). George Mugambe, a twenty-year-old Muganda man, commented, "most of my friends don't care. It's the old people who want to preserve [the Buganda kingdom]" (quoted by Lovgren 1996: 2). Moreover, people from other regions with different political structures than the Baganda have some discomfort about the reinstatement of kingship. Balu Tarubo, from southern Acholi expressed that "As long as the kingdoms remain cultural, I have no problems. But I think the monarchies, especially Buganda, are used for political gains and exist primarily to benefit those close to the king . . ." (Lovgren ibid.). With the present state of kingship, gender is defined in different ways. While the "traditionalists" are fighting to bring women to their former subordinate position, they are faced with emancipatory struggles from, especially, the educated Baganda women. Coupled with no political power, the monarchy cannot enforce a culture that exploited women. While I do not mean to imply that women are fully emancipated, their present situation is improved in some ways compared to the pre-abolition period as will be discussed in Chapter Seven.

THE BAMBEJJA: FEMALE-MEN

In Buganda, the *bambejja* (princesses) were considered men. Although the *bambejja* were biologically female, the Baganda addressed them as *ssebo* (sir), a title designated for men of high status. Augustino Kisitu, a former court drummer during Ssekabaka Muteesa II's reign, explained that the *bambejja* were called *ssebo* because they belonged to the king's royal family, and since the king was also referred to as *ssebo* they are also entitled to the title (interview). In this case, social class subverted the *bambejja's* "femaleness," and accorded them a man gender. The female-*ssebo* took up roles culturally constructed for men, roles that project dominance and control.

For example, Solome Nannyonga, about eighty-eight years old and a *muzaana* (female servant) at Ssekabaka Suuna II's tombs, informed me that "Until Ssekabaka Suuna II's reign [ca. 1832–1856], princesses were never married [male-women never proposed princesses for marriage]; instead, the princesses [proposed marriage] to the male *bakopi*" ("*Okutuuka ku mirembe gya Suuna ow'okubiri, abambejja tebaafumbirwanga, wabula be baawasanga abakopi*").[2] However, Musisi's statement that "princesses were not allowed to marry" may seem contradictory. Musisi used the term "marry" from a Western perspective, which suggests a mutual union between two people and yet, marriage in Buganda is a relation of power. From the Kiganda context and the view of my discussion, her statement simply legitimizes that the princesses would never be controlled under a man's roof. In fact, "it was socially legitimate for them to initiate sexual liaisons with any man [male-woman] they fancied at any time they wished" (Musisi 1991b: 774). Similarly, Kisitu noted that the princesses would house the male *bakopi* they wished to marry although they could still have casual sex outside their marriage. Kisitu said that:

> The princess was the one who asked the commoner to go to princess' place. And when you [the male-woman] came you would sing 'I have come Sir!' And it used to be difficult for the person who was chosen to refuse, because every male commoner felt honored to be taken by a princess. So, when the princess married, he got power over or ownership of this [male-woman]. At times [the *mumbejja*] would not allow this [male-woman] even to go and work, because [the *mumbejja*] did not want any woman to play around with [the male-woman, the *mumbejja* had married]. In Buganda, the princess, in that case, has married you! [Moreover], the princesses were very promiscuous, and always desired to behave as disrespectful as the princes. Because whomever they wanted to befriend [have sexual relations with, the princess] would get her.

> *Omumbejja yeyasabanga omukopi okugenda ewuwe. Era bwojja, ng'oyimba nti nzize 'ssebo.' Era nga kyabanga kizibu omuntu oyo alondeddwa okugaana! Kuba omusajja yenna omukopi yali awulira ekitiibwa okutwalibwa omumbejja. Kale omumbejja bwe yawasanga, yafunanga obuyinza oba obwannannyini ku musajja. Oluusi yamugaananga n'okugenda okukola, anti nga tayagala bakazi balala kumwepankirako. Mu Buganda, awo omumbejja ab'akuwasizza! Abambejja balinga balalu, era nga beegomba nnyo bafaanane abalangira obujoozi, kuba buli gwe baba baagala okukwaana nga bamufuna* (interview).

Likewise, Kaggwa wrote: "And then, a princess named Ndagire Malungu loved very much Tebakyagenda Misanvu Kitunzi [a male *mukopi*] and [Malungu] could send greetings [to Kitunzi] every now and then saying that: 'I love you.' . . . Tebakyagenda agreed to befriend [Malungu] and then [Kitunzi] became [Malunga's] real lover" (1912: 143–144).

As men controlled the sexuality of their women outside the palace, the *bambejja* controlled the sexuality of the male-women they married. While these female-men could easily express their sexual desires to any male-woman, it was taboo for a female outside the palace to approach a man for marriage or even for casual sex. The Baganda referred to such a female as *nnakyeyombekedde*—woman house-owner, master-less woman—referring to one who threatens men's position and subverts the identity of a "proper" woman. It is typical for men to propose to women, whom men must house under their roofs, if they are to be considered husbands. Indeed, the *bambejja* subverted the Baganda women's identity by controlling the sexuality of male-women and keeping them in the home, hence, the *bambejja* strengthened their identity as men.

Therefore, I consider the relationship between these female-men *(bambejja)* and male-women, as a female-husband and male-wives, respectively.[3] To qualify for this marriage, as Kisitu informed me, the female-husband paid bride price, as a male-husband outside the palace, would do in order to qualify as a true husband to the woman. Kisitu said:

> The princess would build a house for the parents of the male-woman ["he"] desired to take into marriage and [princess] offered a lot of gifts to the family where ["he"] married a male-woman. And the princess could afford to give chieftainship to the father of the male-woman ["he"] had married.

> *Mumbejja yazimbiranga ennyumba ewaabwe w'omulenzi gwe yayagalanga okutwala, era yaweerezanga n'ebirabo bingi mu maka mw'awasa omusajja. Era omumbejja yasobolanga okuwa kitaawe w'omusajja gw'awasizza obwami.*

The man gender of the *bambejja* is supported further by the evidence that while the king's wives' movement were restricted; the princesses were able to move about at will. Both female-women and male-women respected the princesses a great deal; "even chiefs bowed low when addressing them in the road and often kneeled to them when they went to visit the princesses at their homes." (Roscoe 1911: 8).

In addition, at one time, the princesses "were barred from having children" although they could at times have children in secrecy and hide them among the *bakopi* (Musisi 1991b: 774). Roscoe points out that although the later kings were more relaxed about the princesses giving birth, the former kings feared that the princesses' children might dethrone the king. According to Roscoe, "if they [the *bambejja*] happened to be with child, they secured the aid of some skilled person to bring about a miscarriage, because it would have been death to the princess, and also to the man with whom she had gone wrong, if a child had been born to them" (1911: 85). J. F. Faupel explained that the prohibition of the princesses from having children was "to ensure that the line of succession should be continued through the princes, who were encouraged to marry and produce heirs in the male line" (1984:2). The princesses' denial of procreation completely "masculinized" them, for a "female-woman" in Buganda is defined by her ability to procreate.

My interpretation of the *bambejja* differs from that of Musisi (1991a) and Tamale (1997, 1999), who have referred to these female-men as "powerful women," and "women of the palace," respectively. Although females, the Kiganda tradition defined them as men. These scholars' interpretations take it for granted that anybody who is biologically "male" is definitely a "man" and anybody biologically "female" is a "woman." While Musisi acknowledges that the princesses were men's equal "addressed by the male title *sebo* (sir), rather than *nyabo* (madam)" (Musisi's emphasis) (1991a: 79) and that the society expected these princesses to behave like men, she still refers to them as "women" (1991a: 78–83).[4] When she elevates them higher, she calls them "extra-ordinary women" (1991a: 38) or "royal women" (1991a: 39, 43). Similarly, Molara Ogundipe-Leslie, a scholar of African gender, has also pointed out the complexity of the term "woman" when used in the African context. She noted that in the West, where the term originated, it "refers to 'middle class, educated white women' while 'woman' in Africa refers to illiterate, peasant, working class or poor women . . ." (1994: 10). In Buganda, the term is even more problematic. It would be a mistake to assume that anyone with protruding breasts and female genitalia is a woman. Although the *bambejja* have female biological characteristics, the Baganda did not consider them women. On the other hand, the male-women have biological features of males, yet within the Kiganda culture, they were considered women. In fact, a Kiganda proverb goes: "Bulikugwa: Obukyala si bumbejja: It will come to an end for you: The standing of a woman through marriage is not the same as the standing of a princess [meaning] The later remains princesses, whilst the former losses her standing" (Walser 1982: 92. no, 1016).

While I agree with Musisi that the princesses had restrictions based on their sexuality, which placed them in a subordinate status to that of the king and other princes, I do not agree that the subordinate position makes them "women." Although women have historically been subjected to subordination, it should not be taken for granted that subordination relates only to women. Domination and subordination are axes within struggles for power that exist in all social relations. To accord the *bambejja* the identity of women because they were subordinates of other members of the royal family, is to ignore the existence of hierarchies between genders; for example, some individuals may be "better" men and "better" women than others. I argue that the princesses were considered men, although at the lowest stratum of the men's hierarchy, especially insofar as their sexuality was concerned.

Although it is irrefutable that these *bambejja* were powerful, I contend that their power was related to the fact that they were men. Moreover, their power changed as cultural and social conditions shifted. The *bambejja* gradually lost their power over the male-women and, when the kingship finally collapsed in 1966, they completely lost their control. The new social conditions enabled male-women to marry the *bambejja*, which put the *bambejja* in a subordinate position. The *bambejja's* man gender was redefined when the male *bakopi* started housing the *bambejja* under their roofs. The *bambejja* ceased to be honored as *ssebo*, the title the male *bakopi* used to call them. There was a gender role reversal when the *bambejja* began kneeling before the male *bakopi*, a role, which was formerly done by the male *bakopi*. The male *bakopi* regained their man gender even in relation to the females of the royal class.

During my first weeks of formal research, my informants challenged me when they suggested contradictory views about the identity of the *bambejja*. When I asked whether women beat drums at festivals before the abolition of kingship, some informants strongly argued that women had been drummers long before the abolition of the Buganda kingdom. On the other hand, there was consensus, especially from drummers and dancers, that drumming was never a role for women; instead, women were the dancers. However, further research revealed that the women drummers referred to were actually the *bambejja*. Although according to the Kiganda custom, they were considered men and, therefore, qualified to beat the drums, my informants referred to them as women because the social structure that constructed them as men had been dismantled. Although culturally they are still recognized as *bambejja*, socially they are reconstructed as women. Even after the restoration of the kingdom in 1993, with a culturally and socially changed Buganda, there is little hope that the *bambejja's* position will be reinstated. After all, the "traditional" position of the king as "man among men" is also still in question.

NNAMASOLE: FEMALE-WOMEN IN THE PALACE

Among the women—male and female—of the palace, the *nnamasole* (queen mother) occupied the highest social position. Scholars have written that the *nnamasole*, unlike other female-women of the palace, had judicial powers, collected taxes, and condemned their own people to death (Lebeuf, 1963; Schiller, 1990). For example, Laurence Schiller argued that the "powers and prerogatives of the *nnamasole* were tangible, superior to that of all other chiefs. On her death, the office would be filled with classificatory mother" (1990:

458–9). Further, Musisi celebrated the *nnamasole's* power and noted, "the Namasole *[sic]* had powers similar to that of the Kabaka and the Prime Minister" (1991a: 76). Musisi related the powerfulness of the *nnamasole* to her access to the taxes of land, ownership of estates, and membership in a court in which she was the "king."[5] Many of my informants also pointed out that she was one of the three important political figures in Buganda. While the celebration of the *nnamasole's* power is somehow justified, we need to reexamine the nature of this power.

A closer examination of the *nnamasole's* power reveals that the Kiganda culture assigned them power when it was to legitimize, empower, and support the king's dominance, which actually left this woman with an empty victory. She did not exercise power on her own, but for the sake of protecting the king. My arguments are based on the following points: first, the chiefs, whom these authors claim had less power than the *nnamasole,* although biologically males, were women. These writers ignored the fact that although they were males, these chiefs were women within the palace and men only outside the palace and in fact, according to the palace hierarchy they were below the *nnamasole.* Moreover, the *nnamasole's* power was derived from the role she had to play as the protector and defender of her son, the king. By protecting the king's position, the *nnamasole* was also protecting the little power she could acquire from the male-dominated society, and which she could only get when her son was the king.

Second, the "privilege" to kill subverted her "natural" role as a procreator, hence robbing her identity as a woman, as defined within the Kiganda society. Moreover, the *nnamasole's* position as a queen mother was recognized only after the death of her husband (the previous king and the father of the present king), and she was not allowed to remarry. If both the *kabaka* and the *nnamasole* were kings, why was her sexuality controlled, while the *kabaka* had sexual access to all women in Buganda? Moreover, until Muteesa II's reign, after enthronement, the *kabaka* was not allowed to see his mother as dictated by the coronation rituals, which Kabaka Namugala introduced in the 1750s (Irstam 1970: 23). One questions why the king had to desert his mother, one who nurtured him, soon after becoming the king. In what sense can a mother of the *kabaka* be considered powerful if she had no access to her son after he became a king? Was it the fear that being the mother of the *kabaka,* the woman's power in her would influence the king?[6] Later in the chapter, I discuss *nnamasole's* disguised identity as a powerful woman as constructed in baakisimba performance context.

SSAABASAJJA: OMWANA W'ENGOMA

Relating to the power of the drum, the *kabaka* is referred to as "omwana w'engoma" ("the son of the drum"). In fact, when the king comes into power the Baganda say "alidde engoma," "he has eaten the drums," which implies that "he has eaten Buganda," he has taken over power. Most important, the *ngoma* symbolizes not only royalty, power and authority of kingship, but also the very existence of the Buganda kingdom. Explaining symbolism in Buganda, Muzzanganda A. Lugira, a Muganda philosopher, notes that: "In the Ganda mentality Symbol *[sic]* is taken generically and includes all that is meant by a sign, a mark or token. It is regarded in one way or another as that which stands for something else" (1970: 133). Lugira argues further that "what the Ganda mind tends to convey through the idea [of] symbolism, is the bringing together of ideas and objects, one of which in a certain circumstance somehow expresses the other" (Ibid.). The Baganda look at drums as those same objects and the ideas they stand for. The symbolism of the drums is inherent not only in the functions the drums perform, but also their shapes and designs, as well as the associated meanings of their sounds.

Nnaalongo Dezideriyo, a seventy-two-year-old woman, stressed that "Buganda is the drum; without the drum, Buganda is non-existent" *("Obuganda ngoma; awatali ngoma, Obuganda tewali!")* (personal communication). In this case, the drum symbolizes Buganda itself, which is under the control of the Kabaka. The mythical origin of the drum explains its symbolic power and high status among the Baganda. According to Katambula Busuulwa, a specialist in Kiganda music and customs:

> The origin of the drum was sacred, meaning that one could find a stone that was shaped like a drum. You would also find two other stones, which function as the mallets. Those who were charged or supposed to beat [these drums] would get the two [beaters] and beat the [stone drums]. When beaten, these drums would sound like the drums made out of animal skins [like the ones we have today]. At times, these drums would beat themselves [they would sound without a visible person beating them]. In other words, the drum would not necessarily need someone to beat them.

> *Kweggamba engoma zaasooka kuba mu butonde, amakulu nti osanga awo ejjinja nga lyeekolera ddala nga bwe wandirabye engoma. Era n'osanga amayinja amalala abiri nga gali awo wabbali nga gy'eminyolo gyago! Era ng'abateekwa okukubako nga bwakwaata amayinja ago ne bakubako.*

Ng'era olukubako ng'evugira ddala nga kati bw'owulira engoma ey'eddiba. Oluusi nga yo yeekuba yokka; kweggamba tebeera awo nti abantu bamale kugyikubako (interview).

Because the stones could sound without anybody hitting them, the Baganda believed that a supernatural power hit these stones to produce sound. Busuulwa stressed that power is inherent in the drum; it was not about assigning meaning through social practice but rather, the meaning was already there in the drum. Busuulwa noted:

> The drums have what we call power that rules the entire Buganda. Actually, those drums have umbilical cords that make them human. In fact, whenever there was any conflict [in the kingdom], the drum just disappeared or it tore or strangled itself!

> *Ngoma zirimu kye tuyita amaanyi agafuga Obuganda bwonna bwonna. Era engoma ezo zibeeramu endira, ezizifuula omuntu yennyini! Kweggamba yo kasita wabeerawo okutabuka kwonna kwonna nga yo ebulawo bubuzi, oba yeeyuza ne yeetuga!* (ibid.).

However, in my view, as Andrew Weintraub has also rightly noted, "power is not something that instruments, images, or sounds inherently possess. Rather, power is a social relation among people that is mediated by the 'language' of instruments" (2001: 198). It is because of the Baganda's belief in the power mediated by the drums that "each successive Kabaka increased the number [of the drums], until, in Muteesa [I's] reign, they numbered many hundreds" (Lush 1935: 9). For instance, Apollo Kaggwa (1934: 48) and Allan J. Lush (1934: 9) reported that Ssekabaka Kimera introduced the *ngalabi* drum called *ttimba* from his maternal family, the Banyoro.[7] Lush noted further that this drum was "highly venerated [and] the Kabaka himself beats timba *[sic]* at his enthronement to declare that he [had] become Kabaka" (ibid.). Further, Ssekabaka Mutebi I introduced *mujaguzo,* one of the most important Kiganda drums of the palace (Lush 1935: 9; Kaggwa 1912a: 44, 49).

Because of the symbolic power of the drum, culturally all Kiganda drums are given due respect and no drum is supposed to be held or placed upside down. This position would mean that "Buganda," the Kingdom and the king, are dead. The drums are only placed upside down when the Kabaka dies, as a sign of mourning. Baaziriyo Nsubuga noted that: "indeed, the drum is very important, and if the drum is put upside down, it means the kingship is also upside down" *("era engoma kikulu nnyo, kubanga engoma bw'evuunikibwa ng'obwakabaka bwonna bwevuunise")* (interview). The drum symbolizes power, *ssaabasajja,* the Man among men.

Ezuliya Nannyonga, a former court dancer, told me that if someone held the drums upside down when the king was still alive, that person was killed, because he either wished the king was dead or wanted to take over power. Roscoe reported that when the king died, Mugema, the chief who took charge of the royal drums, kept them in his enclosures so that no unauthorized prince should confiscate them and have himself proclaimed king (1911: 104). For that reason, no man other than the king beats the drum within the palace. The males that beat the drums are women, since all the female and male *bakopi,* are considered women within the palace. Although Mugema had access to the royal kingship drums and, therefore, access to power, as a male-woman, the cultural emasculation controlled him from installing himself as king. Ideologically, he was made to believe that only men from the royal blood could be "sons of the drum," and ascend to kingship and no woman could ever become a king.

Moreover, Kawula, the head of the *bagoma ba Kabaka* (the *kabaka's* musicians and dancers), was supposed to be a virgin, one who had not yet become a man, since one was considered a man only after marrying and having children. He could not marry throughout his life as long as he served as the head of the *kabaka's* drummers. Because he could not marry, his "manhood" was completely erased since even outside the palace, one was considered a "proper" man only if he had a woman under his roof. In fact, Kawula had his residence within the palace, so as to monitor his sexual behavior.

BAAKISIMBA PERFORMANCE PRACTICE IN THE PALACE

As already discussed in Chapter Three, it is only speculative when baakisimba began to be performed in the palace.[8] Kalyango stressed that while baakisimba existed during Kabaka Kintu's time (ca. 1314–1344), it was not as popular as the *mibala (sing. mubala)* drums (praise drum beats for the king) (interview). He said that the *mubala* drum, "Ggwe musota, ggwe ngo," (you are the snake, you are the lion) which was beaten on a drum with nine bells, was very popular. This drum is related to the power of the king, one that is compared to the fierceness of a snake and a lion. The distinction between the *mibala* drums and baakisimba was that while the *mibala* are beaten with mallets, baakisimba was beaten with the palms. Further, the former simulates only the rhythm of the text, while the latter combines both the rhythm and the pitch. Moreover, while baakisimba drumming can be used to accompany dance, the *mibala* do not accompany dancing.

It should noted, however, that baakisimba played and, to some extent, still plays important roles in both ritual and festive ceremonies of the palace. A number of kings have been noted as great patrons of music in general, and baakisimba in particular. Besides being great patrons of bands of musicians and dancers, it was common for a king to participate in music and perform-ances in general, and baakisimba in particular. Muzaana Namuyanja, a female servant at Ssekabaka Kyabaggu's tombs, informed me that Ssekabaka Kyabaggu (ca. 1754–1764) had a number of occasions, especially when Buganda was not at war, when he beat drums and danced together with the *balangira* and *bambejja*. Omuzaana Namuyanja explained that because of Kyabaggu's great interest in music and dancing, he always organized festivi-ties to inspire dancing.[9] Further, she said, Kyabaggu replaced his original name Muwenda Mutebi, because of his great interest in music and dance. Omuzaana Namuyanja explained that "Kyabaggu" comes from the root word "biggu," which means drum rhythms. And yet, in addition to beating *mujaguzo* (royal drums) and *ntamiivu* (type of drums), *ntaala* (xylophone), and *nnanga* (harp), Ssekabaka Muteesa I is noted for beating the *ngalabi* and singing, especially for baakisimba dance (Kasirye 1959: 58, 83).

Because of their pride, the kings of Buganda wanted to surpass other kingdoms in all aspects.[10] Buganda was known for waging wars with its neighbors, through which it did not only capture "cattle, wives, children, and induced the [captive] to pay regular tribute" (Fallers 1964: 65), but also raided musical instruments, musicians, and dancers (Anderson 1968: 24). Capturing musicians and dancers from other regions illustrates how the Kabaka's dominance extended beyond the boundaries of Buganda. Among all the regions that Buganda conquered, Busoga[11] played an especially important role in enriching the music of the Baganda. The expeditions over the years, especially in the 1800s, not only brought in new instruments, but also new music and musicians as well as dance styles and dancers. More specifically, the Basoga contributed significantly to the palace baakisimba since the mid-nineteenth century, although their influence is traced also to Ssekabaka Suuna's reign (early nineteenth century). For instance, Kalungi traced the origin of baakisimba male-women dancing to Ssekabaka Suuna's reign, in the early nineteenth century (interview). The presence of Basoga musicians in Buganda palace during Muteesa I's reign is well documented (Speke 1863: 297, 323; Wilson and Felkin 1882: 215–216; Ashe 1889: 52, 68, 327; and Zimbe 1939). For example, B. M. Zimbe wrote that, "Muteesa [I] sent for Basoga lyre players, xylophone players, drummers and dancers since he heard that the Basoga had musical instruments that surpassed those of Buganda" (quoted in Anderson 1968: 24).

Another influence from Busoga was the initiation of baakisimba male dancers; the only dance that the male-women participated in was *maggunju*[12], which was invented during Ssekabaka Mulondo's reign. As a matter of fact, the majority of the palace male-women dancers were Basoga. Anderson reported that Balikumbuga, a Musoga [male-woman] dancer, was king Muteesa I's favorite (1968: 23). Consitatino Lwewunzika, Juma Natyole, and Mulyabintu were dancers in Muteesa II's palace (Lwewunzika, interview). And since in Busoga males performed *temenhaibuga,* a waist dance, it is conceivable that they easily learned to dance baakisimba. The Basoga's influence in baakisimba is clearly demonstrated by some similarities in the basic dance movement of baakisimba and *tamenhaibuga.* As in baakisimba dance, *tamenhaibuga* has its basic movement in the waist and footwork; the only difference is that baakisimba has a round waist movement while *tamenhaibuga* has a staccato-like waist movement.[13]

The gradual influence of the Basoga led to the development of three new dance genres, namely *muwogola* ("breaking of bones," a fast dance), *mbaga* (wedding dance, which is relatively a very fast dance), *nnankasa,* named after a drum (fairly faster than baakisimba dance) (Lwewunzika, interview). A quick look at *nnankasa* suggests that the dance is baakisimba, but at a fast speed. In fact, one would agree that there are substantive borrowings from baakisimba. However, while its basic movements are also in the waist and footwork that are closely related to baakisimba, *nnankasa* is less graceful and employs more exaggerated movements. In addition to the accompaniment of the *mbuutu* and *ngalabi,* the nnankasa, a small and high-pitched drum beaten with mallets, distinguishes *nnankasa* dance. *Nnankasa* came to be performed to the king towards the mid-twentieth century (Nakintu, interview). On the other hand, *muwogola* is very vigorous and fast. While this dance is also concentrated in the waist and the footwork and also its music is in 6/8 meter, it is distinct in that it is freer.

The *mbaga* dance, which was always referred to by informants as the *ngoma ey'ebisoko* (drum with many variations), is said to have been very popular during Ssekabaka Chwa II's reign in the early twentieth century (Lwewunzika, interview 2000b; Kalungi, interview; Ggayira, interview; Kisolo, interview). However, some informants trace the *mbaga* as far back as Muteesa I's reign in the mid-nineteenth century, coinciding with the influx of Basoga musicians (Kisitu, interview). All informants said that the dance was first performed in the palace before being performed outside the palace at wedding ceremonies. In the palace, the *mbaga* was performed in the ceremony when the king was appointing chiefs and when he had special visitors. With time, as in the alleged case of baakisimba, the *mbaga* left the palace for the weddings outside the palace. However, it had to be modified first so as to suit the wedding contexts; the dance movement and gestures all aim at projecting Baganda's themes of marriage.[14] In addition to distinct dance movements, *mbaga* includes baakisimba and *muwogola*. In fact, it may be defined as a dance suite, both in terms of the music and body movement. However, the baakisimba movements in mbaga are performed slightly faster, since *mbaga* is a fast dance itself. Although new dances, *nnankasa, muwogola* and *mbaga* were created, baakisimba remained a full-fledged dance, in the palace. This retention positions baakisimba at the apex of Kiganda dance, despite the new inventions. However, after 1993, with the redefined Buganda kingdom, baakisimba began to be performed in the palace as part of a dance suite that combined *nnankasa,* and *muwogola* dances.

However, when *nnankasa* was introduced, the genre, were it was beaten ceased to be baakisimba; rather, it became *nnankasa. Nnankasa* became an independent dance style, although closely related to baakisimba and mainly differed in speed and the exaggerated body movement. Tereza Kisolo told me that although the *mbaga* and *nnankasa* are vigorous dances, they were performed gracefully within the palace. She said, "Our dancing was very peaceful, we did not dance like yours; the way you people are dancing now [in the twenty-first-century]. By the way, whom would you raise the dust for? The king?" (interview). Because the palace grounds were covered with grass, while walking, the king's subjects never lifted their feet in front of the king; least they raised dust for the king.

While other female-women, including the king's wives and the servants, were not allowed to attend baakisimba and other entertainment musics and dances during public functions, the *nnamasole* had her music and dance ensembles. Although the *nnabagereka* (the king's first wife) and *nnamasole* were female-women of the palace, being a mother of the king, and therefore, his protector, the *nnamasole* had elevated power. Writing about his experience at the palace of the queen mother of Muteesa I, John Hannington Speke reported that:

> When the women were dismissed, a band of music, with a court full of Wakungu [chiefs], was ordered in to change the scene. . . . The musicians, dressed in long-haired Usoga goat-skins [skins from Busoga], were now ordered to strike up, which they did, with their bodies swaying or dancing like bears in a fair. Different drums were then beaten, and I was asked if I could distinguish their different sounds (1863: 247).

As a performance of empowering her, she was allowed to have her own musical ensembles. In this case, baakisimba participated in constructing the symbolic power of the *nnamasole*. Being an instrument of power, the ensembles were lost when the kingdom was abolished. Likewise, the *nnamasole* also had to lose her ensemble since they were instruments of power. Although the kingdom was reinstated in 1993, given its redefined political, social, and cultural structure, the *nnamasole's* glory was not restored, and therefore, her music and dance ensembles. While I was able to meet former musician and dancers of Ssekabaka Muteesa II, I never encountered any former musician or dancer for the *nnamasole*.

Moreover, when Milton Obote overthrew Ssekabaka Muteesa II in 1966, Buganda's music also went with the king in exile (Richards 1964).[15] As Anderson reported,

> On May 23, 1966, the central government attacked the royal enclosure, forcing the king and the people who worked and lived there to flee and the Uganda Army occupied the Palace *[sic]* from that time on. Instruments were either sacked or burned during the attack and this proved to be the end of the Royal *[sic]* musical traditions. (A new Uganda constitution in 1967 abolished all Kingdoms and the institution of kingship in Uganda). Since the king eventually fled the country, the musicians were not allowed to play any kind of music because Buganda was mourning (1968: 9).

Does this mean that there were no more music-making activities and dancing in Buganda? Was this the end of baakisimba dancing in the Buganda kingdom since drumming was not permitted in the absence of the king?[16] The old palace baakisimba ceased to exist since its context was abolished; however, people continued to dance baakisimba. As the dance moved away from the palace center, its meaning changed as well, as my discussion will show later in the next chapter.

Although the kingdom was restored in 1993, the twenty-six years of recess was a long period without kingship. By the time I undertook this research, majority of the palace drummers and dancers had already passed away because of age. However, a few former court dancers and musicians are still alive, but many have retired dancing and drumming. The new generation of dancers and drummers has only a vague idea about the kingship, a tradition that seems outdated among the young people. Some former court drummers, including Sulaiti Kalungi and Peter Ggayira, and dancers including Consitantino Lwewunzika, Nusula Namutebi, and Tereza Kisolo, have been trying to teach the young ones, but according to these performers, the original spirit of the *badongo ba kabaka* cannot be retrieved. Kalungi, for instance, noted that although some of his sons are very good drummers, they still lack the skill of controlling the drum. He said that, "they have a youthful pride which does not allow them to beat the drums well!" (interview). Likewise, Lwewunzika complained that some of his dance students are not patient; before they have mastered a motif, they want to perform a new one. He commented that, "they do not have patience like we had. That is what spoils their dancing" (Interview). Besides lacking patience, many of the young people are more interested in cassette-and other mass-mediated music. In fact, a number of wedding ceremonies that I attended where Kiganda music was performed, disco music almost predominated. And yet, baakisimba is mainly surviving in schools as part of the school syllabus, as will be discussed in Chapter Seven. However, after graduating from school, many of these dancers do not continue with baakisimba performance.

THE BADONGO BA KABAKA: THE KING'S ENSEMBLE

The *Badongo ba kabaka* is a generic term that refers to the musicians and dancers of the *kabaka*. There were two types of *badongo ba Kabaka:* those whom the *kabaka* contracted for a specific period of time (*badongo ab'e-bisanja*), and those who were sub-contracted by *badongo b'ebisanja* (none of the informants could provide the title for these sub-contractors). The *bisanja (sing. kisanja)* (contracts) lasted three months, one month, or two weeks. Explaining how he entered the palace, Kalungi, who was one of those hired by the *badongo b'ebisanja*, said that it was his uncle Kayemba who recommended him to Atyeni, the head of the *badongo ba Kabaka*, during Ssekabaka Muteesa II's reign.

The introduction of baakisimba to the palace not only created changes in music and dance performance, but also created a formalized distinction between the performers and the audience, forming the basis for the earliest theatrical performance. Outside the palace, dancing was not formalized; performers constituted, in most cases, the audience and vice versa. One could stand up and dance whenever inspired by the music. However, in the palace, selected and specifically trained performers, whose role was to enhance the dignity and authority of the king, replaced free participation in baakisimba. The palace context created a form of "professionalism" in baakisimba performance. Although the livelihood of the performers did not entirely depend on performing for the king, the *badongo ba kabaka* were auditioned, fully registered, and recognized as the *kabaka's* musicians and dancers. Tereza Kisolo told me that before she was enrolled as a palace dancer during Ssekabaka Muteesa II's reign, she had to be auditioned by a group of chiefs (male-women). She said that there were a number of female-women who were auditioned and those who passed the test were retrained. However, the male-women who auditioned and trained the female-women dancers were not dancers themselves. By auditioning and directing the training session, these male-women were instrumental in shaping and defining female-women's dancing styles.[17] The male-women's power to control the female-women's dancing legitimized the hierarchical strata that existed even among the women of the palace.

Because of the king's authority as the Man, once chosen to perform for the king, no musician or dancer was allowed to perform outside the palace. It is only after the *kabaka's* power greatly receded after the reign of Ssekabaka Mwanga II that musicians and dancers started performing as part of professional performance troupes outside the palace during Kabaka Daudi Chwa II's reign. As already mentioned in Chapter Three, Juma Natyole was the first male-woman dancer to perform formalized baakisimba outside the palace during Chwa II's reign in the mid 1940s.

The remuneration of the king's musicians depended on whether one was in the *kisanja* (contractual arrangement) or whether one was just being sub-contracted on a short-term basis. It also depended on what the Baganda valued at the time. Before the introduction of money and other foreign items, women, goats, cows, and loads of bark cloth were the most valued items in Buganda. Roscoe wrote, "When the king engaged a new drummer . . . he gave him a [female-] woman, a cow, and a load of barkcloths" (1911: 30). In this case, female-women were taken as commodities that could be bartered in exchange for a service. Kalungi confirmed that "The kings used to offer [female-] women as gifts. 'My subject so and so has impressed me,' and he would give him a woman" (interview).[18] However, he noted that none of the drummers of his time that he knew of were given such kind of gifts.

When Christianity and money were introduced, a new mode of payment was adopted. With the abolition of slavery, there were no female-women to be paid to the drummers; Christianity was against the enslavement of women. Money became the mode of payment. Kalungi said that in the 1940s he was paid 1.00 Uganda shilling and, according to him, it was a lot of money at the time. He also said, "The king could give a bicycle, when you made him happy, but there were not many people that got them bicycles." On the other hand, Kisitu, a former court drummer of Kitenga, Buddu County, told me that Ssekabaka Muteesa II gave him the gift to build a tile-roofed house. With great pride Kisitu said: "In the whole of Masaka town, I was the first person to build a tile-roofed house. Ssekabaka Muteesa

II is the one who gave me the money that built this house when I made him happy with my beating of the drum. This house is honored very much!" (interview). And yet, Tereza Kisolo, a dancer, showed me a charcoal flat iron, which Muteesa II gave her. Further, Lwewunzika, a male-woman dancer, was given clothes in addition to a piece of land in Mpigi, where he still lived to the time of my fieldwork in 2000 (interview).

Further, due to the economic hardships of the 1950s because of Ssek-abaka Muteesa II's dwindling power, he could not afford to remunerate every performer. As a result, the number of the king's *bandongo* (musicians and dancers) was cut. The music section was most affected; the number of chorus members was reduced. In order to compensate for the singers' part the *madinda* (twelve-keyed wooden xylophones), *ndongo* (eight-stringed bowl lyre), and *ndingidi* (single-stringed tube fiddle) were added to the drum ensemble for the accompaniment of baakisimba and *mbaga* performance (these instruments are shown in Plate 4). All these instruments were played by male-women since no female-women at that time were allowed to play any musical instrument during festive musical performances. As such, female-women were restricted to dancing alone.

Plate 4. Kiganda musical instruments: *right to left: mbuutu, ngalabi, mpuunyi, nnankasa* (drums), *ndingidi* (fiddle), *ndongo* (lyre), *nsaasi* (rattles), and *madinda* (xylophone).

Since 1993, payment to musicians and dancers is not as clear-cut as it was before the abolition of the kingdom. First, there are no longer permanent musicians. There are no specific ensembles for the palace; established groups are sometimes hired or even perform for free when there is a palace function. Moreover, sometimes school children perform for the king. However, no ensemble that had ever performed before the king was willing to disclose how much they had been paid and instead, argued that it is not a payment, but just a gift. One of the explanations as to why these musicians did not disclose their remuneration as a payment could be because in the Kiganda culture, every Muganda had the obligation to offer free service to the king. It rightly follows then, that the king can only offer a gift, but not a payment.

The king had specifically invited guests that attended the palace functions in general, and baakisimba performance in particular. Describing the kind of audience they performed for, the former *badongo ba kabaka* that I interviewed concurred that attendance at these performances was only by invitation. Guests included mainly princes, princesses, and some favorite chiefs. The princesses attended these performances, because they were like the prince were men and the chiefs, although they were male-women, they were at the top of the hierarchy of women in the palace. All informants agreed it was rare that female-women attended these ceremonies. Kisolo confirmed that: "The women [female] never came out of their quarters. We danced for men and a few male-women. It was once in a while when *nnabagereka* [the king's first wife] came out. The king was with the Prime Minister, the county and village chiefs" (interview). Similarly, Muhamood Kasujja, a former drummer said, "In the past *nnabagereka* could not be seen! It was one time when I saw her in a window, peeping out as we were in the court room performing" (interview).

These performance contexts participated in defining the role of Baganda women and especially the female-women within the palace. Although *nnabagereka* was the first wife of the king, as a female-woman, she was kept in the background and was not allowed to participate in activities that would expose her. One informant explained that the *kabaka* could not attend functions with the *nnabagereka* because, although she was the first wife, all Baganda women culturally belong to the king. This informant revealed that such a custom had to be perpetuated in order to give the king the opportunity to have any woman he wanted. Another explanation to why *nnabagereka* could not attend baakisimba performances or any other festivities was that the customs protected the king from showing any emotional attachment to women in public (anonymous, interview). By sitting next to *nnabagereka* in a performance context, or glancing at her in a way that showed emotion, the king would undermine his power. Similarly, in a video recording of Ssekabaka Mutebi II and Nnabagereka Sylvia Luswata Nagginda's wedding ceremony (27 August 1999), it was evident that the king was always walking a step ahead of his bride, unlike in wedding marches of commoners.[19] One could easily note that although Nnabagereka Nagginda had a wide smile, Ssekabaka Mutebi II rarely smiled.[20] Further, if they at all attend functions together, their seats are always apart.

Tereza Kisolo, who on several occasions performed baakisimba before Ssekabaka Muteesa II, the father of Kabaka Muwenda Mutebi II, told me that it is the practice for kings never to show their emotions publicly. She said, "Ssekabaka Muteesa II never smiled. But when he was very impressed with our performance, he would just beat his thighs; then [we would know] he was happy!" (interview). A number of informants told me that kings were socialized not to be emotional, whether they were happy or not, as a means to enhance their power. Showing emotion was related to being weak. Tereza Nabawanda at Ssekabaka Suuna's tombs told me that the king does not attend any burial rite for fear that he may get emotional and begin to cry (interview). To be emotional is to become a woman, to expose weakness and to loose power.

WHEN FEMALE-WOMEN MUST BEAT THE DRUMS

Until the 1960s, it was unheard of for women, outside the palace, to beat drums in festival contexts, whether in baakisimba or *mbaga* (wedding) dance contexts. However, within the palace, female-women would beat drums at sacred functions. Kalyango reported that Nabukalu, Ssekabaka Mutebi I's wife, was the *ngalabi* performer. Kalyango told me that:

> Once upon a time, Ssekabaka Mutebi I married Nabukalu, who was very beautiful. However, that girl was like a monster. When he took her to the palace, she started beating the *ngalabi*. Then the King decided that she should be killed because she was doing things not meant for female-women. In fact, she was the first woman to beat the *ngalabi* (interview).

A woman who threatens the king's power by beating the drum must be a monster, and since anybody who threatened the king's power was killed, Nabukalu had to die.

In Buganda, like other cultures where women's drumming is regulated, drumming is restricted to private, informal contexts. Similarly, Veronica

Doubleday revealed that in Persian culture, women beat the frame drum in informal musical entertainment contexts that are restricted to women (1999: 117). In addition, among the Akan of Ghana, "The only drums that women were allowed to play and still do play are the *donno* drums which are used during the celebration of puberty rites for girls" (Nketia 1990: 98), rituals that involve initiating girls into their role as adult women. In this case, women's drumming is not for their pleasure, but to facilitate and enhance men's cultural power. Doubleday has also noted that the most legitimate public performance of drums by Persian women is during wedding contexts. As Doubleday rightly argues, "the drum facilitates transfer of a young woman from the control of her father to her husband. . . . [M]en needed women's music to enliven festivities which ensured continuance of the patrilineal social order" (1999: 126). Likewise, Baganda female-women are allowed to beat drums in rituals designed to empower the king, for his pleasure, to appease spirits, or bring about healing. They also beat drums to venerate ancestral spirits in order to strengthen families and clans.

Since the drum is a symbol of power in Buganda, controlling the female-women's potential power involves seizing the drum from them. However, as in the case of Persian culture, men need women to empower them; therefore, they have limited women to drumming contexts necessary for the empowerment of the kingdom, which is the men's terrain. When I questioned why female-women beat drums during rituals, and yet the Baganda customs restrict women to beat any festival drums outside the palace, Ssaalongo Kizza told me that:

> It is possible to beat the drums and she temporarily suspends her being a woman. She participates as a member of the clan because at that point she is going to be used to resolve problems of the clan and that of chieftainship. For instance, if she gets possessed with a spirit and yet she is the one supposed to [appease it] by performing the rituals. She can settle problems, but not to participate as a drummer for pleasure like in baakisimba, where drums are beat for festivity (interview).

The fact that women can beat drums if it is to resolve family or clan problems crystallizes the constructed role of women as those who must provide resolutions for all cultural matters. In Chapter Five, I explain that when a female baby is born, a female tutelary deity, *nnakawala* is called upon to empower the baby with cleansing powers needed during her adult age. By beating the drums during the palace rituals, women are exercising the powers given to them by the *nnakawala* tutelary deity.

Adding to Kizza's views, Sulaiti Kalungi pointed out that the first drum was beaten by women to soothe the angry gods, especially Walumbe, the god of death.[21] According to Kalungi, the first drum descended upon the people of the *ngeye* (black and white colobus monkey) clan at a hill called Kabuye in Butambala County and was beaten by a female. Kalungi informed me that:

> There is a village called Kabuye where the drum descended, sent by God to the Colobus monkey clan. This was a sacred drum and had its own taboos. When Walumbe killed many people, a virgin girl would beat the drum and its sound would reduce Walumbe's anger. After that, the people went to the King, who gave them a cow that they took to Walumbe's shrine and performed rituals [to appease him]. Walumbe then stopped killing people. Girls beat this drum during moonlight. (interview).

Kalungi confirmed that drums have a sacred origin, which is similar to what Busuulwa (interview) and Lush (1935: 9) have reported. Further, the drum was first beaten by females, although mainly as a means to appease Walumbe, the god of Death. In Western cultural contexts, Redmond also reported that sacred drumming was one of the primary skills for women and "remained a powerful tool for communal bonding and individual transformation until the fall of the Roman empire" (1997: 1). The power to appease spirits seems to come not only from the sound of the drum, but also from the performer. Why is it that the Kiganda customs assign women to beat these drums and not men? Examining the contexts in which women beat sacred drums will help to elucidate this point.

The most important ritual for women to beat the drums within the palace occurs when the king pays homage to the royal shrines *(masiro)* of his predecessors. During this ceremony, the symbolic representation of the deceased kabaka, the royal twin, *omulongo wa kabaka*[22]—a stump of umbilical cord taken from the navel, *(akalira)*—is presented to the reigning king. It was customary for the Baganda to set aside also the prince and princess's stump of umbilical cord and to place it in a well-decorated container. C. W. Hattersley reported that: "These frames are extremely beautiful, covered on the wooden frame with a foundation of bark cloth and fibre, with the most handsome many-coloured beadwork . . ." (1968: 15). As Apollo Kaggwa has observed, these umbilical cords are cared for as though they were "the living kings themselves" (1934: 129). For example, Benjamin C. Ray wrote that "Like a human twin, the royal Twin *[sic]* is also wrapped in bbombo vine [a herb] on ceremonial occasions; and like the living king, the royal twin is carried on the right shoulder of its bearer" (1991: 127). Hattersley reported that attendants to these *balongo* frames believed that the moment the king died his spirit entered into this frame (ibid.). The frame was not buried with the corpse, but kept in a secret place in the tomb and carefully watched over. The widows of the deceased *kabaka* who lived in his tomb believed that so long as that frame was in existence, their old lord and master was still with them in spirit; and when these objects are brought out, all the old drummers and singers beat their drums, and sing the old chants and songs, just as they used to do to welcome the approach of their master during his reign. Therefore, when the king pays homage, he is not only visiting these objects, but also his ancestors. To him, his ancestors still live and their spirits are actually present in these '*balongo* frames.' Hattersley has noted, "Women on these occasions beat the drums with hands, and are experts at the work" (Ibid.). As such, men and male power have been challenged and contradicted "in mythical and historical representations in which women and female sources of power are often necessary for the very existence, preservation, and legitimization of male power and culture" (Weiss 1993: 23).

According to Kisolo, she first saw women beating baakisimba drums at Kasubi tombs. However, she noted that their performance was not as energetic as the ones "you see, for instance, at wedding parties. The women's drumming was graceful and their performance was very contained" (interview). When I went to Kasubi tombs, although I never saw women beating the drums, I saw three sets of drums placed directly opposite the tombs of the respective kings. In all cases, the *ngalabi,* were tilted and tied onto poles and covered with bark cloth on their heads while the *mbuutu,* were just beside the men drum, without any covering. When I asked why the drums were positioned like that, I was told that they were in a position ready for performance (see plate 5).

The female-woman attendant told me that they are only beaten by women during a special ceremony; "on this occasion, the king pays homage to his ancestors" (anonymous, interview). When I asked why the *ngalabi* was tied onto a pole, she told me that since it was beaten by women, it had to be tied because women can never put the drum between their legs. She said, "if the *ngalabi* is tied, it gives easy beating posture for the drummer." A male-woman attendant confirmed that only wives of kings or heirs to the former wives beat the drum. He said that although princesses are female, they couldn't beat these specific drums, because they are not supposed to be beaten by men. I found similar drums in three of the six tombs that I visited and in all cases, these drums were guarded by women.[23]

Plate 5. Man and woman drums in Kasubi tombs.

Another performance in which female-women were the drummers is *kifule* dance. This performance was exclusive to the palace and was only attended by the *kabaka* and the *bambejja*. Unfortunately, I was not able to get detailed information about the ritual. Most informants were embarrassed to talk about it and said the dance ritual was very obscene. Efforts to find out whether *kifule* is being performed now since the Kabaka had been restored were fruitless. Although I was not able to get the details of this ritual dance, many informants who requested anonymity alleged that *kifule* was performed by naked female-women, who included drummers and dancers. However, the drumming and dancing styles were similar to that of baakisimba, the only difference being that the female-women dancers had no costumes. One informant confided that:

> There were times when the king was with the women alone and they were the ones beating the drums and dancing. At times the princesses beat these drums. And those dancers used to be naked. From those dancers, the king could choose one whom he desired and when he did, then *kifule* dance would end.
>
> *Waalingawo Kabaka gye yabanga n'abakyala bokka nga beebeekubira engoma ate nga beebazina. Abambejja oluusi baakubanga engoma zino.*

Era abazinyi abo baabeeranga bwereere. Mw'abo abazinyi kabaka yayin-
zanga okulondamu gw'aba asiimye, era bwe yalondangamu ng'amazina ga
kifule olwo gaggwa (anonymous, interview).

The informants interviewed claimed that this performance was mainly for the
king's sexual pleasure, explaining why no males (neither the princes nor the
male-women) were allowed to attend. In this case, women could only access the
drums because the presence of male-women drummers would threaten the
kabaka's pleasure. By eliminating the male-women drummers, the king was
empowered, since he controlled and monopolized the pleasure of seeing the
naked female-women's bodies. Another informant told me that these female-
women dancers were never allowed to perform any dance outside the palace. He
also confirmed that although the king chose some of these dancers for his "sexual needs," he never declared them as his "wives." However, the king never
allowed them to get married. The informant explained that if they got married,
"who would entertain the king? She stays in the palace as the king's concubine"
("ate kati ng'anaasanyusa Kabaka anaaba ani? Olwo abeera mu lubiri nga
mukyala wa Kabaka") (anonymous, interview). Similarly, when I asked Ezuliya
Nannyonga, a female-woman dancer during Ssekabaka Chwa II's reign, to
teach me how to dance palace baakisimba, she asked me whether I was ready
not to get married. She also said that I had to perform certain rituals, particularly, the cleansing ones, in order to be a worthy dancer for the king.

CONTRADICTORY ROLES: CONSENTING AND CONTESTING
THE KING'S POWER

Before the abolition period, the importance of baakisimba went beyond the
specificities of its structure. On the one hand, it was a submission to the
king's power and yet, on the other hand, it was a performance of resistance
behind the backs of the king. The performance of the king's power is not
only shown in the symbolism of the drum, his patronage of baakisimba
ensembles, or even when female-women beat the drums, but also illustrated
by the dance movements. However, it should be noted that the meaning of
the dance movements in baakisimba are fluid; what I offer here mainly
relates to the unsettled construction of gender within the palace contexts.
    One of the motifs in which the king's power is enacted is the
kweyanza/kweyanjula motif. *Kweyanza* means to "say thank you," while
kweyanjula is to "introduce oneself." This motif is usually the first one
performed after the dancers have come on stage and is one of the few
motifs that do not involve waist movements. There are two types of this

Plate 6. Kweyanza/kweyanjula motif.

motif according to the dancer's gender. For female-women, emphasis is put on the hand gestures and a smiling face. While kneeling down on the balls of the feet, folding the hands in a 'prayer-like' position, the dancer moves the hands diagonally to the right alongside each hip, alternating to the left on the first beat of every measure. On the other hand, the male-woman dancer prostrates in front of the king, lying flat on the ground, supporting body with the hands, while moving the head sideways, and the jaw resting on the floor. The dancer lifts "himself" and repeats this movement on the other side of the jaw, alternating on the first beat of the measure, like the woman dancer (see plate 6).[24]

In this motif, female-woman dancer not only expresses her beauty by smiling, but the kneeling position places her below his majesty the king, establishing her subordinate position in relation to that of the king. As Roscoe has noted, in Buganda, kneeling down is both an expression of class distinction between the rulers and the ruled, and a performance of the relations between a man and a woman. He writes, "when any man saw the king approaching, he went down on his knees, and if he wished to be particularly polite, he said 'Nkusiza' which means, 'I worship you'" (1911: 42). On the other hand, when a male-woman dancer prostrates before the king, She completely submits himself to the king. In fact, a male-woman prostrates before the king even outside the dance contexts. Kisolo mentioned that when this dancer prostrates, he declares that he would lay down his life for the protection of the king: "your majesty the king, I will die before you" *("Ayi Ssaabasajja w'oligwa nange wendiggwa")* (interview). Further, while the male-women could never position the drum between their legs when beating it outside the palace, they had to kneel to beat the drum within the palace. Sulaimani Mukwaaya informed me that "even the drummers knelt down and they never showed their backs to the king" (interview). As will be discussed in the proceeding chapters, kneeling is a sign of humility and submissiveness, which signifies a woman gender. The posture that the male-women adopted while beating the drums constructed them as women.

A graceful movement, befitting the dignity of a king, was performed in palace baakisimba. When performing for the king, the dancers were not supposed to lift their feet as in village baakisimba, lest they raise dust for the king; the dancing is flat-footed. With bent knees at body level, the feet make quick accented shuffling on every beat alternately resulting in a walking shimmy, quivering waist, and downward and upward thrusts of the hips with wriggling waist (see Figure11). However, it was more out of respect for the king than a health problem for the subject to raise dust in front of the king. The intensity or vigor of the waist and hip movement depends on the driving force of the drum music: its loudness, speed, and rhythmic figures.

Further, in *nsi eradde mirembe* (Buganda is at peace) motif, the dancer performs the basic footwork and waist/hip movements (as shown in figure 12, Chapter Five), while maintaining a rigid upper torso, the arms of dancer are still, bent, and lifted so that the hands are waist level. The fingers are splayed, palms parallel to the ground with the thumbs pointing to the waistline, which is the point of emphasis (see plate 7).[25]

The male-women and female-women dancers perform the same movements in this motif. The movements are accompanied with the same music as in figure 12. *Nsi eradde mirembe* is named after the arm gesture for greeting. Kaggwa noted that the expression *eradde mirembe* was one of the gestures the Baganda used when greeting each other (1952: 278). Within the palace, the gesture was interpreted as expressing a state of being peaceful. On the one hand, it is a wish for one's peacefulness and, on the other hand, it is a concern to know how a friend or a relative is doing. Since Buganda was involved in numerous wars, baakisimba was usually performed in those times when Buganda was peaceful, to enable the king to enjoy the dance. In the *nsi eradde mirembe,* the dancers had to communicate to the king the status of a peaceful Buganda in their movement.

Figure 11. Kubiibya palace motif.

Plate 7. Nsi eradde mirembe motif. Courtesy of Jean-Jacques Nattiez.

Moreover, the subjects had to show their king that they were happy about his rule and had no complaints at all. In this case, *nsi eradde mirembe* is a motif manipulated to conceal the subordinates' grievance and paint a picture that all was well and that the subjects were actually consenting to their domination. In fact, he Buganda have a proverb: "abatongole bikya bya mbuzi: tibyegaana mugwa, [meaning that], the citizens are like the necks of goats: they don't refuse the rope. [This means that the citizens] may murmur behind the chief's back, but they have to obey" (Walser, 1982: 7 no. 0069). The dance motif and the proverb relates to the time, especially before colonialism, when Baganda could not openly contest their dissatisfaction to the king's rule.

The open arms in the *kusaba* motif, is a gesture of asking for something, or praying among the Baganda. Still maintaining the basic footwork and waist/hip movement, the hands are turned so that the palms face up and the thumbs out. The hands are kept still as are the arms. In Buganda, *kusaba* (to ask or pray) is expressed by a hand gesture where the palms are facing up. Both male and female, within and outside the palace, perform the same movement (see plate 8).

Plate 8. Kusaba motif.

In her explanation of this motif, Ezuliya Nannyonga said that it was common in the palace for all the guests to be served while the musicians and dancers were not served and that at times they could be completely forgotten. As a result, the dancers created this gesture as a reminder that they also needed to be served (interview). In this case, this motif is used as a communication of the actual feelings of the dancers, which was never appropriate in normal discourse, outside the performance context of the palace.

The other palace dance motif that relates to the king's power is *Kuwera*. *Kuwera* means to swear allegiance to the king, a person in a dominant position. There are two kinds of *kuwera* motifs, one for male-women and the other for female-women. When performed by male-women, the left arm is held in front of the body at chest level. The right hand is parallel to the ground, elbow bent in at right angle, facing forward. The right hand takes up "shield." Although the female-women perform similar gestures, they do not take up a position of holding a spear, while the left hand is positioned as if holding a

Plate 9. Kuwera motif. Courtesy of Jean-Jacques Nattiez

"shield"; rather, their hands are open. In both cases, the arms are held rigid. Plate 9 shows Kanyanya Muyinda Ensemble performing *kuwera* motif.[26]

In this motif, the dancers show their allegiance to the king when performing the *kuwera* ("swearing") motif before him. It is a reassurance that his subjects love him and will always protect him. Although the *kabaka* had tremendous power, it was the responsibility of his subjects to protect him.

Moreover, the order was to dance in a straight line facing the king, as it was disrespectful to show the king one's back. Idi Sserunkuuma informed me that the dancers "used to dance backwards, so as not to show their backs to the king because showing their backs to the king was considered obscene in the Kiganda culture" (interview). This dance requirement denied the dancers creativity since the dancers could only move in a straight line and, moreover, face in one direction. When the dancer faces the king, it positions him as the central figure that the dancers must focus on. It also emphasizes the traditional monopoly of the king's power, since he is in direct control of the stage scenery of the dance. Specifically referring to Ssekabaka Muteesa I, Lugira wrote that: "the king was the master and center of everything in Buganda. What he initiated was ipso facto sanctioned, in accordance with the limits of ranks in Ganda society" (1970: 156). In this case, the straight-line choreography crystallizes the king's dominant power. The kind of formations that had to be adhered to when performing baakisimba for the king promoted the idea that the king is a dominant figure and women are subordinate to men.

The king's power as the man was not only shown in motifs performed before him, but also through the song repertoire that was specific to the palace context. The songs repertoire that constituted the accompanying music also point to the empowerment of the king. There are two types of songs, the twin songs and the baakisimba songs whose themes aimed at authenticating the king's power. Like all palace functions, baakisimba performance begins with the invocation of twins. The Baganda venerate the birth of twins; the mother and father, as well as the children, are considered to be sacred. Because of their sacredness, the Baganda believe that twins do not die, instead, "they are said to have just jumped or disappeared" ("babuuka bubuusi"). Because of the belief that twins transcend death, the Baganda accord them a great deal of power. Consequently, the Buganda monarch believes that the stability of the kingdom depends on the established good relationship with the whole realm of the "twins-world."

Therefore, the king has to consult the twins on all matters concerning the welfare of the monarchy, and so singing twin songs at the beginning of a function is to invite their presence (see also Nanyonga 1995: 219). There are always four twin songs sung in a performance.[27] The twin songs, which are always in call-and-response form, usually have short repetitive phrases. Following is one of the songs performed by Tebifaanana Abifuna Nnankasa Group during the Seventh Coronation Anniversary of Kabaka Muwenda Mutebi II on 8 August 2000. This song not only invokes the twins, but also illustrates the power of the king as the "great father of twins."

Ssaabalongo ssaawo amaaso	Great father of twins open your eyes
Bweeza bwa Mukasa	Good luck from Mukasa

Because the king is the man among men, he is more powerful than the father of twins (*ssaalongo*). For that reason, even if he has no twins, the title of *ssaabalongo*—even greater than that of *ssaalongo*—is given to him. Further, the Baganda believe that it is by the power of Mukasa, the god of Lake Nalubaale (Victoria), that people are able to produce twins. The song calls upon the *kabaka* to depend on Mukasa, the fortune giver, for the success of the ceremony as well as his kingdom, in general.[28]

On the other hand, the songs that accompany palace baakisimba narrate chronicles of kings and genealogical histories, which connect the present to the past kingships. This linkage helps to anchor and legitimize the reigning king's right to the throne. Baakisimba songs, like other Kiganda songs of the palace, retell glories, as well as defeats of kings. In this case, these songs participate in reconstructing culture history (Merriam 1964).[29] And yet, these songs exploit the ambiguity of Luganda language, which creates multiple spaces of reception. These songs were voices of what was left unmentioned in ordinary discourse and opened doors to frequently silenced voices. Songs were used to lodge complaints, or plead for mercy from the king. The Baganda greatly feared the *kabaka* and no one would dare confront him directly to lodge a complaint. However, through music, musicians would negotiate for better treatment from the *kabaka*. In this case, songs were used as a vehicle to communicate what ordinary language discourse cannot communicate (Merriam 1964). Although similar songs are still being sung in the Buganda of the 2000s, they are no longer used for lodging complaints. The present cultural, social, and political environments allow people to complain openly to the king. Newspapers, books, and other forms of documentation have become spaces for expressing people's feelings about the kingship.

Despite the change of repertoire, there are certain songs that are still remembered as baakisimba songs of the palace. "Ssematimba ne Kikwabanga" is one of those songs that most former court musicians and dancers still remember. Like all baakisimba songs, it has a call-and-response pattern, although this song has also been performed as a solo piece on a stringed instrument, or on xylophone in three parts (see Kubik 1969; Anderson 1968; Cooke 1970; and Gray 1995). It is important to note that Kiganda songs have numerous renditions because each performer creates his or her version. Justinian Tamusuza has noted that the renditions "are greatly influenced by the interdependency of text and melody. A slight change in either of the two due to the performers' improvisation, would account for the emergence of the many ensuing versions" (1996: 3–4). While the solo parts of this song may vary from performer to performer, the chorus part has to a great extent been retained. Following is the part of "Ssematimba ne Kikwabanga," a rendition sung by Augustine Kisitu during of my field trip in 2000.

Abasiba embuzi basibira bwereere,	Those who look after goats, look after them for nothing,
Laba Ssematimba ne Kikwabanga,	Look at Ssematimba and Kikwabanga,
Abali abangi nsigadde bwomu nze,	We were many, but I have remained alone,
Laba Ssematimba ne Kikwabanga.	Look at Ssematimba and Kikwabanga.

According to Apollo Kaggwa, this song was composed during Ssekabaka Kamaanya's reign (1952: 266–267). Kaggwa wrote that Ssematimba and Kikwabanga were very brave warriors who took part in a number of wars. However, one day Ssekabaka Kamaanya assigned them a raid, but this time they did not survive it. Before they went to war they prepared a big feast where they killed a number of goats to celebrate their victory in advance. Unfortunately, they never had a chance to eat the goat's meat, as it was time for them to leave for the war. They promised to eat their share when they come back. However, they never came back; they died during the war. The musicians composed a song to mourn them. Later, musicians used the song to accompany palace baakisimba dancing as well as playing the song solo on melodic instruments including *madinda, ndongo,* and *ndingidi.*

Although musicians mainly sing historical songs in baakisimba performances, new songs have also been composed. One of the most outstanding female-woman composers is Janet Nadujja. Following is an excerpt of her song "Atuuse Omugenyi Atuuse," which she composed during the coronation of Kabaka Muwenda Mutebi II and was first performed on the coronation day, 31 July 1993 (interview). It is important to note, however, that Nandujja never sings again the same song in the same way. What I have transcribed is part of the rendition that I recorded in 1995 during a field trip.

Atuuse omugenyi atuuse,	He has come, the visitor has come.
Ggwe tubadde tulinda,	The one we have been waiting for,
Wuuno amaze okujja.	He is here. He has come.
Essanyu litutta.	We are filled with joy.
Aliwa obwedda ggwe nninda?	Where is he that I have been waiting for?
Kale nneeyanze abakyala ab'engalo	Oh, I am so grateful to the women who are clapping.
Koona ku ngoma oBuganda bwebuge	Beat the drum so that the Baganda can dance
Olwa leero lunaku lwa nsusso,	Today is a special day,
Okulaba ku kabaka	To see the King.
Ani yali amanyi nt'olidda ku butaka	Who ever knew that you would reign again!
Hmm, nti olifuna eddembe,	Yes, that you will have peace,

There are a number of issues raised in this song, but I will discuss only those issues specifically pertaining to my topic. The song crystallizes the view that Kiganda culture, including the beliefs and ideologies about gender, are contingent on the existence of the kingdom. When Nandujja calls upon the women, she expresses her gratefulness to the women who are clapping. In this case, Nandujja presents the women's role in this performance. Although when she calls for the drums, she does not refer to the men, in an interview, she told me that in her group it is only men that beat drums. I also had the opportunity to attend a rehearsal where only men were the drummers and the women were dancers and singers. In a number of groups, I observed that more often the women's musical contribution to a performance is clapping and singing responses. Moreover, she also emphasized the context of performing baakisimba in Buganda; namely, when Buganda was not at war. By singing, "beat the drums so that the Baganda can dance," Nandujja emphasized the connection between drumming and dancing in Buganda.

While baakisimba was performed before the king as an approval of his power, behind the king's backs, the same dancers could perform *muwogola*, a very aggressive dance, after the king had retired to his residence (Kisolo, interview). *Muwogola* is a more free style dance than baakisimba; it is performed at a very fast pace with correspondingly faster music. Solome Nannyonga told me that it was never performed in the presence of the king because it was not graceful; it was performed after the king had left (interview). It was a performance of relief from the king's dominant power. It was a form of hidden transcript enacted behind the stage as a means of releasing tension created by the king's presence.

Further, the twenty-first-century formations of baakisimba dance exhibit a high level of creativity as opposed to the straight-line formations in the royal baakisimba. In addition, vertical straight lines, dancers adopt vertical straight-lines, semi-circles, and circles. Further, dancers do not shuffle before the present king as they did before the abolition of the Buganda kingdom in 1967. For example, during the Seventh Coronation Anniversary on 8 August 2000, the two groups that performed baakisimba did not shuffle. They raised their feet as they do in baakisimba performances outside the palace. Moreover, the music was faster compared to the graceful and dignified baakisimba of the pre-abolition period. It is not possible to deduce any autonomous meaning from the circles, semi-circles, and letters; however, their resignified meaning is rooted in the historical context in which the dance has been performed, without which, any reading is somewhat invalid. The formations of straight lines, facing the king signified the king's domination as the central figure, the man among men. As such, the post-abolition and post-restoration baakisimba could suggest a level of emancipation from the dominant power of the king. Palace baakisimba illustrates how art forms are alternate vehicle for promoting and deconstructing hegemonic powers.

Chapter Five
Village Baakisimba

BIOCULTURAL CONSTRUCTION OF GENDER: BIRTH THROUGH PUBERTY

Since village baakisimba is shaped by its performance context, it is to this context that we must turn in order to understand how baakisimba articulates with gender outside the palace. I begin with the discussion of gender construction before I examine how gender is connected with baakisimba. The main performance contexts of baakisimba include, beer parties, wedding ceremonies and other village celebrations.

The construction of genders outside the palace begins at birth when a child's sex is known. A male baby is known as "naatuukirira" ("perfect child"), while a female baby is called "gannemeredde" ("failure child; this is not what I wanted") (Naluwooza, interview). Katambula Busuulwa compared the male and female babies to right and left hands, respectively. The right hand is stronger (in a number of cases) and considered sacred, while the left is important only in as much as it supports the right hand.[1] Busuulwa further noted that although it is more important to have male children, female children create a situation of "balance." In fact, a number of Baganda men divorce their wives if they only produce girls.[2] There is a level of "understanding" among the Baganda when men divorce their wives because they produce only girls. As a result, a number of women give birth to as many as ten children is search for a baby boy. According to Busuulwa:

> When a man gives birth to only female babies, he is not happy, because his right hand is not well balanced [because he has no male child]. At times, whatever he does in [the home] does not go well and if he does not succeed in all his work, it is because it is only the left hand [female child] that is functioning.

Omusajja bw'aba azadde baana ba buwala bokka, teyeeyagala kubanga omukono gwe ogwa ddyo guba gukunukidde nnyo. Oluusi ne by'akola tebitereera bulungi mu maka, n'emirimu gye gyonna obutatambula, anti ng'omukono ogwa kkono gwe gwokka ogutambula (interview).

In fact, the importance of male over female babies explains why a male child is referred to as a "perfect child." For women, the "perfect child" offers them security in their marriage; yet for men, it means success and continuity of their lineage.[3] From the time a child is born, gender ideologies take shape and gender roles become more defined as it grows. The girl grows up knowing that a boy is more powerful because he is a "perfect child" and the girl is weak; after all, she is a "failure" child.

A female child is *omwana omuwala* (girl child) and a male child is *omwana omulenzi* (boy child) until just before puberty. Explaining further how the Baganda manipulate language to express their constructions about gender, Busuulwa said that the term "omuwala" is from the verb "okuwala" (to clear, to remove, to cleanse). He stressed that:

> In the Baganda's customs of nature, the female child is the one that cleanses and removes all the problems in the home that have failed to be resolved. Whatever the problems, the female child does not leave them unresolved. She is the one who resolves all issues that have failed; she puts the home in harmony and [brings fortune in] marriages. The female child is the left hand that holds up all the heaviness that may exist and then the home becomes firm. The female child is the one who has *Nakawala,* a tutelary deity that removes all problems in a home.

> *Mu nnono z'obutonde bw'abaganda, omuwala y'awalawo ebikyamu byonna ku luggya ebiba bigaanye, ye omuwala tabirekaawo. Kubanga y'awalawo ensonga zonna eziba zitatuukiridde, okusobola okutereeza awaka n'obufumbo. Anti omwana omuwala gwe mukono ogwa kkono oguwanirira obuzito bwonna obubeerawo, olwo amaka ne gakkalira. Omwana omuwala y'abeeramu omusambwa Nakawala oguggyawo ensobi mu maka* (interview).

Busuulwa described further that when *omwana omuwala* is born, her parents would call upon *Nakawala,* the female tutelary deity to protect and empower the baby girls. The parents pray thus: "never make your friend *[omwana omuwala]* insubordinate, give her all the wisdom to create resolutions about all cultural issues" ("munno tomulalusanga, era omuwanga amagezi agayiiya ensonga ez'obuwangwa zonna") (ibid.). Insubordination, in this case, includes loss of virginity before marriage, disrespect to men, and failure to behave as a submissive woman. The prayer to this tutelary deity is to ensure the protection of the girls' virginity, respect for men, and submissiveness. It is also at this point that the female baby is assigned her future role of being the custodian of culture.

On the other hand, Busuulwa said that when *omwana omulenzi* (baby boy) is born, the parents charge *Kasajja,* the male tutelary deity, with the responsibility for his growth. They pray for the male baby saying, "may you have wisdom. May you be strong in all issues. We want you to be powerful, controlling, dominant in everything" (ibid.). One immediately notices that from such an early stage, boys are expected and indeed prayed for to be dominant and controlling in "everything." The Baganda also have a proverb that legitimizes the boys' dominance and it goes thus: "akaana k'obulenzi: tokaweera mpindi mu ngalo [meaning that] You do not give a little boy beans in a bare hand. You should use a basket or a banana leaf, because he will one day be a man, a ruler, leading the way for women folk" (Walser 1982:19, no. 0197). And yet, girls are initiated into their submissive roles and those of being the custodians of culture. In fact, the women's power lies in their being the custodians of culture, a culture that promotes men's control and dominance and women's submissiveness.

As the children grow, these future roles begin to manifest in the different kinds of games and roles they play and songs they sing. Their roles are inscribed and monitored by parents, relatives, peers, during clan gatherings, and, recently, through electronic mass media. Some of the boys' games include playing with balls, climbing trees, and making toy cars, which are not acceptable for girls. Girls are not allowed to climb trees for fear that "they will become boys!" Sarah Musoke, a seventy-year-old, told me that climbing trees is wrong for girls because "they are not supposed to have anything between their legs because it will affect their virginity before marriage" (interview). When I asked her why girls are not allowed to kick soccer balls, she said,

> Girls were not allowed to kick balls because they would open their legs; a woman does not do that in public. Girls have to be trained from childhood. You know, if you try to shape a grown plant that got deformed during germination, it just breaks! [Meaning that one must be trained as a woman from childhood].

> *Abawala tebakkirizibwanga kusamba mipiira kubanga baawula amagulu gaabwe. Omukazi takola ekyo mu bantu, era abawala balina okubayigiriza*

nga bakyali bato. Anti omanyi nti akakyama amamera bw'okagolola nga kakuze kamenyeka! (ibid.).

Even after the introduction of bicycles in Buganda in the twentieth century, it is rare to find a typical Muganda girl riding one. Restricting girls from such activities is one way of controlling their virginity, preparing them for their future roles as sexual objects for men. Similarly, Musisi noted that virginity was important for becoming a wife of a king or a chief (1991a: 73). Moreover, as Christine Obbo, a Ugandan sociocultural anthropologist, has mentioned "fathers and brothers are expected to guard the virginity of daughter and sisters; husbands should insist on the chastity of their wives" (1990b: 215) even when the husbands are unfaithful.

The girls' games are mainly associated with their inscribed role as mothers and as food providers. For instance, narrating her experience of some of the games she played, Maria Lubega, now in her late thirties, said:

> When we were still young children, we did a lot of cooking in fake pots and tried to imitate how our mother served food; she would give the biggest portion to our father! My brother always liked to be the father. He made himself a table and a chair from a banana stem, and that is where he sat when eating while we sat on the ground as our mother used to do. I also remember playing as a teacher and a nurse (interview).

Lubega, who is now a teacher in a primary school, recalls her past and notes how, to a great extent, it is connected to her present life. Lubega, who is married and has six children, is the sole provider of food for her family. On the other hand, Peter Ggayira, now in his seventies, told me that during his childhood, housework was for girls and, although he also helped in the garden, his parents were never as strict with him as they were with his sisters. When I asked him why he never assisted in the housework, Ggayira said, "when girls are at home and you, a boy, do such things! I only took care of the goats and played *mbiriggo* and *ggoggolo*"[4] Similarly, as John Vernon Taylor noted that "in many peasant homes the man treats his children, especially girls with a mixture of careless and absolute authority" (1958: 148). Even when they grow up, these girls tend to have "both submissive and maternal" (Taylor 1958: 149–150) attitudes to men as they had towards their fathers.

A boy child becomes *omusajja* (a young man) at puberty, a stage when he is eligible to "marry." He is assigned a role of *kusajjalaata* ("being manly"), meaning that he is free to do whatever he wants. On the other hand, a girl at the same stage is assigned a role of *omukazi* ("one who dries the courtyard"), a role that restricts her around the house. At this stage, the mother and the paternal aunts have to make sure that a girl child is trained in domestic chores, in preparation for marriage.

As Musisi rightly noted, in Buganda, like in most cultures of Africa, cultural socialization "orient[s] girls towards 'feminine' mothering and wifely roles while encouraging boys into 'masculine' roles of being aggressive and ambitious and to venture" (1992: 2).[5] While girls spend most of the time with their mothers learning their future roles, boys are with fathers and may be apprenticed to the father or other men, making instruments and beating drums or making bark cloth. For example, Busuulwa, now in his fifties, recalled that, "When a boy child was of age and if his father was a warrior or a hunter, he would go with him to show him what to do" (interview).

GENDERING MARRIAGE AND PROCREATION

A male attains the status of *omwami* (manhood, becoming a man) when he marries a woman. According to one Luganda dictionary, *omwami* is translated as "owner of property, chief or master" (Snoxall 1967: 75). In other words, the title may also be assigned to a male who is not married, but one that has been given a leader's role in a village. Similarly, a woman achieves *obukyala* (womanhood), becoming *omukyala* (a woman), when she gets married to a man. In Luganda, to marry is *okuwasa*. Bonnie M. Lubega, a Luganda linguist, explained that *okuwasa* also refers to *okufuga,* to rule or dominate others (1994: 167). In this case, marriage assigns the man the status of *omufuzi* (head) of the family and the woman, the status of *omufuge,* a subordinate. In fact, men marry (own) and women get married (are owned).[6] Augustino Kisitu elaborated, "to marry is to get something that you have ownership over" *("okuwasa, kwekufuna ekintu eky'obwananyini")* (interview). The Baganda's definition of marriage suggests that when a man marries, he takes, owns, controls, impregnates, and dominates his wife. In other words, omwani, the owner of property marries (owns) a woman, his wife.

Marriage defines a "proper" woman; one is defined as a woman if a man, owns and controls her. The cultural practice—that men "marry" (own) women and women are not expected to "marry" (own) men, but instead to be married—accords men a strong position of power. Marriage, in this case, stresses the subordinate position of women in relation to that of men. Emphasizing the importance of marriage in defining Baganda women, Sulaimani Mukwaya, an elderly man and a musician, said, "I despise a woman that is not married! A woman who is not yet married, even if she is thirty years, is still a girl; she is only a potential wife; but a married woman is somebody's wife. One who is not married can never be counted as a proper woman" (interview).

A married woman is respected because she has a "protector." Mukwaya said that:

> A married woman is feared, she has someone who makes her to be feared, the husband. The husband is like a policeman or a security guard. People say: 'oho! That one, leave her alone; she is somebody's woman.' Further, a proper woman is one who gives respect to her husband. When she sees him from a distance, and welcomes him. A woman who is married and does not give respect to her husband is not a proper woman.

> *Omukyala omufumbo ba mutya, abaako amutiisa, omwami. Omwami akola ng'omusirikale era olugira nti 'oh oyo mumuveeko muka bandi' Era omukyala omutuufu y'oyo awa bbaawe ekitiibwa; era bw'aba amulabye, amulengerera wala eri n'amukulisaayo. Omukyala afumbiddwa bw'aba tawa mwamiwe kitiibwa, tabeera mukyala mutuufu* (ibid.).

Further, kneeling before elders and one's husband identifies a "true" Muganda woman. Nusula Namutebi, in her fifties, stressed that, "a Muganda woman is that one who kneels before elders and her husband" (interview). In fact, a number of informants, both men and women, emphasized the woman's responsibility to respect men; no reference was made to men's respect for women.[7]

Through the payment of the *mutwalo* (bride price), men acquire even more power over women because they can pay and own them. Ironically, some women also take pride in being paid for; some feel it makes them more valuable and respected. In one of my interviews, a woman complained, "A man is powerful even when he did not pay for you; he can control you." In another encounter, I met a couple quarreling and the woman had the following exchange: "You mistreat me as if you bought me! What if you had paid for me? I think I would be carrying you on my head!" (anonymous, interview). This view suggests the men's right to control women, especially if men paid bride price for the women. Writing this about commodification of women through bride price in Buganda, Taylor reported that "the formal acceptance of the beer by the father seal[ed] the betrothal contract . . ." (1958: 171). In this case, women were equivalent to a pot of beer. Taylor revealed further that "sometimes, if he has already been informally advised of the amount, the suitor will pay the whole marriage payment immediately, otherwise a day is fixed for the payment, or part of the payment, and when this has been made over, the father very often will write an official receipt" (Taylor ibid.). Mahmood Mamdani summarized the bride price issue and said, "women were a means of production to be owned, exchanged and distributed" (1976: 25).

Bride price still exists, although in a different way under the guise of *"ebirabo" by'abazadde* ("gifts" for parents). During the *kwanjula* ceremony (formal introduction of suitors to the girls' parents), proposing men are expected to bring gifts of food, clothes, and money to the girl's parents. However, the prospective bride does not send gifts to the man's family before marriage.[8] During several introduction ceremonies that I attended, the suitors were given a letter confirming that they had paid everything and that the parents had allowed them to take their daughters in marriage. As a matter of fact, one cannot be married in the Catholic Church without this "receipt." One of the requirements by the Catholic Church when I was getting married was a consent letter, a receipt to show that my husband had no debt to my family.

Idi Serunkuuma, an elderly man, argued that these gifts "are [just] a sign of appreciation" *("ako kabeera kasiimo")*. However, when I asked him whether the gifts are also considered as a payment that entitles men to "own" women, he answered, "Yes, moreover, there is even an agreement, a receipt. In fact, in the old days, when a wife divorced [her husband], they [parents] would return your money. But if the wife had given birth to children, an understanding person [man] would not take the money back" (interview). In this case, childbirth is a compensation for bride price and, therefore, no refund is made since the husband has already received "interest" from his "investment." Similarly, among the Gusii of Kenya, the return for bride price is children. Thomas Håkansson observed that after bride price is paid,

> All children born subsequently were the husband's irrespective of who was their biological father, unless a divorce took place. If his wife went to live with another man all children born during that time were considered as belonging to the man who had paid the bride wealth (1987: 43–44).

In the case of Buganda, since children were considered as wealth, it makes sense if no refunds are made for a woman with children. In exchange for bride price, women are charged with the responsibility of giving birth, being the custodians of culture, and naming and educating the children about their father's clan. Bride price constructs a woman as a socially defined mother. Inability to satisfy those roles stigmatizes her and completely disqualifies her "womanliness."

As in other African cultures, marriage in Buganda is "taken with a deep sense of responsibility toward both the past and the future generations and, therefore, its objective is primarily to produce children" (Taylor 1958: 169).[9] The new relation achieved through *okuwasa* (marriage) assigns a woman the role of procreator and caretaker. *Okuwasa* is more than housing a woman under one's roof; it also means to "impregnate." Among the Baganda, sex is considered sacred, as it is looked at as the root of procreation. While marriage is a strong qualification for being a proper man or woman, because of the importance of procreation, sometimes, sex before marriage and extramarital sex are tolerated. As Roscoe rightly pointed out, every married woman was, and still is, "expected to show signs of maternity within a few weeks of her marriage. A woman who had no children was [and still is] despised, and soon became the slave and drudge of the household" (1911: 46). Parenthood elevates one to yet a higher level of manhood or womanhood. Idi Sserunkuma stressed, "Giving birth is very important; if one was found unable to give birth, she was returned to her parents and the husband got another one" (interview). However, dissatisfaction with a male spouse did not usually lead to separation; the wife is supposed to be very tolerant, one of the many virtues she is trained in. In Buganda, inability to give birth is attributed to a woman's failure and stigmatizes her throughout her life. Augustino Kisitu, an elderly man added,

> A wife that has not given birth is usually referred to as 'a goat without horns,' because if it loses its rope, it never comes back.[10] A goat without horns, even if you dress it up with a rope, it will remove the rope. This is the same situation with a woman who has no children in a home.[11]

> *Omukyala atazadde mwana batera okumuyita 'embuzi enkunku'; anti bwe yeeyambula omuguwa tedda. Embuzi eterina mayembe, ne bw'ogyambaza omuguwa gutya, egweyambula. Kale kyekimu n'omukazi atalina mwana mu maka* (interview).

In this case, "Women's biological role as child-bearers is regarded as their primary social role and defines their social worth" (Obbo 1989: 81). The woman's reproductive role defines her as "a proper woman" (Obbo 1989: 79). Because of the importance of giving birth, when twins are born, the father and mother are raised to yet a higher status. They are given new titles namely, *ssaalongo* and *nnaalongo*, respectively. *Ssaalongo* is no longer *mwami* (a man); he is above that status. Similarly, *nnaalongo* "surpasses all women" *("aba ayiseewo mu bakyala bonna")* (Kisolo, interview). Sserunkuuma said that God blesses *nnaalongo*; and it is God who raised her above other women. And because of this sacred title and honor, *"Nnaalongo* does not kneel before anybody except her *ssaalongo*, other fathers of twins, her father and mother in-law" (interview). He said that although a woman is expected to kneel before all her in-laws and of course all elderly persons, when she gives birth to twins, culture excuses her of that expression (ibid.). *Nnaalongo* and *ssaalongo* gain what I have called "cultural immunity." They surpass all cultural taboos, to which people who have no twins are susceptible. The cultural immunity that *nnaalongo* acquires enables her to behave in a way contrary to the expected behavior of other females outside the palace. Although women generally do not beat drums, as I will mention in the coming sections, one of the few outstanding women drummers that I met was a *nnaalongo*. However, usually *nna/nne* are feminine pronouns and *ssa/sse* are masculine pronouns. The syllable *nna* refers to *bugonvu* (softness), while *ssa* means *busukkulumu* (powerfulness) (Naluwooza, interview). Although *ssaalongo* and *nnaalongo* contribute to the birth of twins, it is still *ssaalongo,* the male, who is considered more powerful than *nnaalongo*.

In sum, the biocultural construction of gender in Buganda points to patriarchy, which emphasizes the importance of sons and the absolute authority of the father in the family who controls and owns the woman and her productivity.[12] Children are named after the father's clan and, therefore, belong to the man's clan. The man is *ssemaka,* the head, supervisor, and owner of the household. Childbearing and domestic work define a typical Muganda woman; inability to satisfy those roles disqualifies her from being a proper woman. Emphasizing the basic role of a Muganda woman, the Baganda have a saying "Nnantaganyula: ng'omunafu omugumba [meaning] A useless person: like a lazy woman who is barren. [Such a woman] does no work and cannot produce any children" (Walser 1957: 294, no. 3272). Indeed, as Musisi rightly points out, "among the Baganda . . . productivity and reproductivity [are] so linked . . . that barrenness, a major cause of divorce . . . render[s] a wife a positive danger to the fruitfulness of the garden" (1991a: 66–67). It is the responsibility of the woman to grow the food to feed her children, her husband and the entire household, while the man is the overseer, responsible for supervising the woman's activities. Indeed, the Muganda woman's role as the food provide is emphasized in a proverb, which goes: "Eka egwana mukazi ne bba: atalina mukazi azimba ekibanja? [Meaning that] In a home there should be a wife and husband: does a man with no wife put up a plantation?" (Walser 1982: 115, n0.1256). Surely, such stereotyped expectations of the sexes that are held by men and internalized by women help to perpetuate gender inequalities in societies in general (Hunt 1990; Walker 1990; Hansen 1991), and Buganda in particular. These internalized power relations between men and women form the basis for roles assigned to particular genders in musical and dance activities as well.

In the next sections, the gender role prescription will become evident in my examination of the ways in which baakisimba defines gender and how gender shapes baakisimba. Baakisimba is one of the means through which a woman is prepared for marriage. I analyze baakisimba as a factor in defining Baganda's gender through marriage.

VILLAGE BAAKISIMBA PERFORMANCE PRACTICE

Baakisimba ey'omukyalo (village baakisimba), as many of my informants referred to it, is that one performed outside the palace, but not in schools or churches. It should be noted that many of the changes that happened in the palace were subsequently readapted for the formal village baakisimba since, to a big extent; the *badongo ba kabaka* controlled the development of the dance outside the palace. Although baakisimba and all the other palace dances were submerged after the abolition of the kingdom, dancing outside the palace context enabled the exploration of new possibilities, as discussed in the following sections. There are two broad kinds of village baakisimba, sacred and secular. The sacred ceremonial baakisimba is performed during *kumala balongo* (ceremonies of twin rituals), *kusamira* (indigenous worship), and *kwabya lumbe* (last funeral rites). On the other hand, secular baakisimba is performed during *mbaga* (weddings), *mu birabo* (at beer parties), graduation parties, and other festivities. My focus is on village baakisimba performed in secular contexts. I have categorized secular village baakisimba into two; "formal baakisimba" and "informal baakisimba." However, formal baakisimba and informal baakisimba are not strict categorizations; they are fluid and overlapping is possible depending on the performance contexts.

Music and dance specialists perform formal baakisimba. By music and dance specialists, I refer to performers belonging to a formally organized group (to which they have membership), which could be hired to perform at a social function. In such groups, each member has a clearly designated performance role as a drummer, singer, or a dancer. Such performing groups are characterized by creativity and innovations in terms of choreography and costume designs mainly prompted by competitions among groups. Because these performers do not depend entirely on music and dance performance for their livelihood, I refer to them as semi-professionals. On the other hand, informal baakisimba refers to a context in which people spontaneously join in the performance. Informal baakisimba is more free and participatory since no prior performance roles are assigned to individuals. There is a lesser degree of distinction between performers and audience in informal baakisimba compared to formal baakisimba. Some people beat drums and dance in turns while the rest clap and sing. If some of the audience members wish to dance, they can grab the *mpina* (skirt made of banana leaves), a jacket, or a strip of cloth, tie it to their waist, and then dance. Except in a few contexts, especially at beer parties, men rarely dance even in informal contexts; they beat the drums and women dance. Because of the free participatory dancing, the performance stage scenery is usually circular; there is no separate stage for the performers. The performers dance inside the circle, while the "audience-performers"—those clapping, singing, and appreciating the dancers—surround the core performers. However, the circles are not fixed; they can be broken when people get excited and create new stage designs. While informal baakisimba still exists, it is not as common as formal baakisimba.

Until the 1940s, there was no formalized baakisimba performance outside the palace. However, when the *badongo ba kabaka* (king's musicians) began to perform outside the palace, and especially in the 1960s after the abolition of the Buganda kingdom, some formalized groups emerged. Notable of these groups was the Heart Beat of Africa, a national troupe. The Heart Beat of Africa, which was founded in 1963, had music and dance performances that "aimed at the emphasis of the national outlook as opposed to the individual cultural performance. The Basoga performed Kiganda dances and vice versa" (Kasozi 1979: 57). The context that the Heart Beat of Africa presents exemplifies my argument that meaning in baakisimba is not static; rather, its meanings are contingent on existing social, political, and cultural structures of which it is a part. The creation of the Heart Beat of Africa was an "attempt to preserve valued elements of ethnic culture [of Uganda], enhance its national pride and unity, and project its image to the outside world" (Hanna and Hanna 1968: 42). Judith Lynne Hanna and William John Hanna summarized the role of the Heart Beat of Africa as "a 'renaissance' of African culture" because the European colonizers and missionaries had for a long time managed to suppress the local music and dance of Africans. The Heart Beat of Africa performed not only music and dance from Buganda, but also from other parts of Uganda. Likewise, the Baganda dancers and musicians learned music and dances from other parts of the country. Baakisimba, like other dances and musics, became resignified as a "creative art."

Baakisimba ceased to be performed as a full-fledged dance; instead, it became part of a dance suite. Baakisimba was combined with *nnnankasa* and *muwogola* to create *baakisimba-nnnankasa-muwogola* dance suite. *Muwogola* being the fastest of these dances, builds up the climax from *nnnankasa*, which is faster than the slow and graceful baakisimba. In addition to modified choreography, costumes were also changed. Tereza Kisolo, a former member of the Heart Beat of Africa and a Muganda, told me that the colors of the Uganda flag (yellow, black, and red) dominated the colors of the costumes. As such, baakisimba became a national dance, representing national symbols rather than ethnic identities. Moreover, the dance was performed outside of the traditional contexts of festivity, which excluded drinking and eating (interview). So, when the Heart Beat of Africa performed baakisimba, it became an art form and ceased to be an intimate and vital aspect of living among the Baganda as before.

Because of the unfavorable political situation from the 1970s till the mid 1980s, the establishment of new performing ensembles was minimal after the Heart Beat of Africa went into recess. Moreover, since the mid 1970s, foreign dance music (disco) predominated the festivities of the Baganda. With the great influx of Western, especially American popular music, there was no room for "outdated baakisimba," as one informant called it. Moreover, because of the expansion of Kampala (the capital of Uganda) due to rural-urban migration in search for better jobs and social amenities, baakisimba became somewhat irrelevant in a cosmopolitan community. Because of the need to create new music that would appeal to the nature of emerging audience, *kadongo-kamu,* a music genre that blends mainly Western and Kiganda musical materials, especially baakisimba rhythmic figures, which had developed earlier in the 1950s, became an alternative entertainment.[13] Some of the musicians behind this recreation of baakisimba include, Dan Mugula, Herman Basudde, Fred Ssebatta, Paulo Kafeero, Matiya Luyima, and Willy Mukaabya. However, since the late 1980s, towards the restoration of the Buganda kingdom, a number of Kiganda ensembles were revived, while new ones were created. Among the outstanding performing groups are: Sulaiti Kalungi Nnankasa Group, Tebifaanana Abifuna Nnankasa Group, Nandujja and the Plates, Ssenkubuge Nnankasa Group, The Samads, and Bazanya n'Engo Cultural group, and Agaly'awamu Cultural Group. It is evident from the names of these ensembles that *nnankasa* is part of their identity. While they perform baakisimba in their repertoires, *nnankasa* and *mbaga* dances are their trademarks. One informant explained that they had to repackage baakisimba to attract a new market. He explained that they could not name their ensemble with baakisimba label because baakisimba is graceful. He noted that using *nnankasa* label is attractive because *nnankasa* is fast, and therefore, exciting. Nonetheless, baakisimba is part of their repertoire in addition to *nnankasa, mbaga,* and other dances. It can be inferred, therefore, that baakisimba, like any other performance arts, is fluid and as such; elicit a multivocality of meanings.

MEN AS DRUMMERS: GUARDING DEAR SPACE

Carol Meyers has observed that: "certainly female percussionists exist; but, whether for rock combos or symphony orchestras, we tend to think of men, not women sitting with drumsticks in hand" (1993: 49). What Meyers has observed is also true among the Baganda. Even within families of drummers and dancers, drummers are in the most cases men. Although some women now beat drums in baakisimba and *mbaga* dance performances, their performances can only be tolerated in certain contexts, mainly schools, churches, and occasionally during ceremonial contexts. In fact, 70% of the membership of Sulaiti Kalungi's group is his children, grandchildren, and other relatives. Within this musical family, almost all the men are drummers (only one is a dancer) but all women are dancers. When I asked him why all his female relatives are dancers and none of them beat the drum, he said, "aha! [with an expression of incredulity] those women are only dancers" (interview). Kalungi implied that all that women can do is to dance. Buganda is not the only African culture where women are not allowed to beat drums. For instance, in the late 1950s, Kwabena Nketia reported that among the Akan of Ghana, women did not as a rule beat drums (1990:98). L. Jafran Jones also observed that among the Tunisians of North Africa, "instrumental music and music creations remain the domain of men" (1987: 77).

Based on the view that at one point in time women may have been rulers before Kintu, the first King of Buganda, ousted them, I suggested to Busuulwa the possibility that women could have beaten drums as well. I argued that since there were no gendered roles in the pre-Kintu time, women and men could have beaten the drums without any gendered restrictions. I suggested that drumming could have been one of the empowering activities lost when women lost power to men. Although Busuulwa agreed that it could be a possibility that women beat the drums before, he explained that beating the drums, especially in festival contexts, was a role assigned by God and that drumming was certainly not one of the roles given to women. He stressed:

> It could be that drumming was one the things that were lost. But of all the drums I have known, which belong to the Kabakaship, it seems men beat them all. It could be that women were given their own roles. In fact, when you examine them, they are many; but certainly, drumming is not one of them (interview).

Busuulwa's argument that no known palace drums are supposed to beaten by women is not enough to support the view that men's role of beating the drums was assigned by God. Besides, the monarchical institution was created only after men had overthrown women's power to rule. If women lost the power to rule, certainly they had to lose the privileges of beating the drums. Since the drum is believed to be a symbol of power for kingship, women's access to the drum had to be controlled and, therefore, no drum is supposed to be beaten by women. One would argue, therefore, that before kabakaship was instituted, women might have beaten the drums, as much as they could have been rulers.

One would then ask: "why do men regulate women's access to the drum?" Why are women not allowed to beat or touch the most valued instrument of the Baganda, one that is central to their self-identification? In Buganda, each clan is identified by a drumbeat and when one beats his or her clan beat, he or she is actually identifying with his or her roots of ancestry. Therefore, restricting women's access is refusing their identification with their roots. Baaziriyo Nsubuga explained that the aim of restricting women's drumming was to control any possible gender subversion. He said that it "could have happened because men never wanted women to beat the drums, which would make women become men" (interview). How do the drums symbolize men? To this question he answered that "the drum is beaten by a strong and energetic person, and yet a woman is not supposed to have such energy to beat drums!" (ibid.). Similarly, Tereza Kisolo, one of the few female *ngalabi* performers, said that if a woman beat drums, it was thought that she wanted to compete with men. People who are strong beat the drum, and yet a woman should be very calm and graceful (interview). When I asked Nsubuga why a woman should not be strong, he answered that "because a woman is a flower for us men; [she] is not supposed to strain in such activities" (interview). Although Nsubuga agreed that in reality women can be strong and can actually beat drums, he argued that "if she beats the drum, her palms will harden as those of men, and yet her palms are not supposed to be like that!" (ibid.).

Kisolo and Nsubuga's views suggest that men must regulate women's access to the drum because when women beat the drum, they challenge the Baganda's worldview of femininity, which is based on being soft and calm. Since women are supposedly flowers for men's pleasure, it follows that, men would rather see women dancing than drumming since drumming projects more power and energy than beauty. Nsubuga's view is a hidden transcript especially if it is public knowledge that Baganda women are involved in more "hardening" domestic activities than beating the drum. Women's major occupations—including growing food and its preparation, fetching water (a couple of miles away from home), collecting firewood from the forest and cutting the grass for thatching new and old houses (Mukasa 1938: 6; Nsimbi

1956: 28)—do not leave their palms as soft as Nsubuga claimed. In fact, women's palms are often harder than those of men.

On the other hand, Nuludin Ssekitto argued that women are just not interested in drumming (interview). One wonders why women would be interested in an activity they are not allowed or forbidden to do anyway. However, my research revealed that a number of women would have liked to beat the drums, but they are discouraged and are never given access to the drum from childhood. According to the prescribed roles for a woman, it is not important for a woman to learn the drum, because it is not of any use to her; after all, she is expected to be married. Most of the time was spent preparing her for marriage, especially in domestic chores, and no leisure time is available for learning the drums. Once married, the woman would not have time to learn the drum because domestic work occupied her day.

Further, Ssaalongo Kizza asserted that women's access to the drum is controlled because of their menstruation periods. He said:

> The Baganda have taboos: a woman is not allowed to beat drums because she goes into menstruation, and because of that, she is completely denied to touch the drum. In their thinking, the elders in the palace took it that women's menstruation is unclean. It would also be difficult to determine who is in menstruation and who is not menstruating [clean]. That is why a general rule was made for all women at all times not to touch drums.

> *A Baganda balimu emizizo. Omukazi takkirizibwa kukuba ngoma kuba ye agenda mu nsonga, era bw'atyo, ne bamugaanira ddala. Mu ndowooza yaabwe abakulu mu lubiri baakitwala eky'abakyala okugenda mu nsonga okuba nti si kiyonjo. Kyandibadde nakizibu nnyo okwawula agenze n'atagenze mu nsonga, bwe batyo ne bakibagaana eky'okukwata ku ngoma* (interview).

Similarly, Nketia also observed that the Akan women of Ghana were never allowed to beat drums "because in the past it was thought that a woman might defile the drums, particularly those of the state, since some of the important drums, like other things, were not to be touched by a woman in her monthly period" (1990: 98).[14] It is not only the drum that women cannot access while in menstruation. According to Roscoe, when the Ganda king's or chief's women were menstruating, they were not allowed "To touch any of the husband's weapons or implements . . . [it] was equivalent to wishing him dead or working magic to compass his death" (1911: 96). Similarly, Nancy Bonvillain's cross-cultural study has emphasized, "In societies characterized by male dominance, women are often thought to be ritually impure and contaminating. Women's sexuality is considered dangerous and must be controlled by men" (1998:246). Women's menstruation does not affect the menstruating women alone, but also the people around them. For instance, among the Nyoro from western Uganda, "a man [could] not visit the king if ... his wife was menstruating" (Irstam 1970: 78).

What is so powerful about women's menstrual blood that makes men fear it? Is it really because women's blood is unclean? In my view, menstrual blood is not unclean, as claimed, because in Buganda, for instance, no man would want to marry a woman who does not menstruate; that would mean she cannot have a child. In Buganda, it is common that most men want to marry young women (of menstruating age). In fact, if some one approaches the age of thirty-five years before being married, her chances of getting married become small. While young woman's physical appearance is attractive, it is most crucial that she belongs to an age where her chances of giving birth to at least four children are high. Roscoe noted that "A girl who did not menstruate was looked upon askance, and if a man married such a woman, then every time that he went to war he wounded her with a spear sufficiently to draw blood; otherwise he would be sure to fall in battle" (1911: 80). In this case, female blood is regarded as power to protect the man during the war, to the extent that a non-menstruating wife would be a threat to a warring man.

Given the importance of children among the Baganda, how can the only means through which children are brought into being be unclean, and yet the products (children) are considered sacred and, indeed, belonging to men? I have already discussed how the very act of procreation defines the *mukyala* ("proper" woman). In this case, menstruation is a sign of reliability for a woman's motherhood. Similarly, Gilbert H. Herdt has noted that among the Sambia of New Guinea, "a woman's periods are so steady and visible that they serve as constant notice of a powerful force alive and operating within her" (1981: 190; quoted in Hauser-Shaubin 1993: 91). Sulaimani Mukwaya provided a clue to the blood taboo and the women's drumming. When I asked him why women should not beat the drums, he stressed that, "The woman is taken to be the mother of a nation. The mother should not touch the drum, the drum is for men" (interview). Mukwaya established one point clearly: one can either be a mother or a drummer, but not both. Women cannot be allowed to take up these two important and powerful roles of the Baganda concurrently. Allowing them to do so is to assign women extra power. And since men lack the natural procreative powers, they must exert their "creativity externally, 'artificially,' through the medium of technology and symbols" (Ortner 1974: 75) and in this case, through the drum. Thomas Buckley and Alma Gottlieb explained that "Because menstrual blood and menstruous women are perceived as dangerous, taboos have been devised to contain their energies and keep [them] from spreading beyond a limited place in the order of things" (1997: 150). Similarly, Carol E. Robertson argued that men try to keep women from certain music-making activities because they hold power and knowledge that would make women even more powerful. Consequently, "the prohibitions of performance often apply specifically to the use of certain instruments—often drums . . ." (Robertson 1987: 228).

On the other hand, Busuulwa attributed the control of women's beating of drums to the posture that is adapted when beating drums. The drummer adopts a number of postures when beating the *ngoma*. When beating the *mbuutu*, the drummer sits in such a way that the drum is between the legs. This position gives the performer full control of the drum and one does not get tired so quickly. On the other hand, since the *ngalabi* has an open-ended bottom, tilting it between the legs enables not only full control of the drum, but also provides a better timbre as well as a louder percussive sound. In a number of performances that I attended, the *ngalabi* performers also beat the drum from their armpits or at times leaned the *ngalabi* against a chair or on the *mbuutu*. In addition to comfort, these postures are adopted for technical reasons in order to produce the right sound. Plate 10 shows the postures used when drumming.

Plate 10. Beating the *ngalabi* between the legs. Augustino Kisitu demonstrates the *ngalabi* as a young *ngalabi* performer looks on. Peter Mubiru Beats the *mbuutu*.

Busuulwa explained:

> I think women are not allowed to beat these festival drums because of the
> sitting posture. If women sit like that, then they are naked. That is why I
> think drumming was denied them. Moreover, even those women that I
> first saw beating drums—Tereza Kisolo, the Nayigas—they first had to sit
> down, and then they beat the drums. Their drums used to be short; they
> never beat the long ones we have these days. You can also see that such a
> drum does not afford you to beat well; you get tired very soon (interview).

Defending Busuulwa's view, Paulo Kabwama emphasized that:

> A woman was not allowed to put anything between her legs; that was a
> woman's honor given to her. Moreover, the way women dressed in the
> past was in such a way that they had nothing beneath [underwear],
> other than the bark cloth, so she could not put the drum between her
> legs. It was not possible for a woman to put anything between the legs
> that would inconvenience her.

> *Omukazi teyakkirizibwanga kuteeka kintu kirala mu magulu. Kyali nga*
> *kitiibwa kya mukazi ekyamuweebwa. Ekirala, enneesiba ey'edda ku*
> *bakyala, zaabanga mbugo zokka nga munda tebateekamu kantu kalala*
> *konna, kale nga tayinza kuteeka ngoma mu magulu. Omukyala kizibu*
> *okweteeka ekintu mu magulu, ekimutawaanya mu magulu* (interview).

Kabwama stressed that a woman cannot use such a posture because of her
honor. However, it is my contention that the taboo aims at protecting the
men's social space. Kabwama raised two important points: 1) women should
not beat drums because of the posture; 2) women should not beat drums
because of the nature of their dressing.

At the beginning of this chapter, I discussed how roles assigned to
women are dependent on the guarantee that their virginity is not endan-
gered. While it may be possible that a woman may lose her virginity if she
puts things between her legs (like riding a bicycle), it is not true that she
would lose it by putting the drum between her legs. Men are even more vul-
nerable than women. Because women's organs are internal, accidents of any
sort are not likely to occur when they beat the drums between their legs. It is
more likely for men, since their organs are external, to have an accident if
they beat the drums between their legs. In fact, when I discussed this issue
with Ssaalongo Kizza, a drummer and a lecturer in music at the Institute of

Teacher Education Kyambogo, he agreed that the position of the drums, especially the *ngalabi,* is very dangerous for men. The question is: "if men have continued to beat drums and actually put them between their legs, has there ever been a casualty?" In his answer, Kizza said, "If you talked with people who have performing groups, and if these people are sincere, you would find that three, four, or five of them would reconsider the posture of putting drums between the legs" (interview). Similarly, Ibrahim Ggayi and Badru Ssebumpenje, both fluent drummers, agreed that putting the drums between the legs is very risky and can make one lose his manhood (interview). In fact, I observed that men used to put the drums between their legs only when they were beating the drums softly and when the music was slow. They would put the drums between their legs at the beginning of a dance or when accompanying a song without dancing, but as they accelerated at climatic points, they changed the drum and put it under their armpits. When I asked the men drummers why they put the drums under their armpits, the majority of them said it is just a style. Others said they just did what they had learned and practiced what they had seen other drummers doing. On the other hand, Ssebumpenje explained that present-day *ngalabi* are smaller and lighter than those of the past, so they can easily be put under the armpits.

However, Kizza revealed that Bakongola, a former *ngalabi* performer during Muteesa II's reign, introduced the style of beating the *ngalabi* from the armpit as a form of protection. Kizza said that this position was adopted among the drummers of *mbaga* (wedding) dance since their music is very fast and performed with a lot of drama. He explained further that the *ngalabi* performed in the baakisimba motif of the *mbaga* is very fast and, therefore, requires the *ngalabi* to be beaten under the armpits. Putting the *ngalabi* between the legs—especially when they are beating the drum very fast, moving vigorously, falling down, and moving sideways (as most dramatic drummers do)—is risky for men. Kizza strongly agreed that the men drummers use the armpit posture as a means of protecting their organs. The above discussion suggests that given their biological construct, men should not beat the *ngalabi* between their legs. In fact, it is biologically more secure for women, rather than men, to beat the *ngalabi.*

On the other hand, Augustino Kisitu stressed, "a woman to beat the drum while it is between her legs is sexually immoral" ("omukazi okukuba engalabi ng'agitadde mu magula buba bukaba" (interview). By putting the drum between her legs, the woman drummer encroaches on a "naturally" allocated space for men. Another man informant emphatically stated that having the drum between a woman's legs is equated to her having sex, which is immoral if performed in public. In this case, men must regulate women's bodily contact with any object in fear of any possible tactile stimulation.

I now return to Paulo Kabwama's second point, that women should not beat the drums because of the nature of their dress. Actually, other men drummers also complained that women's dressing exposes their bodies, especially the thighs and legs, since they have to pull up their dresses in order to put the drum between their legs. The typical Baganda women used to wear a *suuka* (a sheet of cloth neatly wrapped at the chest with a sash around the waist), which was initially made out of bark cloth and later cotton linen. In the twenty-first century, a respectable "traditional" Muganda woman would put on a busuuti (also called *gomesi* or *boodingi*), a wrapped sheet of cloth with gathered or pleated top sleeves. With the nature of the dress design, one would certainly need to pull the clothes up in order to place the drum between her legs. When I suggested to Kabwama that women drummers could put on trousers while beating drums, since they would not have to pull up any clothes to expose their bodies, he would not hear of a woman dressed in trousers. He stressed that trousers were meant for men and not women. He argued that it is only "spoiled" women, who have copied foreign cultures, who dress like men. Europeans who specified them for men only introduced trousers in Buganda in the late nineteenth century. Putting on trousers is to be a man and therefore, considered to be an act of women's subversion.

However, Kizza argued that it is even more risky for men to beat drums in tight trousers because of the nature of their fashion. And yet, men usually dress in fitting trousers, which may not be appropriate if they put something between their legs, in this case, the drums. He explained that when Bakongola introduced the dramatic beating of the *ngalabi* in *mbaga* dancing, he made a very wide trouser, which gave ample room for his movements. Kizza said:

> Bakongola had sewn a trouser made of woolen material with patches between the legs, which created more room for his men [male organs]. The trouser was not tight and when he fell down as he dramatized his drumming, he would put the drum on the sides or in the armpits and would never put it between his legs (interview).

The problem is not the nature of the women's dress, but the issue is that when women beat drums, they encroach on the men's space, a strong reason for men to regulate women's drumming. It is the power to control and possess women's bodies and their virginity that is at stake, rather than the physical danger of the drum to the women's lives. The baakisimba drums, especially the *mbuutu* and *ngalabi* are used to construct the Baganda's world-view of gender. In this case, the baakisimba drums are cultural "instruments of struggle" through which gender is configured.

HOW MEN CONTROLLED WOMEN'S ACCESS TO THE DRUMS

As Robertson has argued, "mythical explanations are given to show why women should be excluded from the dominant power structures and why men fear and must regulate the behaviour of women" (1987: 228). In Buganda, one of the most popular myths used to regulate women's access to the drum was the threat of death. As Roscoe reported, "No woman might touch a drum . . . she had to keep at a safe distance, lest it should kill her, and she should defile the drum" (1911: 30). The threat of death should not be taken literally; Kizza explained that what is referred to, as "death" is actually barrenness. Women were told: "If a woman beats drums, she does not give birth. As a result, there was no woman who would dare touch the drum, because women knew very well that their identity as ["proper"] women depended on their ability to give birth" (interview). However, Janat Nakitto, a dancer, demystified the myth and argued:

> I think there was discrimination during the times of our ancestors. Women were suppressed; that the women cannot do that thing and yet, they could do it. Now, what has happened to the women who ride bicycles? What has happened to those women who beat drums? I have never seen anything happening to any of them or seen anybody who has changed! (interview).

The true transcript about the drums, however, is not that the drum could "kill" the woman that touched it. As a matter of fact, one of the most renowned woman drummer I got to know during my research was a *nnaalongo* (mother of twins), the highest status a woman outside the palace can ever achieve. Many drummers and dancers referred to Nnaalongo Nazziwa (RIP), who was a member of the Kasangati Women's Cultural Group, as a fluent drummer. In fact, although I beat the drums, I gave birth to twins. By Kiganda cultural standards, I am considered a powerful and successful because I gave birth to twins. How can this myth of barrenness be reconciled with a woman who beats drums and is still able to have twins? It is clear that the threat of death was one of the ways men used to consolidate and control women's power. The drum taboo, in the case of Baganda, mediates men's power over women (Nannyonga-Tamusuza 1999).

The second myth is that God assigned the role of beating the drum to men; like the "power" to rule women, the "gift" of beating the drums was given to men. For instance, describing the drum as a gift from God, Kalungi said:

> This drum is inherited; I am convinced it was the anointment from my ancestors because I was never taught to beat the drum. My drumming just happens because it is inherited; someone pushes me to beat this drum; it is spiritually inspired. Even when I imitate a motif from some one, it is a matter of adding to what I was given by the spirits. But even then, when I learn this motif, I beat it in my own way (interview).

Kalungi was not the only drummer who claimed that the ancestral spirits inspired his drumming. Actually the majority of drummers told me that their drumming was a "blood thing" ("kya mu musaayi"). However, none of the informants could explain why only the men, and not the women could inherit a "blood thing." Probably being men, these drummers had closer contacts with fellow men drummers than women and so, they could learn easily to drum. As already mentioned, the young men always apprentice in occupations of older men. The woman can only learn those skills similar to those of the women with whom they apprentice. As Blaziyo Kalyango explained, since women could not be allowed to mix easily with men, there was no way they could learn the drums. He said, "In the past, women used to be by themselves and men on their own" (interview). Similarly, Sserunku- uma, who was supported by Muhamood Kasujja, said, "In the past, women used to remain at the back of the house and rarely would they come out. Only during special ceremonies would women join the men, and after serv- ing food and drinks they would go back [to their hiding place]" (interview). However, when I revisited the question of his training in drumming at my next visit, Kalungi mentioned that his brother and uncles were drummers in the palace. He also noted that his great grandparents were drummers at Kabaka Suuna's palace. He admitted that whenever his uncles had rehearsals at home, he would help carry the drums in and out of the house and his pay- ment was to be allowed to beat them. It is, therefore, evident that Kalungi learned some of the drum skills by imitating his relatives.

The third myth is that by controlling women's access to the drum, men are honoring women and indeed some women believed so. Badru Sse- bumpenje explained that "since a woman is a mother, that is an honor not to beat the drums. Because when you beat the drum, you definitely have to sweat" (interview). Although he agreed that even when you dance you sweat, he insisted that there is a difference between the sweat from dancing and that from drumming. He stressed that the sweat from drumming is disrespectful for a woman. Similarly, Tereza Kisolo, one of the few women *ngalabi* drummers, noted that it was considered disrespectful for women to beat drums. She said: "Women of the past used to respect themselves a lot and they never wanted to see a woman doing such things [beating drums] and if you beat the drum, you would be called names such as *nnakawanga,* because you are like a man" (interview). Both Ssebumpenje and Kisolo confirmed that it was disrespectful for women to perform roles "traditionally" assigned to men.

Another way in which men have controlled women's access to the drums is through training. In most cases, men are the drum teachers and so, they can control what they want women to learn and consequently, what women perform. My Kiganda music teachers, who had been mainly men, had always discouraged me from learning how to drum, but always praised me as a highly talented dancer. I remember, when I was in high school, I asked a fellow student (who was a male) to teach me what he had performed in the previous rehearsal. He dismissed me and said there was no way I could ever learn to beat the drums since I was a woman. He said it was a "men's thing" to drum. Similarly, during my field research, as part of my research methodology, I had to enroll as a drum student. One of my drum teacher's could not overcome the fact that a woman wanted to learn how to beat the drums. However, because I insisted and I actually paid him his fees, he could not refuse me any longer. Nonetheless, he thought he could discourage me by teaching me differently from the way he had taught the men students. I do not rule out the fact that he was primarily a performer and not a teacher, but it was very clear at the beginning that he was not interested in my learning the drum. First, I was told never to put the drums between my legs. Therefore, he could not allow me to beat the *ngalabi* since I had to tilt it between my legs in order to get the right sound quality and better control. Although I was allowed to beat the *mbuutu,* I could only do so by beating it from the sides. This position was not only tiring, but it was also very difficult for me to control the drum; it was moving as I beat it. In fact, all the men drummers I interviewed agreed that beating the drum from the sides was not only tiring, but could easily lead to the injury of muscles in the arm.

Second, the pace of instruction was so fast for any student to learn. I tried periodically to ask him to reduce the speed, but all my effort was in vain. Since I had to act as if I had never beaten the drums before, I pretended to be slow at learning during the first two sessions. The third time I went back, he was surprised that I had returned, because he thought, with certainty that I would give up. This time, I wanted to show him that I had

"learned" what he had taught me the previous two sessions. He acknowledged that I had improved and introduced more motifs at an even faster
pace. He suggested that I should practice those motifs before I met with him
again. This time our session was shorter than the others. My experience with
this drum teacher made it clear to me why few women can learn the drums.
In fact, if I had not had prior knowledge of drumming, and if I did not have
an objective beyond learning, I would not have been able to learn even a single motif.

A similar incident occurred when I visited Kirimuttu Women's Group
in Kyotera, Buddu County. My contact with this women's group was through
a very talented and accomplished drummer whom I later learned was actually
the teacher for this group. We had agreed that I was going to meet his group,
Ssenkubuge Nnankasa Group (a well established semi-professional group of
men drummers and women dancers), as well as Kirimuttu Women's Group.
However, after meeting with his group, he suggested that I should forget
about the women's group. He said, "What these women are beating is nothing." It is only when I saw them perform and learned that he was actually
responsible for teaching them that I understood why he never wanted me to
see them. After introducing me, he excused himself and only returned after
the women had finished their performance. He feared embarrassment since
he was their teacher. This group was poorly prepared. And yet, these women
drummers seemed very enthusiastic and had contributed money to learn to
beat the drums. After listening to their drumming, one could not believe
that this fluent drummer was actually their teacher. The group told me that
they had been learning drumming with him for two years and were meeting
at least once a week. The most striking thing was that although I had just
seen him beat the *ngalabi* between his legs (when his group performed the
previous day), he actually instructed the drummer to beat the *ngalabi* while
in an upright position. This position not only affected the sound quality of
the *ngalabi,* it was evident that the *ngalabi* drummers got tired early because
she had no control of the drum. Plate 11 shows Kirimuttu Women's Group
singing and beating the drums; note that the ngalabi is beaten in an upright
position.

Further, men have discouraged women from drumming by completely
dismissing women's drumming as mere "tin-beating"; women beat tins and
men beat drums. Men describe women's drumming as being weak and only
suitable for accompanying simple and casual singing, but not "serious" dancing. They argued that women cannot beat drums because, they are naturally
"weak" and drums require a lot of energy if one is to beat them well. For
instance, a man drummer, who believed that women are weak, also believed

Plate 11. Kirimuttu Women's Group Performing baakisimba.

that their drumming sounds equally as weak. I argued that women are not weak, especially since they can dance for long periods of time (from thirty minutes to ninety minutes or even more). When I asked this drummer whether a woman could dance for one hour if she was not energetic, he answered that "she is energetic, but she mainly uses more of her legs and the heart is working hard. Yet, the drummer uses the chest and the hands" (anonymous, interview). Based on experience as a drummer and dancer, I am convinced that one has to have a certain amount of energy for both drumming and dancing, but drumming certainly does not require a kind of energy that women do not have. Similarly, Sam Kimbugwe, a drummer and xylophone performer stated that, "if a woman can beat the drum [and if] she has her energy, I think there should be no problem" (interview). He also associated drumming with energy, but not one's gender.

However, Nakitto rejected this allegation and pointed out that, "I do not think women are weak. I think they just despise themselves, 'how can a woman beat drums? It should be done by a man!'" (interview). She argued that, "although men may be stronger, women have enough energy to beat drums and beat them well. If Nnaalongo Nazziwa could beat drums at weddings, then she was a strong woman! What about Nnabanoba of Luwafu Women's Group?" (interview). She pointed out further that her father,

Sulaiti Kalungi, does not exert a lot of energy when beating the drum. She noted that, "when my father is beating it, he does not seem as if he is beating a drum; you do not see him straining. Drumming depends on one's skills but not the amount of energy one has. My father's drumming is in the hands. When you look at him without seeing his hands, you may not think he is beating anything!" (interview). Indeed, when Kalungi is beating the drum, he is so relaxed that even after performing, you can never see him sweat. I have also heard similar comments about his drumming from the audience. Among fellow drummers, Kalungi is referred to as the "grandfather" of drummers *("jjajja w'abagoma")*. For instance, Ggayira noted, "Kalungi is the best amongst all drummers. And he leads us; he is the grandfather for drummers" (interview). The title of grandfather denotes knowledge and skill, which Kalungi possesses. In this case, as a grandfather, he is looked upon as the model drummer whom other drummers desire to emulate. Kalungi's case helps to explain that drumming does not require much energy; rather, skill and knowledge are most important. It follows, then, that if women were given the opportunity to gain skills and knowledge of drumming, they would be better drummers. This discourse about performance practice suggests that the prohibition against women's drumming is connected to social relations of power and not women's physical attributes. Since the drum is symbolic of power and beating it is connected to both physical and spiritual power, I would contend that the process of disempowering women involved banning women's drumming.[15] By controlling the drum, men constituted themselves as agents for dominating women.

NAKAWANGA DRUMMERS: MANLY-FEMALES EATING THE FORBIDDEN FRUIT?

Richard Lubega informed me that in 1959 Ssekabaka Edward Muteesa II visited a girls' school in Villa Maria, Buddu County, where girls beat drums and danced to entertain him. In appreciation, the *kabaka* gave a scholarship to the best *ngalabi* performer (interview). Further, Tereza Kisolo told me that she started beating the drums, especially the *ngalabi,* in 1960 (interview). Although more women began beating baakisimba drums after the abolition of the Buganda Kingdom in the 1960s, the existence of women drummers has been recorded before this period. Walabyeki Magoba wrote that "although in the past [before 1960] Buganda women only sang, Nabukalu refused that; she would beat the *ngalabi* and *mbuutu* as if it were people speaking!" (1999: 27).

The changes in the social, political, and cultural structures in Buganda since the 1960s influenced the performance practice of baakisimba. The men's control over women's access to the drums in the public arena could not be sustained. After the abolition of the monarchy, the custodian of Kiganda customs, and with increased accessibility to Western education; Baganda women could no longer accept being passive receptors of culturally constructed gender identities and roles. More women began to beat the drums as a form of resistance to the symbolic construction of women as weak and subordinate beings. Beating the drums helped them to redefine themselves as active agents of cultural and social change. Richard Nsubuga explained that women began beating the drums because the monarchical institution that was limiting them is no longer in existence. He said: "Because of the changes women should also beat drums in order to help preserve the tradition. This is so because even the era when we used to go to the palace is over!" The discussion thus far, confirms the view I began with at the beginning of this book that the stability of the kabakaship is very important in the sustenance of customs and Baganda men's hegemony.

There were mixed attitudes toward women drummers; some Baganda, both men and women, believe women should beat drums like men, while others insist that drumming has never been and should never be a role for a woman. Many men with whom I interacted were not happy with music festivals that required women to beat the drums.[16] And when a woman performed well on the drum, they would call her all kinds of names to insult her. For instance, on a number of occasions, I have been called "maama Nalukalala," meaning an assertive, aggressive female, one who threatens the social order. Similarly, Sulaimani Mukwaya, a member of Kalungi's ensemble, laughed when I asked him what he thought of a woman drummer. He said such a woman is "kyakulassajja" ("manly-female") and "when you see a woman beating drums you can imagine that if she was a man, she would have been very powerful and aggressive; one who is feared!" (interview). While Mukwaya view may sound positive, but he actually despises the idea of a woman drummer.

Likewise, Augustino Kisitu said, "a woman who beats the *ngalabi* is called *nnaluwali* [aggressive person] and she is *nnalukalala* [an intrepid person]. In fact, men used to fear the home where such a person came from; they would rarely marry from there" (interview). Given the meaning of "okuwasa" in Buganda (to marry is to control and own) few men, if any, would like to marry a woman that they cannot control. Of course a "womanless" female, *nnaluwali*, a woman who can not be tamed, would certainly threaten any man who may want to control her. When I asked Ssekitto, a drummer, whether he would consider marrying a woman who is a drummer, he said he would, since he is also a drummer. He noted, however, that if he were not a drummer, he would fear her. He argued "My dear, if she can beat the drum, then she can also beat me up! You know my friend, drummers have a lot of energy; their hands are very strong!" (interview). This manly-female drummer subverts the constructed concept of women being weak, and thus threatens the "naturally" strong men.

Interviews with some of the best women drummers revealed that they are either still single, separated, or divorced. Tereza Kisolo told me that she began to beat he drums only after she had separated from her husband. Likewise, by 2002, Nnabanoba, another fluent drummer, was still single. I also observed that the schoolgirls who beat drums usually do not continue when they get married; if they do, they perform mainly in churches or as teachers in schools but not on a public stage. In the next paragraphs, I present the voice of one of the most musically fluent women drummers, Rehema Nnabanoba.

In 2000, I had the opportunity to watch Nnabanoba beat the drums in a performance of forty-five minutes and later interviewed her for two hours. My interview was timely, because I conducted it towards the end of the first phase of my research, so some of the questions I asked Nnabanoba were actually based on my interpretation of the data so far collected. Nnabanoba was one of the informants I used to check and tease out what I thought were the main issues of my data. And yet, Nnabanoba fluently communicated the views of a number of women I interviewed about gendered drumming in Buganda. I present only the salient issues of our interview. Plate 12 shows Nnabanoba beating the *mbuutu*, with Margaret Nanziri providing the basic beat on the *mpuunyi*. I took this photography when Nnabanoba was practicing a new *mbaga* motif she had learned the previous day.

To some people, especially men, Nnabanoba is called *nnakawanga*, ("she-cock"); others call her *kyakulassajja* ("manly-female"), while to others, she is known as *nnabyewanga* (a man impostor). Nnabanoba, who is in her late twenties, started drumming when she was about twelve years old, while in primary school. Due to financial constraints, Nnabanoba could not continue school and later joined a women's group called Kiwafu Women's Club, through which she has excelled as a drummer. Nnabanoba performs almost all the drums, but her favorites are the *ngalabi* and the *mbuutu*. She performs baakisimba, *nnankasa*, *muwogola*, *mbaga*, and *ssenkubuge* drum styles. Although she is also a good dancer as well, Nnabanoba has focused on drumming since 1989. Nnabanoba strongly disagreed with the construction that women cannot beat drums as well as the men do because of women's biological construct, as most men drummers have argued. Nnabanoba contested the view that only men can inherit drumming, and argued that men only have more opportunities to beat the drum than women. Nnabanoba reacted thus:

Plate 12. Manly-Females beating the drums: *left to right:* Margaret Nanziri, Rehema Nnabanoba.

It is not true! It is not in blood [inherited] that a woman cannot beat drums. They are just lying; they want to eliminate us from sharing the queen ant! Those are some of the old taboos where a woman would not be allowed to eat chicken and eggs. But nothing ever happened when women began eating the eggs. The reason they give that a woman will not give birth if she beats the drum is a lie too. Although I have never given birth to a child, there are women who beat the drums, and yet have children! In fact, we have a woman drummer who has a child of one-year-and-a-half. Moreover, she got married after she had become a drummer!

I told Nnabanoba that men drummers give the excuse that women are "naturally" weak, so they cannot beat the drum. Nnabanoba rejected the view and argued that if women are given equal access and training they are capable of excelling in drumming. Nnabanoba said:

Women are not weak! Beating the drum is a result of wanting to do it and actually getting the opportunity to learn. There may be a man who is actually strong, but when you give him the drum, he may fail to beat it. And yet a woman would beat it and surprise you! Therefore, I cannot say that it is because of being weak that women cannot beat the drums; women are not weak. Drumming is like desiring something and then you give it a trial. Women can beat drums and in fact, they beat them. During the competitions (of Makindye division) that I have told you about, it was only women; there was no single man! And yet they beat very well, although some groups were better than others.

Nnabanoba believed that it is lack of exposure and the lack of opportunities to learn, rather than women being weak, that account for the few women beating drums. She was convinced that practice makes one a better performer; "the drum is tiring, if you do not regularly practice; you can get a muscle injury." Nnabanoba contended that drumming does not necessarily require a lot of energy, but rather, skill and perseverance. She believed that "if one loves what she is doing, she can persevere." Nnabanoba compared drumming to a marathon; a runner is not merely strong, but has to have the stamina and the desire to finish the race. She argued that if women get the exposure to the drums at an early age, like boys, and cultivate the interest and desire to beat these drums, they too could excel. Nnabanoba said that in performance she usually beats the drums for an hour, but in most cases, it depends on the requirement of the host and the context of the performance.

Explaining further why there are not many women beating drums, she said that women are usually discouraged and at times completely dismissed as people who cannot perform well on any musical instrument. Nnabanoba explained further that many women believe the mythical construction of women and as a result, they have low self-esteem and are always shy to try out anything that is "coded" for men. Sharing her own experience, Nnabanoba told me that it took time and courage to beat the drums in front of an audience. She said:

> Even after I had learned how to beat the drum, I could not perform on stage, even if my teacher had allowed me. At that time, I was very shy; I used to fear people seeing me when I beat the drum. I used to beat the drum by myself without anybody seeing me.

Nnabanoba noted further that the kind of names given to women who beat drums or who may do things usually done by men discourage women from getting involved in the so-called men's activities. She shared with me what she called the most humiliating occasion of her life as a drummer. When Nnabanoba had her first big show, at a village women's festival, she had to be subjected to a physical examination to prove that she was a female. Moreover, since Nnabanoba is a person of small stature, most people in the audience were suspicious of her being a man. She had to endure the loud shouts of *kyakulassajja, nnabyewanga, nnaluwali* and others. She reported that:

> The majority of the audience initially refused to believe that I was a woman; they thought I was a man. Our first competition (I have forgotten the year) was at White Nile Theater. These were competitions for women, for the Makindye division. In fact, the audience and the adjudicator reached a point of wanting to take me outside and check whether I was a woman. It is because they disagreed on my gender; 'oh that is not a woman!' They checked me and tried to feel whether I had breasts on my chest. In fact, they almost undressed me [she laughed]. Because we were dressed in Kanzu [men's robe], it was difficult to tell whether I was a woman or not. Finding out that I was actually a woman, some people applauded me and others confirmed that I was indeed *kyakulassajja*. Some women were happy to see a fellow woman beating the drums, while others were not. All the people were very surprised and a number of them gave me a lot of money. In fact, it is us who won the women's competitions in Makindye division. We won three consecutive times and they gave us the trophy for good. They were indeed shocked to see a woman beating the *ngalabi* as I did.

Unlike many women, Nnabanoba has never been discouraged by the disapproval of people, especially men. She is now very proud that she is a drummer. Nnabanoba recounted:

> I feel very good. In fact, sometimes when I have a lot of thoughts, or things that has annoyed me, I go and get my drum (because I live very close to our practicing place) and I beat it. All the thoughts go away. The drum takes away all thoughts; it relaxes me!

In Nnabanoba's case, the drum is not only a symbol of identity, or an object of power, but it is connected to her psychological and emotional well-being. Denying her the access to the drum would be to restrict her the right to release her tensions and anxieties. Nnabanoba is being challenged: on the one hand, beating the drum robs her identity as a "proper" Muganda woman; on the other hand, the drum helps her release tension.

Explaining how her family background helped her to realize *her* abilities as a woman drummer, Nnabanoba said:

Our father loved the drum, although we never had a drum at home. At
times we used to beat tins and dance, because I loved drumming. We
used to sing and would see that our father enjoyed it. He liked what we
were doing. In fact, he often came to see us singing at school.

Nnabanoba was lucky that she had the support of her father. A number of people, both men and women that I interviewed admired and wished to be musicians, but their parents discouraged them. In my case, my mother wanted me to
become a lawyer and initially was disappointed that I studied music. When I
asked Nnabanoba who taught her to beat the drums, she said:

> I taught myself. Because we had drums at school and boys were beating
> them, my heart desired to beat them. When I tried them out, I found
> myself learning. I started beating this drum when I was still young. I
> think when I was about twelve years old. But of course, it seems I had
> the talent. At the beginning, I was just imitating, but later I learned to
> beat the drums. I joined a women's group called Luwafu Women's Club,
> which is in Makindye [Kyaddondo county]. The man who mainly
> trained me, especially teaching me more motifs, is called Ronald
> Kayondo, who also lives in Makindye. But he found me when I knew
> how to beat the drums; he only taught me more motifs [or variations].
> By the time he began to teach me, I knew well how to beat baakisimba,
> *nnnankasa,* and *muwogola* styles.

Nnabanoba was particularly articulate about the Baganda beliefs that men
fear marrying women who are drummers and the myth that when a woman
beats the drum she can "die." I asked Nnabanoba whether her drumming
does not reduce her chances of getting married, let alone failing to give birth,
the only means through which she is defined as a proper woman. Nnabanoba answered:

> Men are always there, but in our group we try to control ourselves. Oh
> yes, there are many! Imagine, he may come to give you a money tip, but
> encloses saying: 'after the performance, find me in such and such a
> place; I have something to tell you.' You can always get a man even if
> you beat the drums. There are many who want to propose and you see
> they have actually fallen in love, but my dear, because of the rampant
> disease [AIDS], it is not worth the risk. Moreover, he may take you
> [marry you] and then refuses to let you beat the drum again. Ha! I do
> not know whether I can ever leave the drum. Even if it is for a man, I do

not know! Indeed, I fell in love with the drum! Probably, I can leave it; but I do not know!

Nnabanoba informed me that, in fact, the majority of the members of her group are married. However, she argued that initially there were problems because a number of men did not want their wives to be away from home. Men feared that if their wives interacted with other women, they would learn 'bad behaviors' and stop respecting their husbands. She said some men would follow them to the places of performances, and hide in order to spy on them. But later after they had gained confidence and trust, they let go. According to Nnabanoba, to beat the drum is to be alive; the drumbeat is a heartbeat to her. Nnabanoba said:

> When you have learned the drum and someone tells you to stop, in fact, it is like [he/she] wishes you death! In fact, when you learn the drum very well, it enters into your heart; you get to like it. If someone tells you to stop beating [the drum], that person is indeed a killer!

Nnabanoba joins many voices of Baganda women who believe that there is nothing wrong with women beating the drums. In fact, denying women the right to beat drums, as Nnabanoba stated, means "killing" the woman. Of course, a person who is denied access to his or her own identification is as good as "dead." Until women can freely access their symbolic identity as Baganda, they will remain in the background and be, indeed, "dead." Concluding our interview, Nnabanoba had this to tell the women. She said: "The only thing I want to tell the women is to stop being shy. They should stop saying, 'how will so-and-so see me?' They should stop despising themselves. Most women despise themselves. That is what I have to emphasize to them."

By proposing that women gain access to the drum, Nnabanoba is not advocating women's dominance over men or even agitating for "equality"; rather, she is claiming her right to co-exist with Baganda men. The right to self-identification, empowerment, and pleasure are symbolically derived from beating the drum and its sounds. Since the drum is central to the identity of both women and men, beating the drum is to be a Muganda. By beating the drum, women rediscover and thus redefine themselves.

BAAKISIMBA AT VILLAGE WEDDING CEREMONIES

The most outstanding secular contexts in which village baakisimba was performed were at wedding ceremonies. Baakisimba was mainly performed at the *kasiki,* the eve of the wedding and the wedding day itself. At these ceremonies, baakisimba was not only used for entertaining the guests and bidding farewell to the bride and groom, but it was also used as a vehicle to prepare the couple in their new roles as "proper" man and woman. Participation was free and both the bride and the groom used this ceremony to join relatives, friends, and neighbors in baakisimba dance, especially during the *kasiki* (eve of the wedding day). Baakisimba performance at a wedding ceremony crystallizes gender differentiation among the Baganda. It should be noted immediately, however, that baakisimba's role in marriage ceremonies was stronger before the influx of disco music in the early 1980s. Peter Ggayira told me that until the 1970s, baakisimba performance was part of every wedding festivity. Especially since the 1990s, disco music and dancing replaced baakisimba performance at many people's functions. However, I do not mean to say that baakisimba is never performed at marriage ceremonies; while it is not as popular as before, baakisimba is still performed and some people still treasure it as an important part of the marriage ceremony.

When the *badongo ba Kabaka* introduced the *mbaga* (wedding) dance outside the palace, baakisimba began to be performed as a movement within the wedding dance. Because the mbaga dance is very fast and vigorous, when baakisimba was introduced in the wedding dance it began to be performed at a faster speed. Despite its inclusion, baakisimba maintained specific distinct features in the musical accompaniment, choreography, and costume.[17] Besides being retained as a dance motif in the newly created mbaga dance, baakisimba came to be restricted to *kasiki* (wedding eve) only. Moreover, dancers had to be hired for the wedding dance performance and free participation was restricted to the *kasiki* ceremony. At that point in time, a "big" wedding was not only characterized by the number of *maato g'omwenge* (barrel of Kiganda local beer), but also the presence of hired dancers (Kabwama, interview). Paulo Kabwama, in his early seventies, told me that people would say " so and so made a great wedding ceremony; he also hired four dancers!"

Since procreation is the main aim of marriage among the Baganda, the bride and the groom are given special training so as to achieve what the Baganda consider a successful sexual life. A successful sexual relationship is related to childbirth. That is why a woman and a man who give birth to twins, *nnaalongo* and *ssaalongo,* respectively, are considered to be sexually powerful. Although the training for a successful sexual life may begin early in the bride and groom's lives, on *kasiki* and the actual wedding day, music and dance crystallize this training. While baakisimba is performed on both ceremonies, it is most important at the *kasiki* when it is performed at the bride's home. While the *kasiki* ceremony is meant to bid farewell to the bride, it is at this time that parents, and indeed the entire village, came to judge the softness of the bride's waist. The softness of the waist is associated with a successful sexual life, which is related to childbirth.

One informant told me, "A woman who did not have a soft waist was never married" (anonymous). He said that at a certain point, during the *kasiki,* baakisimba was performed and the bride was supposed to dance alone. If the bride's waist was not soft enough, the paternal aunt spent the whole night training the bride. He told me that the groom's family would also send spies during the bride's *kasiki* to prove whether she was appropriate for their son. During my research, I had the opportunity to attend one *kasiki* where only Kiganda music and including baakisimba, was performed for the bride.

25 December, 1999, was not only a day to celebrate Christmas, since Peter Ggayira is a Christian, but was also a day to bid farewell to his daughter; it was the eve of her wedding. He told me that as a Kiganda musician he could not allow his daughter to be sent away with disco music. Preparations began very early in the morning and the ceremony began at around 5:00 P.M. with a big meal. By 9:00 P.M., Agalya Awamu Cultural Group, the ensemble that was hired, was already on stage amid shouts and applause. After the first round of dancing, which lasted for almost two hours, the general audience was ready to join the stage. Ssaalongo Benedicto Kansamba, who beat the *mbuutu,* performed a slower baakisimba to which the general audience could easily dance. After that round of "general happiness," the official dancers were ready to do their second round. Behind the house, relatives of the bride were busy giving her their last words; teaching her about her new role as a wife. Paternal aunts were particularly at the center of the training.

By the time the second round ended, it was approaching 1:00 A.M. It took one and a half hours. After an exciting dance, with the audience applauding and giving money to the "soft" dancers, the tipsy audience started demanding that the bride should dance. One man shouted: "where is the bride? We have seen these ones [the official dancers]. We want that one who brought us [here, the bride]" *("Omugole aluwa? Bano tubalabya, twagala oli eyatuleesa!").* Then a drunkard woman shouted back, "you have helped us sir, it is good you have spoken. For us we came to see the bride" ("otuyambye ssebo! Olyose n'oyogera, ffe twazze kulaba mugole"). More people joined this woman to lodge their complaints about the delayed dancing of the bride. Because of the noise, from the audience, the musicians were forced to stop drumming. Amid shouts and applause, eventually the bride emerged and treated the audience to a slow and graceful baakisimba. Her dancing lasted for about three minutes before she was taken back to rest. It is at this time that people went to greet her, to give her their blessings and gifts. From the audience's reaction, it was apparent that they were impressed with the bride's performance. I could hear, audience members especially men, commenting about her soft waist. There was another dance session for the relatives and this time, a song entitled: "Kuzaala Kujaagaana" accompanied it. While this song is usually sang at most occasions when celebrating the success of one's children, it is commonly sung on the eve of a wedding. It is also common for such a song to be sung at other occasions, for instance, at a graduation party. For the sake of the discussion, I only transcribe part of the song text here.

Kujaagaana	To be proud
Ng'azaala akuza	Like one who gives birth and his or her children grow
Nze naayita ani	Whom shall I call
Nnyabo okuzaala kujaagaana	My dear, giving birth is pride
Yee	Yes
Nnyabo okuzaala kuzibu nnyo	My dear giving birth is not easy
Ngalo, ngalo bazadde bannange	Clap, clap fellow parents
Nnyabo omuzadde asaana mbuzi	My dear a parent deserves a goat
Siba muzadde ne ndya dduma	I cannot be a parent and I eat food without stew.

At the beginning of this chapter, I discussed how giving birth defines one as a proper man or woman. However, it is even more prestigious when a parent sees her or his children grow up and eventually get married. In this song, parents (and in this case, Ggayira and his wife) celebrate the successful nurturing of their daughter, which they believe, enabled her to find a man who could marry her. Further, the song reaffirms the commodification of daughters and women. The issue of bride price is referred to in the song when the parents sing: "my dear, parents deserve a goat. I cannot be a parent and I eat food without stew." Further, the "goat" in the text is also a metaphor for virginity, which is a sign of respect for the bride as well as the parents. If parents protect their daughter's virginity, they are given a goat in appreciation of taking good care of their daughter. One informant told me that at least until the 1940s, brides would be sent back home if they were not found not to be virgins (anonymous, interview). However, this practice is less prevalent in the twenty-first-century

Buganda. This song illustrates that in addition to dance motifs, the Baganda use song texts as a vehicle to communicate roles assigned to men and women in marriage.

Besides having a successful sexual life in marriage, women must be successful food producers in order to keep their families strong and healthy. Baakisimba dance helps to crystallize the Baganda women's role as the food providers. As Kwakwa has observed, "work movements involved in daily female chores form a basis for the organized movements in women's dances" (1994: 11). She mentioned, for example, that "pounding, grinding, winnowing—which a woman performs lend themselves easily to dance movements because of their inherent rhythm" (ibid.). Similarly, Peggy Harper has noted that, "work movements involved in Tiv farming activities form a basis for many stylized movements in Tiv dance (1970: 7). In Chapter Three, I explained that the term "baakisimba" is derived from the phrase, *abaakisimba ekitooke* (those who planted the banana plantain) and, therefore, relates to the production of food. As M. B. Nsimbi has noted, "The main occupation of women in Buganda was the growing of food and its preparation. . . . It was considered a very bad thing for a man to do cultivation or to prepare food. . . . Young boys were strictly forbidden from going near the cooking place in the house" (1956: 28).

Baakisimba draws on movements from the daily routines of women as the food providers. The *kubiibya* motif, the basic footwork and waist movement in baakisimba, relates closely to the planting and preparation of *matooke* (bananas) and *mwenge bigere* (local beer). The basic body movement in this motif is in the waist and hips as directed by the footwork. Most activity is in the lower torso, while the upper torso (head, chest, shoulders, and arms) is still. The dancer stands at a low level, with bent knees, chest high and forward, and buttocks outward. In figure 12, I transcribe the basic footwork and waist movement. This transcription is not based on one single performance, but a collection of my observations in the field and my own experience as a dancer and drummer.

The transcription of the music is for two basic baakisimba drums, *ngalabi* and *mbuutu*, and clapping. As illustrated in the transcription, the dancer begins with both feet flat on the ground. While maintaining the weight on the left leg, the dancer shifts her weight to the ball of the right foot in front of the body. When the dancer lands on the ball of the right foot, the right hip is lifted before dropping. Meanwhile, the left foot and hip move in the opposite direction. When the right hip is lifted, the left hip is dropped. Because these hip movements happen so quickly, the effect is a shimmy of the bottom as the entire waist wriggles. Like the basic baakisimba musical motif, the basic dance motif is completed in one measure.

Figure 12. Kubiibya basic footwork and waist/hip movements in village baakisimba.

The dancers' movements, from flat foot to the ball of the feet, alternately simulate the planting of the bananas. The posturing on the balls of the feet imitates the hoe when it is dug in the ground in order to create a hole for the plantain. On the other hand, by stepping with a flat foot, the dancer imitates the planting of the banana tree; after digging a hole of about four feet, the farmer puts the banana tree in the hole and pulls the soil to cover it. Then, she stamps around the plant to make it firm. The footwork and the waist movements in *kubiibya* motif can also be related to the preparation of *matooke* food (cooked bananas). The alternation of the flat feet-and on the balls of the feet-flat feet movements relate to the movement of the hands in the kneading of the bananas.[18] In making beer, sometimes the Baganda use their feet, producing what is called *mwenge bigere* ("beer of the feet"). Similarly, the soft-round waist movement seems to imitate the ripe bananas and how they are squeezed to make the beer. Baakisimba being a women's dance helps to crystallize women's roles as food producers.

DANCING BAAKISIMBA: PERFORMING SEX IN PUBLIC?

Baakisimba is a site through which Baganda women are constructed as sexual objects. Since the Baganda women are defined by the full realization of their sexuality, baakisimba is at the core of their identification process. However, discussing baakisimba, as a sexual dance may seem to be another eroticisation of Africa women as Kariamu Welsh pointed out:

> Many historians and critics have interpreted the role of women in African dance as erotic, exotic, and sexually aggressive. . . . It is not an accident of history or an aesthetic anomaly that the image of females in African dance is most often barebreasted women dancing in an ecstatic frenzy. The cultural legacy that these images spawned continues to determine and prescribe how African women are defined (1994: 16).

Of course, I am not intending to over-sexualize the dance, but the performance practice of baakisimba—contexts, the choreography, costuming—strongly suggest that sexuality is an integral part of baakisimba. The women's position in baakisimba is defined not only by the many aspects of baakisimba production including dance movements, costume, dance training, position within the performing group, as well as the audience's responses to women's dancing, but also by the complex sets of historical and cultural factors. While Western scholars have been criticized for "over-sexualizing" African dance, relating specifically to baakisimba, the view of the dance as being sexual is not unfounded. Although I may be criticized for perpetuating a colonial legacy as cited by Welsh above, my research confirms that baakisimba is strongly embodied in women's sexuality. The majority of the Baganda that I interviewed confirmed, either directly or by implication, that the dance emphasizes the objectification of women's sexuality, based on their gender.

In order to proceed with this argument, let us first examine the term *okuzina,* which is the equivalent of the verb "to dance." While *kuzina* generally means to "shake one's torso" (*"okunyeenya ku galiba enjole"*), its deeper meaning is to have sexual intercourse. As a matter of fact, dancing is so much associated with sexuality that dancers are in most cases referred to as prostitutes, not necessarily because they indulge in prostitution. Sam Kimbugwe, a xylophone player, told me that he could never marry a dancer, although he is a musician himself. As a number of informants, he said that "people despise dancers; they call them prostitutes" (Interview). Likewise, Kisitu informed the author that dancers are referred to as prostitutes because when they dance, they entice the entire audience" (interview). And yet, a number of informants who were not performers also believed that dancers are prostitutes. As a matter of fact, a number of informants stressed they can never allow their daughters to join dance troupes. These informants suggested that a good dancer would definitely perform sex better and that many people would approach her for sex.

One informant confided that he had a casual relationship with a dancer, but stressed he would never marry a dancer. He argued, "a woman that dances is not yours alone. Remember that other [men] also admire her as you do" (*"Omukazi omuzinyi taba wuwo wekka. Kimanye n'abalala bamwegomba nga ggwe!"*) (anonymous, interview). He expressed that as she dances, she is actually having sex with every man in the audience. He said, "You can actually tell by the way the men [in the audience] react when there is a very attractive dancer on stage!" (*"Era ekyo okirabira ku ngeri abasajja gyebeeyisaamu nga balabye mu ddiiro omuzinyi omulungi!"*) (ibid.). In fact, one dancer complained that some members of the audience, especially men, treat them as if they were prostitutes. She narrated that it is common that when men come to give money tips, as applause, to women dancers, they include notes of love proposals, which men put in the women's bras. In so doing, the men are able to touch the women's breasts. She noted, however, that with the present Acquired Immune Deficiency Syndrome (AIDS) scourge, men are scared to approach her any more because they do not know her health status (anonymous, interview).

Further, an ensemble leader confirmed that women dancers are looked at as sexual objects. He said:

Men want women dancers. You can also see that [he laughed]! At times someone may hire you and say: ' Do not bring me any men dancers.' In other cases, someone may hire you and say: 'do not bring me a dancer that does not look beautiful.' They want beautiful dancers, ones with good-looking faces, even if they do not dance so well, as long as they have good-looking faces (interview).

When I asked him why patrons want beautiful dancers, he said, "you can just see that, if someone says 'I do not want a dancer that does not have color [not beautiful],' he wants one that he can use; one he can have a relationship with!" (ibid.). Looking at women performers, especially dancers, as prostitutes, is not unique only to Buganda. L. JaFran Jones has noted how the *qayna* female musicians of Tunisia "served as gifts between the wealthy and the powerful. . . . sometimes with the legal status of concubines" (1987: 70–71).

Because of the implicit and, at times, explicit statements of sexuality in baakisimba, "dancing requires someone who is not shy at all" (Kalungi, interview). Janat Nakitto told me that although her mother was a great dancer, she could not dance because she was shy (interview). In fact, because children tend to be innocent, the majority of the dancers I interviewed began dancing when they were young. For instance, Nakitto began dancing when she was only six years old (interview). As a child, one may not understand the implied meanings of the dance and simply replicate what she or he is taught. For instance, when I asked Sarah Namutebi, one of the dancers, why she knelt at the beginning of the dance in *kweyanza* motif, she said, "I do not know. I was only taught what to do" (Interview).

In the following paragraphs, I examine how the choreographic features and costuming in baakisimba help to crystallize the construction of sexual objects. In every dance, dancers project certain parts of the body, while suppressing others. Why are certain parts of the body emphasized more than others? Most specifically, why is the basic movement of baakisimba in the waist and hips? Why do dancers have to expose these body parts, yet among the Baganda, the waist of the woman, among other parts of the body, is usually concealed and rarely exposed in public discourse? Most of the women dancers that I interviewed were too shy to discuss the issue. Nonetheless, all the dancers interviewed agreed that a good dancer is one who dances with a smile, has a soft wriggling waist, and does not move the upper torso. On one occasion, a man from the audience, who requested anonymity said, "When a woman dances with a very soft waist, it is exciting to us [men]. That is the foundation for one's pleasure.

You can also see that!" (*"Omukazi bw'agonda ennyo ekiwato ffe kitusanyusa. Awo we wali entabiro y'obulamu, ekyo naawe okiraba!"*) (anonymous, interview).

Further, one drummer argued that the waist is the most important part of the woman and that is why it can only be exposed in dancing contexts. He explained that: "People consider you a great dancer by looking at your waist. To be able to separate the upper torso from the lower one and then you quiver; that is when they praise as being a great dancer. In fact, some people are even given herbs in order to be soft" (anonymous, interview). Ezuliya Nannyonga, a former palace dancer, confirmed that she was given some herbs in order to develop very soft waist. As a matter of fact, she had agreed to give me some herbs if I was seriously considering becoming a palace dancer.

Further, Kisolo explained why the thumb points to the waist in *nsi eradde mirembe* motif (see plate in Chapter Four): "We want this place [the waist] to be distinct: 'you see how I was designed!' And another thing, the other parts of the body are still, so that when a dancer turns, it enables the audience to see how the other side of the waist rotates or wriggles" (interview). When the thumb points to the waistline, it stresses the focal point of the dance. The thumb draws ones attention to the beauty of the dancer.

Further, the Baganda have an acceptable code of dressing for women. If a woman does not follow this code, she is disregarded as a "proper" Muganda woman. Alexandria Nanono rightly noted that clothing is influenced by "environment and climate . . . social, *[sic]* ritual and convention" (1977: i).[19] Baaziriyo Nsubuga, an elderly and very conservative man regarding Kiganda customs, described the "correct" code of dressing for women in Buganda to me. He said:

> A Muganda woman should not dress in a way that exposes her legs and calf of the legs. In Buganda, that is obscene, that is what we call nakedness. But she needs to dress in clothes that cover her legs and if it is a dress, it should be long. Therefore, *boodingi* [dress style] is the best. In fact, the *boodingi* is very good for a Muganda woman; it covers her very well and keeps her warm. Because we [men] have many things we would not like a Muganda woman to expose, what the Europeans call, in public. Furthermore, when a Muganda woman is dressed in *boodingi,* she has to walk gracefully, because all the time we [men] need her to be like a flower. She should not move fast (interview).

Similarly, another informant related the appropriate dressing of the Baganda women to *omuwumbo gw'emmere* (mass of cooked banana food). In the preparation of cooked bananas, the Baganda, wrap the peeled banana in many banana leaves before steaming the bananas. These leaves are not only intended to give flavor to the bananas, to facilitate even cooking, but also to keep them warm. This informant emphasized that a woman dressed in *boodingi* covers herself properly; she is protected from dust and keeps warm for her husband. He stressed the fact that women's dressing is to protect and keep warm the men's controlled space.

Considering the acceptable code of dressing in Buganda, the dancers' costumes through history can be considered close to nakedness. Since village baakisimba was informal until the 1940s, the costuming at the time was also informal. An excited person would just pick a banana leaf and make into strips *(mpina)* and tie it around her waist and then dance. Later, the formalized baakisimba dancers adopted the palace costume. They wore a strip of cloth around their bust, a kind of bra, and a sheet of cloth beginning from the waist line, leaving the stomach or the belly exposed. They tied a sash and on top of it they tied an animal skin. It was not until the mid-1940s that dancers began to put on costumes that covered their stomachs. While it was and still is a requirement that women should cover themselves to the toes, it was not questionable that the dancers to dressed in a fashion that not only exposed their chest, but also their stomachs. The Baganda consider exposing one's stomach as sexually provocative and, therefore, one is not supposed to do it in public.

Although petticoats were invented later to cover the stomach, it was mainly because the dancers' stomachs were not sexually appealing. The majorities of these dancers had given birth to children so their stomachs had stretch marks and were a bit flabby which was considered not sexually exciting. Explaining why petticoats were introduced, Lwewunzika expressed that it was embarrassing for women to expose stomachs with stretch marks. He said that "these stretch marks on the stomach were showing that the dancer was older, had children, and so she was no longer sexually attractive" ("mugaba yali alaga nti omuzinyi mukulu nnyo, era yali yazaalako, kale nga tasikiriza") (interview). Nonetheless, the petticoats are very light and although they concealed the stretch marks, the stomach was generally exposed. In this case, the costume was used to protect the beauty of the dancer, by concealing those body parts that were not attractive and exposing only those that were exciting sexually.

And yet, the invention of the petticoat as a dress for the public stage conflicts with the perception of it as underwear. In fact, in contexts outside dancing, if one's petticoat protrudes, she is considered naked, and people reprimand her. If one happens to be walking on the streets of Kampala (the capital city of Uganda), and her petticoats protrude, men call her all sorts of names qualifying her as a prostitute. However, within the dance contexts, nobody questions exposing the petticoats. Justifying the use of a petticoat, one dancer said, "but it is not embarrassing. Moreover, it is the only thin cloth on the body that is not warm. Further, it does not get creased when one puts it on and it is soft" (anonymous, interview). When I asked one man who was in the audience what he thought of the costume, he said "you go there [to the performance] knowing what to expect. After all, that is the expected uniform for the dancers!" Ironically, Nsubuga, the conservative man regarding dress, pretended he had never noticed that petticoats exposed women's stomachs. He exclaimed:

> Does the stomach show through the petticoats! Ha! Because of the excitement, we do not see that! But even then, that is the dressing for dancing. It is not embarrassing, because it is known that dancers dress like that when performing. In reality, the dancer looks nice in a petticoat when she is dancing! (interview).

In this case, the general rules of dressing do not apply when women dancers are on stage entertaining men. Nsubuga showed that rules are not fixed, they are fluid, and one needs to understand the context to know when to apply them. He does not see anything wrong with the costume since it is meant for men's sexual pleasure.

Likewise, Sarah Namutebi, a dancer, argued that if a dancer does not expose her waist, she cannot dance well (interview). When I suggested dressing in a tee shirt, Rose Namusisi, another dancer, reasoned, "a tee-shirt would not be bad, but it does not show the waist well because it has a straight fashion and made of a harder material than that of a petticoat. After all, the dance is in the waist; this is where the dancing is and that is what we should expose" (interview). Similarly, Lwewunzika argued that, "a tee-shirt is hard, yet the petticoat is soft. So, the dancer's softness is enhanced when she puts on a softer cloth than that one which is hard" (interview). In this case, petticoats facilitate the exposition of the softness of the woman's body.

Furthermore, the costumes in baakisimba aim at projecting the idealized beauty of a Muganda woman. Explaining why dancers put on a dancing skin and some kind of raffia skirt, all dancers I interviewed told me that both the dancing skin and the raffia skirt help to exaggerate the quivering of the dancer's buttocks (see plate 13).

Plate 13. Costuming in village baakisimba.

The Baganda, I interviewed, contended that someone with big but-tocks dances better, so many dancers put on extra clothing to create bigger buttocks. Apart from facilitating the waist movement, the raffia skirt and the dancing skin also add beauty to the dancer. Among the Baganda, a woman with big buttocks is considered to be beautiful. Writing about fashion in Buganda, Nanono noted, "it is understood that ladies even went to weaving blankets inside the *busuuti* in order to create . . . a pronounced steatopygia [*sic*]" (1977: 3). Likewise, Sarah Ntiro noted that even before the invention of cloth, women dressed in a number of bark cloth sheets to acquire big bot-toms. She noted:

> Under the bark cloth would be several bark clothes tied round the waist to add to the fullness of the figure . . . a large rounded figure was and still is a sign of beauty. Among the Baganda, big bottoms were or are still secretly highly celebrated. As one man put it 'I like her hips to hyp-notize me.' In fact, it was considered to be seductive (1977: i).

Therefore, the raffia skirt and the dance skin in baakisimba performance, reconstruct the idealized beauty and sexuality of a Muganda woman.

BAAKISIMBA: DEFINING SUBORDINATE AND EMPOWERED BAGANDA WOMEN

Apart from the baakisimba motifs performed in *mbaga* dance, the perform-ance of baakisimba as a full fledged dance, or a suite of baakisimba-nnnankasa-muwogola, begins with *kweyanza* ("thank you") motif (refer to plate 6 in Chapter Four). In Buganda, kneeling is a sign of respect. As such, a "proper" Muganda woman is not supposed to greet a man while standing; and "if a man greeted a woman thus laden, she would answer: 'I am unable to answer, because I have a load'" (Roscoe 1911: 8). One of the important aspects of training a girl-child as she grows up is respect for men and elders. A woman being prepared for marriage is told never to address her husband or in-laws (especially men) while standing. "Men" in this sense include even younger boys who are related to one's husband.[20] Therefore, the kneeling motif emphasizes the women's position in relation to the hosts and the men in the audience.

To examine the ways in which baakisimba defines women as men's sub-ordinates, it is also important to analyze the hierarchies of power within the performing groups during and outside the performance contexts. Although music and dance are highly integrated in baakisimba, the drummers control the flow and duration of the dance. Because the drum music defines the type and length of the dance motifs, men, as the drummers, control the women's dancing. It is the drummer, mainly the *ngalabi* beater who provides the signal for change to the next motif. On a number of occasions, I observed that when men drummers enjoyed the "soft" wriggling of women's waists, they would prolong a motif until the dancers performed an intermediary and relaxing motif. The relaxation motif communicates to the drummers to change to a new motif. If the drummers delay to change to another motif, dancers cannot change to the new motif because the drum music is essential for performing the motif. One dancer complained that when a drummer is excited by a specific dance motif, he could beat it until you just stop to dance without waiting for the signaling drum. Men control the women's dancing through the role and relationship between the drummers and the dancers. According to the stage design, men drummers perform while facing the dancers. Although this position enhances good coordination because the dance motifs depend on the drum motifs, the drummers are in direct gaze of the women's wriggling waists. While the drummers and dancers depend on each other for a successful performance, in most cases, the men drummers control the dance.

Further, I observed that when men and women dance together, men are usually given the leadership positions. Whenever there was one man in the dance ensemble, he usually led the dancers. In instances where there were two men dancers, I observed that one man led from the front and the other from behind. These two positions are leadership positions; besides leading the dance formations, dancers in these positions lead the other dancers on and off the stage. Dance leaders are responsible for guiding the others and in groups of only women dancers, the best dancers are chosen for these positions. However, on a number of occasions, the men dancers chosen were not always the best dancers. Because the first dancer introduces the dancers and the last dancer concludes the dance, these two dancers tend to be prominent. Explaining why men lead, Lwewunzika, a former male-woman dancer said that " in daily life, men are always the leaders, so they must also lead in the dance" (interview). Nakitto mentioned that men usually want to lead the dance because the dance leaders are more prominent since they lead the changes of motifs (interview).

In addition, in most of the ensembles and schools I visited, the majority of the dance teachers were men. In fact, all my baakisimba teachers have been men, except Hajati Nakintu, my field teacher. However, even when Nakintu was the teacher, on many occasions, the men drummers prescribed how I should dance. I was surprised that at one point, my teacher lost complete control of the class; and drummers dominated the teaching as she looked on. These drummers always commented as I danced; they criticized me when I moved wrongly, in their opinion and praised me whenever I danced the way they had instructed me. Hasifa Nakayiza, a dancer, suggested that women are usually shy to teach dancing (personal communication). I contend, however, that leadership roles have never been made available to women. Rather, leadership positions are reserved for men, and this is one of the reasons why they have been able to control and manipulate women's dancing. Relating dancing (*okuzina*) to playing sex, one informant argued that since it is the men that are supposed to propose sex to women, it is understandable that the men teach the women how to dance. He argued that since men gain pleasure in women's dancing, they should, therefore, determine the movements that give them pleasure.

Further, in a number of ensembles that I visited, men drummers held the positions of power, except in all-women ensembles. They administer the ensembles and determine how much money to pay the performers. In most cases, the men drummers are paid more money than the women dancers. The women dancers told me that money tips from sympathetic audience members is the only boost to their meager payments. Moreover, when men perform the dance with women, in many cases, they are paid more than the women. This imbalance in rewarding a similar activity emphasizes women's secondary position in the dance and in the Kiganda society in general.

Moreover, the recruitment of musicians and dancers also offers a space for performance of power relations between men and women. The recruitment, whether for men or women, depends on the nature of the group. However, when one is recruited, the performance roles are assigned according to gender; men are assigned to be drummers, and women are assigned roles as dancers, except in all-women's group. Further, one's physical appearance, especially for women, is sometimes important for one's recruitment. Peter Ggayira told me that beautiful women dancers are preferred since patrons are attracted not only to good dancing, but also to the dancer's beauty and sexuality. He told me, however, that such requirements do not accrue to men (interview).

Moreover, it is common to all groups that I interviewed, that the recruitment of a women member has to be endorsed by a man, either a husband or a village council leader (local council chairman), who in most cases are men. As part of my research methodology, I joined Bazannya n'Engo Cultural Group. Hajati Madina Nakintu, the leader of this group, set the following requirements for my recruitment. The first and most important requirement was a letter from my husband consenting to my enrollment, without which I would not have been accepted.[21] This letter had to be accompanied by two endorsed recent passport photographs also endorsed by my husband (see Appendix 7 for the consent letter my husband wrote).[22]

The second requirement was the training fee, equivalent to $15. The third requirement was that I buy a full dance costume before I could become a member. I asked Hajati Nakintu whether I would have needed a letter from my wife if I were a man. She told me that men do not need a letter, neither from their wives nor from the local council chairman. Explaining why women must have this letter, Peter Kigozi, one of Nakintu's drummers and one of my drum teachers, said that:

> It is because a woman is like a child at home. She needs a letter from her husband because he is the one who is responsible for her. Now, if your husband refuses to give you this letter, we cannot allow you to join our group (personal communication).

Explaining why men are not required to have permission from anybody, Ssaalongo Benedicto Kansaba, the head of Agaly'awamu Nnankasa Group, told me that: "when a person becomes a man, he does whatever he wants without restriction. A man controls himself, yet a woman has to be controlled by a man" (interview). Emphasizing Kansamba and Kigozi's view, Hajati Nakintu, who is married, narrated to me how it was difficult to convince her husband to allow her to create this group. Although by the time her husband proposed marriage to her she was a dancer, it took him six months to honor her request to start her own group. She told me that the continuity of her group still depends on her husband (interview).

Social relations of power are always a site of contestation and negotiation. Although baakisimba participates in constructing women as sexual objects and submissive human beings, it also contests those very structures. As mentioned in Chapter One, the multivocality of baakisimba affords these kinds of multiple meanings to emerge in performance. First, the actual dancing of baakisimba contradicts the cultural construction of women as being weak. Although the duration of dancing varies from context to context, the majority of the ensemble dancers I interviewed usually spend at least an hour on stage for a single round. The duration of dancing proves that indeed women are strong, enduring, and physically fit. Dancing, to some extent, is a physical exercise, which can only be survived if one is strong.

Second, the style of moving only the lower torso requires skill and concentration. I base my argument on my experience as a dancer and what I observed during my own dance classes. I have noted that one of the most difficult movements for my dance students is to be able to separate the lower torso from the top one. Usually, when they try to wriggle their waists, the chest also moves. While my students have been able to learn other dances from Uganda, baakisimba has been the most challenging.

Third, baakisimba provides a space in which women control and manipulate men's sexual desires. One male informant revealed that the success of a woman dancer is to leave all men in the audience aroused. In this case, the women's power is embodied in "their sexual allure. Since females are sexually desirable, and since sex is perhaps man's strongest desire, males wish to have sexual intercourse with them" (Spiro 1993: 327). Although when dancing the woman dancer has only an indirect sexual contact with the men musicians as well as the men in the audience, she sexually controls them. A number of dancers interviewed testified that on many occasions when men bring tips to them they include small notes suggesting an appointment after the performance. On a number of occasions, I have observed men putting tips in the women dancer's bras, touching the breasts and having a sharp gaze at their wriggling waists. I have also observed men holding the dancers' waists as they dance. In fact, most men who preferred women dancers to men related to this sexual satisfaction that they get when women dance.

Fourth, despite the negative portrayal of women as sexual objects, baakisimba performance provides one of the few arenas in public life that affords women the opportunity for self-expression. During the meetings of my clan, which I attended during the research, there were many women who also attended; however, the men dominated the discussions. I noted that even the few women who dared to raise their hands were not given a chance to speak. Paulo Kabwama told me that women were never allowed to talk in any gathering. He said that even though a woman sued her husband in court, it was her brother or paternal uncle who spoke on her behalf (interview). Further, as mentioned at the beginning of this chapter, no woman could dare propose marriage to a man or invite him to engage in casual sex. In this case, dancing is one way through which women dancers can indirectly communicate their physical presence as well as their sexual desires in society of suppressed women voice.

Chapter Six

Baakisimba in the Catholic Church

CATHOLIC CHURCH REDEFINED KIGANDA GENDER

While Islam was the first foreign religion to come to Buganda, Christianity, which came later, had, and still has, the greatest influence in Buganda. Moreover, Christianity had the most impact on gender and baakisimba. However, the greatest church influence on baakisimba is from the Catholic Church. While the Catholics have fully embraced songs of baakisimba style in their liturgy, the other Christian denominations are yet to incorporate the genre in their worship music. Most especially, Protestants did not consider "traditional" drumming and dancing appropriate for religious purposes. As such, my discussion, in this chapter, will focus on the Catholic influences on the gendered performance of baakisimba. In order to situate the context of my discussion, I first examine the contribution of the Catholic Church in the reconstruction of the Baganda's gender.

Historians have argued that Ssekabaka Muteesa I invited the European missionaries through Henry Morton Stanley, who arrived in Buganda in 1875 (Gray 1947: 88; Taylor 1958: 19; Ward 1971: 15). The Catholic missionaries came in 1879 (Pirouet 1995: 104) led by Père Lourdel and Brother Amans (Faupel 1984: 17).[1] Although the Kabaka showed great interest in Christianity, he was not converted; "Yet he readily allowed his chiefs to adapt the new faith and encouraged them to read in missionaries' classes" (Taylor 1979:19). One of the obstacles to the conversion of the Kabaka was the Christian requirement to have only one wife. Choosing one wife among eighty-five wives (Kaggwa 1952: 75–78) was not only a difficult choice, but also a threat to the king's power since more wives for the king symbolized greater power.

Christianity, in general, challenged the king's position as the absolute authority and changed the subjects' attitude towards the monarchy structure and the king's power. Commenting on the effect of Christianity on the king's power, Robert M. Maxon mentioned that, "the new religion had caused change and turmoil which undermined the foundations of the kingdom, most notably the power of the *kabaka,* which declined steadily after 1885 . . ." (1994: 123). It was after the introduction of Christianity that the King's subjects, especially the pages, who had been converted in large numbers, started to question their relationship to Ssekabaka Mwanga II to the extent that they were willing to die for their new God. Further, after being baptized in the Protestant Church, Princess Nalumansi denounced the customs of her culture. For example, "contrary to the old Kiganda traditions, which forbade princesses of the blood to marry [see discussion in Chapter Four], she became engaged to Joseph Kaddu, a Catholic baptized in 1880. She was married, with dispensation for a mixed marriage and, later, two days after Easter in 1886, she was received in the Catholic Church, taking the name Clara" (Faupel 1984: 129). The princess's action was not only insubordination to the customs of the land, but also a recreation of her female-man power into a woman gender. It is only women who must be married, owned and controlled for fuller identity as women. Being a female-man, she was the one to marry, control and own a male-woman, a commoner. By challenging the social order, the princess threatened *ssaabasajja's* absolute authority, which, to some extent, was dependent on the hierarchical structure of gender constructions. Challenging her status as the female-man was also to defy the king as the Man among men, both male and female.

Another influence of Christianity in general, and Catholicity in particular that impacted not only on gender, but also baakisimba is the gradual erasure of superstitions about the Kiganda culture in general and, the Kiganda drums in particular. After the introduction of the Christians' one God, the Baganda's beliefs and dependence on indigenous gods receded; new beliefs emerged.[2] These new beliefs in some ways restructured the Baganda's view about gender, while in other ways crystallized existing gender ideologies. Because of Christianity, the palace gradually lost its role as the custodian of the customs of Buganda.

As a result of the dwindling Kingdom and Kiganda gender construction, the Catholic Church was able to introduce celibacy, a way of life, which was taken up by people specifically set aside for sacred purposes. Males could become either *bafaaza (sing. Faaza)* (fathers—priests) or *babulaaza (sing. Bulaaza),* brothers, while females could become *basiisita (sing. Siisita),* sisters. The first Catholic Seminary in Uganda was established at Lubaga (Kyaddondo county) in 1891 before being moved to Kisubi (Kyaddondo county) in 1893 (Kiregeya 2002: 24). The first priest, the late Bishop Joseph

Kiwanuka, a Muganda, was ordained in 1913 (2002: 10). As the number of young boys who desired to lead a celibate life increased, "in 1947, the Rt. Rev. Louis Joseph Cabana . . . immediately started planning to build a [minor] seminary at Kisubi; since Bukalasa Seminary in Masaka (Buddu county) could no longer take in the ever changing number of candidates (Kiregeya 2002: 24). There are two outstanding congregations of religious brothers in Buganda and these are namely; Brothers of Christian Instruction of Kisubi (Kyaddondo county), which was started in 1926 and the Bannakalooli Brothers of Kiteredde Bikira Parish (Buddu county), which was introduced in 1927. On the other hand, there were three congregations of religious sisters that was introduced in Buganda: Bannabikira (Daughters of the Virgin) of Bwanda (Buddu county), the oldest congregation of religious sisters in Africa, which was established in 1910; the Little Sisters of St. Francis, in Nkokonjeru (Kyagwe County), established in 1923; and Sisters of the Immaculate Heart of Mary Reparatrix, Ggogonnya established in 1948 (Pirouet 1995: 65).

However, these new Catholic genders strongly challenged the Baganda who had embraced the new faith with enthusiasm. According to the people I interviewed, there were mixed views about Catholic celibacy even among professed Catholics. A number of Catholics, that I interviewed, expressed that they could never accept their children to become *bafaaza*, or *babulaaza* or *basiisita* because of the requirement to live a celibate life. Celibacy "involves a profound self-dedication that goes to the root of human personality, in as much as sexuality is inherent in our very identity" (Shorter 1998: 13). This vow of chastity in a society that views marriage as essential to adulthood, and sexual activities as a continuation of humanity, contributes to the challenges of living a celibate life in Buganda. As Pirouet has noted, *basiisita* challenge the "traditional way of life among the [Buganda] in which there [is] no place for women outside marriage" (1995: 65).

One sister whom I interviewed confided that some members of her family did not want her to become one. In particular, her *ssenga* (paternal aunt) was very concerned about the bride price and the grandchildren she was going to miss if her niece became a sister.[3] This sister told me, "I had to hide from my aunt whenever I went home for holidays, and soon I felt it befitting to stay in the convent while my other friends went back to their homes" (anonymous, interview). And yet, some of her mother's friends could not take in that nonsense. One of her mother's friends asked, why should you give in your [beautiful] daughter? She would give forth grandchildren that look very beautiful" (anonymous, interview). To them, this sister was too beautiful not to have children, not to be a woman.

Another sister, who also requested anonymity, told me she has always been confronted by men and women alike, who have challenged the celibate life she chose. The sister said:

> I remember one time when I was coming from the village and going to the road to catch a bus to go to Kampala [capital of Uganda]. When he reached me, a man who was driving a car thought I was a Hajati [a Muslim woman, because of the veil] and he wanted to give me a lift. But when he reached me and saw that mine was a sister's veil, he got very annoyed and said, 'I thought she was a woman! These are the sisters [in a diminutive way] who kill their eggs within their wombs!' He drove past me and left.

> *Nzijukira lumu nali nva mu kyalo nga ngenda ku luguudo okulinnya bus nzigye e Kampala, Omwami eyali avuga emotoka bwe yantuukako yali ampita Hajati era n'ayagala okuntwalako. Naye bwe yantuukako n'alaba nti eyanga vero, neyeesooza nnyo n'agamba 'mbadde ndowooza na mukazi! Bwe buno obusiisita obuttira amagi mu mbuto zaabwe!' n'avuumuula emotoka ye n'agenda* (anonymous, interview).

To this man, a sister is not a woman, but a "sister." Ironically, it is common to hear people in Buganda say, "I met a sister and four women at the bus stop." Because sisters vow to disassociate themselves from the cultural process of becoming Baganda women, they are not referred to as "proper" Baganda women. They are assigned a "sister gender." Likewise, the celibate life that priests and brothers vow to uphold form the basis for the assignment of the *faaza*, "father" gender and *bulaaza*, "brother" gender, respectively.[4] As discussed in Chapter Five, when a child is born, the parents as well as relatives, and friends begin to assign genders dependent on the baby's sex. A male baby is given a man gender, while the female is allocated a woman gender. Parents, relatives, and friends begin to inculcate into the child the expectations of the respective gender. According to this study, none of the parents and relatives of the religious people that I interviewed ever expected their children to become fathers, sisters, or even brothers. As such, whether parents, relatives, and friends consent or not, the father, sister, brother, genders are subversions from the expectations established at birth; a justification given for not considering fathers and brothers as men and sister as women.

While the Catholic Church introduced new genders, it crystallized, in practical terms, the relations between males and females as those existing outside the palace. Priests, who are only males, hold a higher status than the sisters, who are only females. By controlling the sister's access to priesthood, the fathers control power. A sister, who requested anonymity, confided that one of the reasons why females cannot become priests in the Catholic Church is because they menstruate (anonymous, interview). Likewise, Modupe R. Owanikin has pointed out that the "opponents of women's ordination advance the argument that because [women] are occasionally unclean women [during menstruation] (when compared to men who always maintain a constant biological state) cannot be qualified to serve as priests" (1992:211). Similar myths about menstruation used to control the female power outside the church contexts are adopted within the church contexts. Moreover, patriarchal interpretations of the Holy Scriptures have been used by the Catholic Church to hinder women from becoming priests and to emphasize their subordinate positions. For instance, I Tim 2:11–13 states that: "Women should learn in silence and all humility. Do not allow them to teach or have any authority over men; they must keep quiet" (American Bible Society: 1080–1081). Further, I Cor 14:34–35 reemphasizes and states that:

> The women should keep quiet in the meetings. They are not allowed to speak; as the Jewish Law says, they must not be in charge. If they want to find out something, they should ask their husbands at home. It is a disgraceful thing for a woman to speak in a church meeting (American Bible Society 1992:10432).

Kenneth E. Bailey reminds us that it is important to examine these Scriptures (like any other text) within their right historical and cultural contexts. He argues that, "As known, the NT [New Testament, where these two quotes are found] is deeply influenced by its first century middle Eastern cultural settings [and therefore, one] must discern the fabric of cultural assumptions . . . [a]s a supplement to other historical concerns. . . ." (1994:7). It should be remembered that these cultural settings perpetuated the dominance of men over women. Yet, the Bible clearly identified women in the leadership roles of the church. It affirms women as teachers; in Acts 18:24–26, Apollos is referred to as a teacher about Jesus, but knew only the baptism of John. However, "When Priscilla and Aquila heard him, they took him home with them and explained to him more correctly the way of God" (American Bible Society 1992: 1001). Further, In Rom 16:1–2, Phoebe is referred to as a deacon: I recommend to you our sister Phoebe, who serves the church at Cenchreae. Received her in the Lord's name, as God's people should, and give her any help she may need from you . . ." (Good News Bible 1992:

1029). In order to perpetuate the male dominance, the great vision of Christianity, as affirmed in Gal 3:28 has to be ignored in practical terms. The Scripture says: "So there is no difference . . . between men and women; you are all one in union with Christ Jesus" (American Bible Society 1992: 1058).

As such, as has been the case in other African cultures, when the missionaries introduced Christianity in Buganda, it also "meant further male domination for females who were already experiencing unfair treatment in various spheres of their lives" (Fanusie 1992:140). Like their fellow females outside the palace, the sisters position is mainly in the private arena. While a number of congregations have tried to educate their sisters, the contributions of these educated sisters in mainly within their congregations. The sisters are yet to play any significant role within the structures of the Catholic Church. One sister lamented that 'you cannot believe we do not have any substantive representation on any council or committee governing the church, not even at parish level" (anonymous, interview). The sisters' contribution to the running of the church is to work in churches or chapels and manage the kitchens in most parishes. During their fiftieth anniversary celebration, the Kisubi Seminary community acknowledged the services of the Immaculate Heart of Mary Reparatrix Sisters and wrote:

> Kisubi Seminary Convent was opened to offer catering services to the Priests *[sic]* and seminarians and to take good care of the chapel and sacristy. . . . . The I H M R [Immaculate Heart of Mary Reparatrix] Sisters are acknowledged for providing a motherly ambience in a community, which is by common estimation male dominated (Kiregeya 2000:27).

By relating to the sisters as providers of motherly care, the priests and seminarians of Kisubi Seminary are recapturing the role assigned to females outside the church and palace. This assignment reinforces the fact that rules are flexible and can always be broken if they benefit the major actors. When the sister denounced to be women, they deplored the traditional roles of being women and mothers. However, since this male community needed motherly care, being females, the sisters were assigned the role.

Further erasure of the sisters' woman gender was to limit their contribution to even those women who wanted to procreate, a Catholic Church policy which came with the introduction of sisterhood in Buganda. Although the Franciscan Sisters of Africa initiated one of the first nursing training school in Buganda and Uganda in general in 1903, the church could not allow them to establish a midwifery section until much later. Paul G. D'Arbela reported that: "Midwifery could not be started at the inception, as at that time nuns were barred by the Holy See from practicing that trade. It was only very much later on in 1919 when they were disbarred that a mid-wifery section of the Hospital *[sic]* was opened" (2003: 24–25). One would wonder whether the church feared that if these nuns involved themselves in assisting mothers giving birth, they would be interested in getting their own.

Outside the religious gender structures, both Kiganda myths and beliefs and patriarchal interpretations of Biblical quotations were and still are being used in the celebration of men's superiority over women. The Baganda immediately adopted Christian beliefs, which were closely related, by implication or by men's reinterpretation, to those already existing in the Kiganda society. And yet, differing beliefs were reinterpreted to conform to the Kiganda culture. In some instances, new beliefs created new gendered structures while, in others, they legitimized already existing ones. For instance, as already mentioned in Chapter One, the Baganda integrated the Biblical creation story of Adam and Eve with that of Kintu and Nnambi to legitimize the inferior position of women (Kaggwa 1951:115). Most of the informants, both men and women, contended that men are more powerful than women because God created a man first, and therefore men should lead women. Explaining why men should dominate women, for instance, Sulaiti Kalungi said:

> It was instituted by God. Because God first created a man. After a long time, because the man was very lonely, God created a woman, his assis-tant. You can also see that it is indeed suitable for the man to be the head; and the king is supposed to be a man (interview).

This theory of creation legitimizes the men's dominant position over women within and outside the palace. A number of informants used this theory to explain why the king is the son of the drum and why only men should beat the drums and outside the palace. In Chapter Four, I have provided the detailed discussion of the issue.

SACRED BAAKISIMBA? MUSIC AND DANCE IN THE CATHOLIC CHURCH

When Christianity was first introduced in Buganda in the last quarter of the nineteenth century, missionaries insisted that "traditional" music was one of the cultural practices of the Baganda that had to be eliminated. Most impor-tant was the elimination of baakisimba music and dance. A. B. K. Kasozi noted:

> The early [missionaries] thought that [Kiganda music] was so much
> intertwined with pagan customs that it was better to forget it com-
> pletely and replace it with 'Christian' music. This music was played on
> the organ, the piano, the flute, the violin and sometimes the guitar. As a
> result, [Kiganda] traditional music began to die out gradually. The old
> men who could play it or make musical instruments began to disappear
> through death and there were no others to replace them (1979:64).[5]

Besides the fear of the drum being satanic, the missionaries were afraid of the
drum's power to communicate, which was greatly exploited by the Baganda.
The Baganda used the drum to communicate danger and joy, among other
situations. Whenever the drum sounded every member of the community
was obliged to respond appropriately. When "Ggwanga mujje" sounded it
communicated trouble, war and yet baakisimba conveyed joy. One priest
explained,

> Our drums could beat rhythms these missionaries could not under-
> stand. For example a drum rhythm like "Ggwanga mujje," ["Nation
> come"] whenever it sounded then people would come with sticks and
> any weapon for protection. Then the missionaries feared that may be
> any time these drums any sound when they want to attack them.

However, the Bible frequently refers to the "dancing and drumming for the
Lord." For example, in the Book of Psalms 150:1–5 and especially in verse 4,
it is written: "Praise him [God] with drums and dancing" (American Bible
Society 1992:573). Further, in II Sam 6:5, it is written, "David and all the
Israelites were dancing and singing with all their might to honor the LORD
[sic]. They were playing harps, lyres, drums, rattles, and cymbals" (American
Bible Society 1992: 269). And yet, in the Exodus 15: 20, "The prophet
Miriam . . . took her tambourine, and all the women followed her, playing
tambourines and dancing" (American Bible Society 1992: 62). Since the
Christian missionaries claimed to use the bible as a basis for their teachings,
why did they refuse the Baganda to drum and dance baakisimba in the
church? Why was it "appropriate" to play piano, organ, guitars, and violins
and not the Kiganda drums? It is clear that when the Christian missionaries
came to Baganda they did not only bring Christianity, but also a form of cultural imperialism. They forced their musical culture onto the Baganda as a
form of cultural control. This cultural imperialism, to a greater extent,
accounts for the lack of strong indigenous church music tradition in
Buganda and Africa in general.

Since the introduction of Catholicism in 1879, through the mid-1970s, a large part of the music repertoire of the Catholic mass was sung in Latin. Although the faithful did not understand Latin, the Gregorian chants were the liturgical songs of the mass. Because of the need to improve the congregations' participation during mass, the Western hymns were translated into Luganda. However, as Rev. Fr. Joseph Namukangula, a composer himself, explained, the adoption of pre-composed European melodies for texts in Luganda (a tonal language) altered the meaning of the text (interview). The literal translation of English text into Luganda "did violence to the natural rhythm, stress and tonal pitch of [Luganda] and the words often became meaningless in the process" (Kakoma 1964: 35).[6]

Besides the Luganda text, the other Kiganda aspect was the retention of the *kiribaggwa* drumbeat, which was used to call people to worship in the *masabo* (shrines). According to one informant, *kiribaggwa* was a drum signal for *lubaale* (gods). He said, "Kiribaggwa was beaten when they [the church] were calling people to worship" (anonymous, interview). When I asked why the church retained this drum style, I was told that it was because the missionaries thought that since this drumbeat was not used at beer parties, or wedding festivities, so it had no associations with heathen practices.[7] Further, because of the power of the drum to communicate, and since people at that time had no clocks or watches to tell the time, it was the drum that the church could use to call the people to worship. Another informant told me that this specific drum rhythm had to be appropriated because it was known to the people as a call to prayer or worship, although the people were called to worship another God (anonymous, interview). This informant argued further that it was not possible to compose another rhythm since the White priests did not know the Baganda's compositional style. The priests also feared that people would not respond to the new drum signal. Although this drum style was retained, baakisimba drumming could not be tolerated in the church.

However, *Kiribaggwa,* the call to prayer drum rhythm, was recreated by the altar boys and given a new onomatopoeic words which expressed their attitude towards the White Fathers, as they were called at the time. One of the former altar boys, now himself a priest, recalled that because the White Fathers had long beard and big stomachs, the altar boys created a hidden transcript about them. They recreated the phrase text of the call to prayer drum beat to relate with the rhythmic structure of the phrase that teases the fathers as having big stomachs. The text goes thus: "Basosodooti balya bulungi, balya bisiike, nebamala bagejja" ("priests eat every well; they eat fried food and then they become very big").

Despite the Church's negative attitude, baakisimba drumming and dancing survived in Buganda outside the church contexts in villages among nominal Christians. They could go to church and sing Western Christian music and thereafter, be entertained with traditional music and dance at a wedding ceremony, for instance. It was impossible to uproot drumming and dancing in Buganda; instead, dance and drum traditions underwent transformations and acquired new meanings. As such, when the Catholics embraced baakisimba in their repertoire as part of the church revival spearheaded by Vatican Council II, musicians could still remember to compose and perform baakisimba music. When Vatican II of 1962 called for the renewal of the Catholic Church (Flannery 1997), in Uganda, the clerics worked to bring the church closer to the people. One of the ways to bring the church closer to the people was the indigenization of its music.[8] However, at the beginning, baakisimba drums were only adapted to accompany singing and dancing was deemed unacceptable.[9]

Baakisimba drumming was first performed in the Catholic Church at the St. Peter's Basilica in Rome on October 16, 1964. The Pope was canonizing twenty-two Uganda Catholic martyrs, who were persecuted by Ssekabaka Mwanga II in the late nineteenth-century. As part of the celebration, Joseph Kyagambiddwa, was commissioned to compose songs in Kiganda musical style, depicting the story of the Uganda martyrs. He composed twenty-two songs, which he entitled "the Uganda Martyr's Oratorio."[10] The twenty-two songs were to honor each of the twenty-two Catholic martyrs. In addition to composing the songs in *biggu* style (Kiganda musical style in 2/4, typical for Kiganda worship music), Kyagambiddwa composed songs in baakisimba styles, in 6/8 with a *ggonno* vocal style. He even suggested the possibility of dancing to some of the songs (Kyagambiddwa 1964).

According to one informant, who actually performed the Uganda Martyrs Oratorio in the Basilica, a group of African students in Europe mainly Ugandans, Kenyans, and Nigerians—were brought together to perform the Oratorio. This performance was not only the first baakisimba music performance in the Catholic Church, but also the first time that women performed music in the Basilica. This informant said: "Kyagambiddwa brought together black students and all the Baganda [students] in Europe and he made them into a choir, which sung on the day of canonizing the martyrs on the 16th of October 1964. And that was the first time for women to sing in the Church of Rome, the Basilica" (anonymous, interview). When I asked him why women never performed in the Basilica before, he said it was a church tradition to restrict women's participation in church activities.[11] He explained that women were able to perform the Oratorio in the Basilica because, "When Kyagambiddwa was looking for singers, Ugandan and other Africa sisters were the people available. The Ugandan sisters were the ones who could sing in Luganda; they were the pillar the other Africans could depend on when singing" (ibid.). In this case, if there had been enough men who could sing in Luganda, women would not have sung in the Basilica.

Although the performance of baakisimba in the Basilica formally introduced indigenous music in the Catholic Church, it was initially received with resistance in Baganda. For instance, when the Oratorio was first performed at Kitovu Cathedral (Buddu County), it was performed outside the Cathedral. Christians disagreed as to whether the drums were appropriate to enter a sacred place like the Cathedral. Later, a consensus was reached, but only based on the precedent that the oratorio had been performed first in the Basilica. One informant narrated that "if people beat the drums in the Basilica, then why can't we beat them in the Cathedral? And the drums were brought in the church." The Christians accepted the drums in Kitovu Cathedral only because the Pope had accepted the drums in the Basilica, the supreme Cathedral of the Catholic Church.

Although the drums finally entered Kitovu Cathedral, there was also resistance to introduce the drums in the dioceses and parishes among the bishops and priests. The most receptive clergy members were those whose home backgrounds were characterized by festivities and beer parties, where drumming and dancing was common. One of the priests, who requested anonymity, confided in me and said

> As for me, at my home, we used to beat the drums in the village and people danced. In my primary school we participated in a number of festivals. For instance, when the parish priest or a teacher celebrated his feast day, they would call us to perform. At home, my family members were beaters of the drum and they also tuned [or made] the drums. So, the idea of bringing the drum into the church, to me, was delayed! We had wanted it very much! (anonymous, interview).

Before the drums were introduced in other churches, the clergy decided to first conduct an experiment within the church institutions. Katigondo Major Seminary (for priests), Banakaloli Brothers of Kiteredde (for the brothers), and Bwanda Sisters' Convent (for the sisters) were the experimental institutions. It was thought that by making the experiment within the church institutions, the church would have control over what would be appropriate for the church before it is taken up by the congregations in their parishes. This experiment exposed the drums to females of a sister gender, for the first time.

Although many church parishes welcomed the "new" music, some completely rejected the drum. One priest narrated to me the following story:

> There is a certain parish in Kampala, where one priest loved the Kiganda songs and drums so much that he made a choir. However, the Christians did not like it. They used to call the drums satanic, because of their former use before religion came. They also said that those drums were for drunkards. One day, when the priest was celebrating mass with his choir singing, a member of the congregation threw an artificial snake in front of the choir. Ho! Everyone got dispersed and they said 'the snake has come, Satan has come out of the drum.' Then they scattered the drums (anonymous, interview).

When I asked why the people rejected the drum and yet they still beat them during weddings and other festivals, the priest said:

> The people did not understand, because when the religion came, they were told, 'leave the drums, they belong to Satan.' And now, you are the same people bringing the drums back. And another thing, religion was brought by White fathers, who did also discarded the drums and yet, those who are bringing back the drums are Baganda. The poor people got confused. Might they have been the White priests who had re-introduced the drums, it would not have been difficult for them to accept the drums in church! (anonymous, interview).

However, when the other instruments—the *madinda* (xylophone), *ndongo* (bowl lyre), *ndingidi* (tube fiddle)—were introduced in the church, during the mid-1990s, they met no resistance whatsoever. One choirmaster said that since these instruments are foreign to the Kiganda culture (it is alleged that all of them came from Busoga), their symbolic meaning is not known to many Baganda. Moreover, very few people can play these instruments, so it is prestigious for a choirmaster to have his choir perform in this style (Muyinda, interview).

As the baakisimba repertoire increased, Kiganda music became popular in many churches and a number of choirs sprang up. For instance, in 1978, a Catholic national choir, the Catholic Centenary Memorial Choir (CACEM-CHO) was founded. Kyagambiddwa and Achilles Bukenya, among the other founders of CACEMCHO, spearheaded the performance of traditional music, especially from Buganda, in addition to classical church music. In addition to the oratorio, Kyagambiddwa composed new pieces. Later, a number of priests and lay people joined Kyagambiddwa including, but not limited to, Rev. Fr. Joseph Namukangula, Rev. Fr. Vincent Bakkabulindi, Rev. Fr. James Kabuye, James Makubuya, and Justinian Tamusuza.

However, the church has not registered many women composers; mainly sisters have participated in the composition of this new music, although they are also a few. While there are other factors contributing to the poor participation of females (women and sisters) in the composition of the Catholic Church music, the church has not fully participated in encouraging them. For instance, in the Vatican Council II of 1962, it was stated, "composers and singers, especially boys, must also be given a genuine liturgical training" (Flannery 1997: 48). In fact, while priests in formation have a music course, as part of their curriculum, it is not a requirement for sisters to be trained in music (anonymous, interview). One sister told me that "for us, we do not have [music] trainers; we teach ourselves. We just imitate, but we are not given any training" (anonymous, interview). Majority of the priests who are fluent musicians that I interviewed had some musical background from their homes in addition to the training they got from the seminaries. They had a musical training in both Kiganda and Western music. The sisters are very unfortunate; they never had access to the drum while still at their homes and yet even as sister, such accessibility is not available.

As the revival of the Catholic Church become more embraced, especially since the late 1980s and early 1990s, baakisimba dancing became part of the church repertoire. However, the other Ugandan ethnic groups had already incorporated their dances in the mass. Baakisimba began to be performed during offertory and thanksgiving sections of the mass. Explaining why dancing was not introduced when baakisimba was first introduced in the church, one priest argued that because the basic movement is in the waist, wriggling it in a liturgical context was not appropriate. In comparison, the other dances, especially those from Ankole (western Uganda) did not involve waist movement; a dance like the *kitaagururo* involves mainly the footwork and the hand gesture. This informant noted further that there is no creativity in baakisimba, "because when the baakisimba drum [sounds], it only tells the waist to wriggle and nothing else. You can not substitute the waist movement" (anonymous, interview). One priest told me that there was a huge debate whether baakisimba should be performed during a high mass celebrated by the Pope when he came to Uganda in 1993. Because majority of the members on the liturgical committee that organized this mass were from Buganda, they had wanted to perform for the Pope a dance from their culture. However, the dance could not pass all the liturgical tests and *analeyo,* a dance from Karamoja (northern Uganda), which is basically jumping up in the air, was performed instead.

The question is: what is a liturgical baakisimba and how different should it be from that performed outside the Church? In order to appropriate baakisimba for a liturgical purpose, one priest suggested that, only young girls should perform it and at a slow tempo. He argued that, "the young children do not have so much of a problem. Instead of using old women, or old girls, or young men, let us use the young girls; that is tolerable!" He suggested further that the costume and the dance style should also be recreated to suit the liturgical context. He disagreed, that petticoats should be used, and instead suggested T-shirts. He also suggested that "the drums should also be neat, not like those ones beaten at beer parties and wedding ceremonies. You can decorate them. In fact, some choirs dress them in a uniform similar to what the choir members are dressed in." However, one choirmaster and layperson contended that it is impossible to make everyone adhere to the defined liturgical baakisimba because the drum dictates that the waist should wriggle. The choirmaster said, "Ha! To make the church baakisimba to look different from that of the village is not an easy task. The beating of the drum is betraying the cause, unless it is beaten slowly, but even then it is difficult to adopt a liturgical baakisimba." (Muyinda, interview). Michael Mukisa, the Choir Conductor of the Catholic Centenary Memorial Choir, said that a liturgical baakisimba must be dignified and graceful rather than fast and vigorous, such as baakisimba performed at weddings (interview).

I observed during my research, however, a tendency for performers to get excited at climactic points of songs and get carried away, losing the supposedly graceful liturgical baakisimba mood. In all the church performances that I attended, the music would begin slowly and gracefully, but as the song went on, it accelerated, as in the case of baakisimba performed outside the church. Musically, there is little difference between the two contexts besides the liturgical text. Further, the dance motifs are more or less the same as those performed outside the church. For instance, the dance movements that were performed during the Uganda Martyrs' celebrations at Namugongo (Kyaddondo county) Catholic Shrine on June 3, 2000, varied from shuffling (as formerly done in the palace) to kicking in the air. In plate 14, I illustrate, *kindere,* one of the motifs that was performed by St. Charles Lwanga Secondary School.

Plate 14. Performance of kindere morif at a high mass during the Uganda Martyrs' celebration at Namugongo in 2000.

Kindere (relaxation) is a comparatively slow motif, usually performed as a means of relaxation within the dance; it is a loose-limbed motion of skipping on every first beat, while the arms move loosely in alternate directions with the skipping legs. There is minimal waist and hip movement; it is mainly jumping. However, as they jump, the dancers spray their legs. The movement of spraying legs in this motif is mainly borrowed from mbaga wedding dance (see Nannyonga-Tamusuza and Nattiez 2003). In an interview with one mbaga dancer, she said that when they spray the legs they are communicating to the bride to open up to her husband. As such, while it has no waist movement, the spraying of the legs challenges liturgical relevance of baakisimba in church.

GENDERING IN CHURCH BAAKISIMBA

Gendering in church baakisimba is evident mainly in the assignment of roles of performance. While the recruitment of choir members is not gendered, the assignment of roles to these members, to a greater extent, is contingent on one's gender. Choir members are recruited based on one's musicality; ability to read music is an added qualification in big choirs like the Catholic Centenary Memorial Choir (CACEMCHO). Besides one's musical ability, most choirs require that the recruit is a member of the church that houses the choir he or she wants to join. In a number of choirs that I visited, the choirmasters audition the new members. Although the recruitment of members is not based on gender, in the majority of the choirs that I visited, women comprised the majority of their membership. As is the case with baakisimba performed in the village and schools, I observed that in most cases, although both men and women sung, men were the drummers and women the dancers. One brother argued, "it is embarrassing for a man to dance in church; dancing is for women." Similar views as those outside the church contexts form basis for assigning women to dancing roles and men to drumming roles.

On the other hand, the sisters beat drums when they are the only ones that constitute the choir. However, if they perform with laymen, fathers, or brothers, they do not beat the drums, instead, the males beat them. During my research, I observed that although the sisters could not beat the drums equally as good as the men do outside the church contexts, the sisters had better access to these drums than their female counterparts outside the

Plate 15. Drums spread upside-down in the Sisters' convent chapel.

church. There are three explanations to why sisters beat the drums; first, since their institution is based on the erasure of basic Kiganda customs, they have no respect for taboos that restrict females' (outside the palace) access to the drum. Moreover, while it is taboo for Kiganda drums to be held up side down (see discussion in Chapter Four), on a number of occasions, I observed drums put drums up-side-down, both on stage and off the stage during storage (see plate 15).

In Chapter Four, I have discussed how one would be killed if he placed the drums up side down. While in church sometimes, the drums are placed up side down so as to improvise for a high-pitched drum. When I inquired why the drums are stored up side down, the sister in charge of these drums said, it was to protect the top surface, which is beaten so that the skin does not wear out. She also mentioned that this position protects the drum from loosing its pitch. The sister, however, confessed that she was not aware of the associated taboos. Nonetheless, the sister expressed lack of concern for cultural taboos and argued that those are some of the Kiganda customs that she denounced at baptism. Because the sister denounced any kind of superstitions and indeed their community life enables them to uphold this commitment, they attach no symbolism to the drum, besides its musical value.

The second explanation to why sisters beat the drum is that, since drumming is an issue of power relations between men and women, the sisters are not involved in such power struggles. One sister argued that their marriage is not with a 'jealous' man. The sister said, "Our husband, Jesus, is too powerful to consider our drumming as a threat to him. It is these worldly men that feel challenged if women beat drums" (anonymous, interview). Of course, one cannot ignore the contexts in which the sisters perform their drums, let alone the low intensity of their drumming. In most cases, they perform among themselves in their convents and rarely do they perform for the general public. Moreover, most of the singing they accompany the drums with is in a "liturgical" context, which calls for gracefulness and not the aggressive drumming, as is the case when drums are beaten at a dance festival outside the church. For the sisters to drum is female emancipation in a culture (both within and outside the church) where females hold a subordinate position.

Despite the fact that the organ is a Western instrument, it accompanies baakisimba songs in addition to drums. Being a Western instrument, one would expect the instrument to have no gendered restrictions among the Baganda. Nonetheless, very few women play the instrument. Moreover, even few sisters that play the instrument rarely perform it beyond their convent gates. Since priests have formal Western musical training as part of the curriculum in priesthood formations, they have more opportunities than the sisters to learn and perform the organ. As such, when the organ was exported to Buganda, it was brought with the Western gendered ideologies of the nine-teen-century.

Further, it is apparent that men hold most of the leadership positions in these choirs despite the fact that majority of the membership to these choirs are women. Apart from the sisters, there are few choir mistresses. Majority of the choirs that I visited had men conductors and it was apparent that women had no space on the conductor's podium. As a member of a choir (CACEMCHO) for a long time, I noticed that men, and women too, tend to despise women conductors. For instance, as part of training during my Masters in arts (music) course, I had to train a choir and conduct a number of pieces before I could graduate. Being a member of the Catholic Centenary Memorial Choir, I thought this choir would be the best ground for my training. However, I was received with a lot of resistance and mainly from women. While they did not question my ability (I was already a voice instructor), they rejected me on the grounds that women can never be choir conductors. It is now apparent to me that I was rejected because being a conductor positions one into a leader's role, which among the Baganda was never assigned to women, especially when men were present. My research has revealed that the assignment of roles in choirs has a lot to do with the generally low position accorded to women not only outside the church, but also within the church.

RELIGIOUS SISTERS DANCING BAAKISIMBA DURING MASS: A LITURGICAL CRISIS?

While sisters may perform baakisimba in public, the church restricts their performance in church contexts during mass (anonymous, interview). However, sisters perform baakisimba and other dances, outside the church contexts, among themselves during feast days and other convent functions. What meanings are mediated when sisters perform baakisimba in the church? In Chapter Five, I have discussed the ways in which baakisimba defines women as sexual objects and how the dance induces men's sexual desire when women perform the dance. What messages are communicated when baakisimba, a site for sexual desire, is performed in a Catholic Mass and most especially by sisters who vowed to celibacy? Does the sisters' performance of baakisimba dance in church create a liturgical crisis?

Informants, both lay and religious had divided views' about the sister's dancing. I had the opportunity to attend the annual commissioning functions of two sisters' congregations, where baakisimba church songs were part of the mass repertoire. However, only one congregation performed baakisimba dance during thanksgiving, after Holy Communion. Performing baakisimba after Holy Communion, was very appropriate since it was after "eating and drinking," taking on a similar context adopted when village baakisimba is performed. The other congregation performed other Ugandan dances although baakisimba songs were also part of the mass repertoire. The choir mistress of the congregation that did not perform baakisimba dance told me that they usually do not perform the dance during such a public function. This sister explained that, "it does not look nice for sisters to wriggle their waists, especially, in front of men" (anonymous, interview). However, the sister confided that they perform the dance among themselves. Generally, most of the elderly sisters I talked to were convinced that dancing in church was not inappropriate for religious sisters. As a matter of fact, these sisters did not agree to the performance of the dance during the celebration of their twenty-fifth and fiftieth anniversary although the youthful sisters wanted to perform it (anonymous, personal communication). The elderly sisters argued that the celebration should focus on prayer and thanksgiving; dancing would interrupt their devotion time. On the other hand, the youthful sisters consented to dancing as long as the dancing sisters performed in their veils and habits and as long as the movements were decent (anonymous, personal communication). According to these sisters, decent dancing does not involve kicking in the air and has a less vigorous waist movement.

On the other hand, some of the priests to whom I talked believed that baakisimba is not appropriate for church contexts, whether performed by sisters or other people. They argued that baakisimba has explicit sexual connotations. One priest said: "It is not appropriate for women to wriggle their waists while the intended audience is supposed to be meditating about God's message" (anonymous, interview). Like the laymen that I interviewed about village baakisimba, this priest confided that when women dance baakisimba, they excite the men. He was open to say that much as they are priests, they are sexually normal and as such, they have to be very conscious of their environments so as not to lead themselves into temptations. This priest finds baakisimba especially inappropriate when performed during the procession that precedes the Gospel reading. He was reacting to the performance of baakisimba dance that preceded the Gospel reading during the Uganda Catholic Martyrs' Celebrations at Namugongo in 2000. The secondary schoolgirls, who were in their adolescent age, performed the dance following behind a priest who held the Holy Book where the Gospel was to be read. Being schoolgirls, they did not mind the sisters' views of dancing less vigorously. They performed as if they were indeed on stage to attract their audience. Meanwhile, the congregation, which attentively watched their wriggling waists, clapped and applauded as the dancers proceeded to the podium from where the Gospel was to be read. However, majority of the priests agreed that the dance in itself is not bad as long as it is performed by the right people and in the right contexts including weddings or other secular functions. From these priests' opinion, we can gather that the gender of the sisters makes their performance of baakisimba inappropriate; these priests had no problem with women, other than the sisters, performing the dance outside the church contexts.

According to some priests and lay people, mainly the youthful, they did not see it as inappropriate for the sisters to perform the dance. They based their argument on the Bible and especially Psalm 150:4, "Praise the him [God] with drums and dancing . . ." (American Bible Society 1992: 573) They argued that if baakisimba is the dance for Baganda and we perform songs in baakisimba style, why shouldn't we accompany it with the dance? They argued further that the second Vatican Council allowed the church to indigenize its worship. While they agreed that indigenization of the church involved evaluation of what should be adopted from the indigenous culture, they stressed that baakisimba does not conflict with the liturgy. However, when I asked them about the cultural significance of the dance, they were ignorant about the dance's role in preparing girls for a successful sexual life in marriage, for example. All they knew, like me before research, was that baakisimba was created at a beer party and that it was a celebration dance. In fact, some priest stressed that baakisimba is very appropriate after Holy Communion, since the dance was created after the Baganda had eaten and drunk at a celebration; it is a thanksgiving dance. Yet, other priests argued that since baakisimba was performed before the Kabaka, it is appropriate that it should be performed before the overall Kabaka, God, who is the King of all kings. They proposed that the palace baakisimba is very suitable for church context. Apparently, priests and brothers do not dance in church and if they dance outside the church, it is private and among themselves. While I attended a number of functions for the priests, there was no single function that I observed a priest dancing or even a brother. When I asked why they do not dance, majority of the priests argued that baakisimba is for women. One would wonder whether God appreciates only when the women dance. Is the sister's dancing an interpretation of Psalm 150, where the dance is assigned to women and sisters and trumpet, harpists, and flute playing, and drum beating is allocated to men and fathers?

What message is communicated when sisters perform the dance in church? When sisters perform baakisimba, they redefine their sister-gender into that of the women since baakisimba is a women's dance of sexual objectification. Sisters recreate the woman gender through the dance choreography, formations, and costumes. Like the woman-gendered baakisimba dancers, these sisters' dancing focuses on the waist. Although the sisters suggested dancing in subtler and less vigorous ways, the wriggling of the waist, whether subtle or vigorous is a suggestive sexual action. Although the sister dancers perform with lesser vigor compared to women dancers, to an observer, the sisters' dancing would be interpreted as just dancing, unskilled.

Sisters mainly perform the following motifs: *kweyanza, nsi eradde mirembe* (see plate 16), *kusaba,* and *kusoma,* a prayer-like motif. Among all these motifs, *kweyanza* is fitting because it does not involve any waist wriggling. On the other hand, the *ensi eradde mirembe* motif somehow revokes the sister's identity as non-sexual objects (see discussion in Chapter Five). By pointing to the wriggling waist, the sisters invite all males (men, fathers, and brothers) attending the mass to admire how soft their waists are ("how they were created") and thus, alluding to their sexual ability. In *kusoma* motif, while the arms or palms are folded in front of the chest, the waist movements as, in *ensi eradde mirembe* re-emphasized the sister's sexual ability. In fact, the

Plate 16. Sisters dancing baakisimba during thanksgiving in a mass celebration.

audience is more likely to focus on the waist other than prayer-like hand or palm gesture. From my interviews, there was no confusion about what the waist movement would mean; all the informants, including most religious persons were able to associate it with sex.

Further, when dancing, sisters put on *bikooyi* (Indian fabric) *bisenso* (straw dancing skirts) and *buliba* (dance skins) on top of their habits. While their habits, do not expose their waist outline, as is the case when a dancer puts on a petticoat, because they are usually made from hard materials, still the waist movement is evident. Moreover, when the sisters wear *bisenso* and *buliba* they exaggerate the size of their buttocks as well as their quivering, an act that redefines the sisters as objects of men's sexual desire and pleasure.

One would wonder why the sisters particularly dance during the mass and yet, their participation in the liturgy of the mass is minimal; it is mainly singing. On some occasions and especially when the congregation is big and yet the priests are few, sisters give out Holy Communion. I have never observed, in any Church in Buganda, throughout my life experience, when a sister reads out the Gospel. Of course they take readings from other books of the Bible, but not the Gospel. Is it to emphasize that much as they recreated themselves as sisters, being females outside the palace, they are flowers, whose waists are to be admired? I have discussed how the waist movements are metaphors for sexuality and how the Baganda use these movements in the preparation for a successful sexual life for a new couple. Because of the connection between baakisimba and sexuality, sisters dancing baakisimba seems to contradict their vows to celibacy. Moreover, as discussed earlier in Chapter Five, dancing has been regarded as prostitution among the Baganda. From this stance, when sisters perform baakisimba, they revoke the vow of celibacy. The woman gendered dance redefines them as sexually objectified women, which contradicts their sister gender. As such, one needs to question the liturgical correctness of baakisimba dance performance in church, and especially by the sisters.

Chapter Seven

School Baakisimba

EUROPEAN EDUCATION AND GENDER CONSTRUCTION AMONG THE BAGANDA

While baakisimba dance and music have been historically redefined, probably the school performance context made the greatest contribution. Baakisimba is performed in primary schools, secondary schools, high schools, tertiary institutions, colleges, and universities. The impact of school education has been in terms of the ideologies one is instilled with while still in school and those he or she acquires as a result of going through the education system. On the one hand, the education system has contributed to the legitimization of the Kiganda gender constructions, while on the other hand; it has facilitated the creation of new views about gender. In order to examine the ways in which school baakisimba relates with gender, it is paramount to examine the effect of school education on the redefinition of Baganda's gender.

Missionaries and colonialists introduced European education to Buganda in the late nineteenth century, although the missionary education predominated until 1918 (Musisi 1991a: 256; Kasozi 1979: 9). However, "the majority of [these] schools were mainly for sons and daughters of more influential families who, it was assumed, would sooner or later hold positions of responsibility as chiefs, for example" (Lugumba and Ssekamwa 1973: 47). Among the first missionary schools were Namilyango College (1902); Mengo High School (1903); Gayaza Girls' High School (1905); King's College Buddo (1906); and Kisubi St. Mary's College (formerly, St. Mary's College, Rubaga) (1906). As such, the girls did not have a place in the early missionary education, since there was only one girls' school. Lugumba and Ssekamwa have noted, "Throughout the period 1900–60 there was great disparity between the numbers of boys and the numbers of girls attending school . . ." (1973:90). They reported further that by 1960, while there were

354,027 boys, only 161,721 girls attended primary school. Yet, only 456 girls among 3,360 boys attended the top three classes of secondary school (1973: 91).

Besides the few opportunities for girls to attend school, "it was not until much later that girls were offered education of a comparable academic standard to that of the boys' schools" (Pirouet 1995: 138). The girls' education was geared towards preparing them to become better housewives and domestic workers, crystallizing their traditional roles as Baganda women (Obbo 1976; Musisi 1991a, 1992; Tamale 1999). In her report, the Woman Inspector of Schools, A. B. Robertson wrote that "In more *fortunate* [my emphasis] schools under European headmistresses . . . [there is] suitable emphasis on such subjects as housewifery, cookery and laundrywork *[sic]* in the senior classes of primary schools as well as secondary schools . . ." (1939: 63). She was proud to note further that: "Amongst other encouraging features of the work in girls' school . . . [are] the variety and excellence of the handwork done and the attempts to keep alive the traditional crafts of certain tribes . . . and the closer relationship between school arithmetic and such real-life problems as those encountered in needlework, shopping, gardening and house decoration" (Ibid.).

On the other hand, the boys' education prepared them for clerical work and administrative jobs, reinstating the customary role of men as leaders and supervisors. As Musisi has observed, "The main difference between missionary education and traditional education was the fact that missionary education was taught by foreigners or people trained by foreigners, with foreign tools of instruction, including the technology of writing, in a classroom environment" (1991a: 260). Both missionary and colonial policies emphasized a type of education for women that confined them to domestic roles and denied women access to the intellectual skills needed to participate in other domains of social, cultural, and political life of the changing Buganda.[1] The European education maintained the traditional curriculum that prepared women as mothers, child-care takers, food providers, and subordinates of men.

However, as Musisi has also noted, European education "functioned in a complex and contradictory manner; it liberated women from the particular subordination inherent in their roles in traditional society by introducing them to new careers and earning power, yet it limited them to subordinate roles in the newly emerged social structure" (1992: 186). As such, it should not be claimed that European education had a completely negative impact on women. For instance, European education postponed the age of marriages for girls, giving then more time to pursue activities outside marriage including career building.

Although the colonial powers handed over the management of the education system after independence in 1962, it was almost mere change of administration; the girls' plight changed only slightly. While the number of children attending school increased, "Most of the pupils were boys whose figure was about four times that of girls" (Kasozi 1979: 32). Nonetheless, changes in the construction of the Baganda's gender are evident. As Tamale has rightly mentioned, "higher education and other extra-domestic activities expose women to alternative values which can overshadow childhood socialization" (1997: 77). Moreover, by interacting with other people in schools and at colleges, men and women were resocialized, opening them to new possible views about their own gendering. As more women became educated and made contacts with the outside world, the struggle for emancipation from the men's dominant power and the agitation for equality emerged. Moreover, educated women began mobilizing disadvantaged women, especially in rural areas, in the struggle for gender equality and emancipation. However, gender equality in Buganda and Uganda in general, means different things to different people, and these meanings do not always coincide with the Western meaning of the term. To some of the women I interviewed, gender equality meant being able to control their money from sales of crops, which men controlled in the past. To some men, it is allowing women to be involved in wage-earning jobs, but also requiring the women to use the money for the benefit of the whole family. Yet to the most radical, especially women with college education, gender equality means liberation from cultural bonds of submissiveness and being part of decision-making in public and private arenas, as well as equal opportunities for all genders. As a woman informant expressed, "we can hold on to our natural roles as procreators, but share the role of bringing up these children." On the other hand, some men as well as women interviewed contended that gender equality involves sharing societal and cultural roles depending on the abilities of the individuals. However, Nuludin Ssekitto, like a number of young men interviewed, said that, "Although I agree that a husband and a wife should have income-generating jobs, I disagree with the sharing of the domestic roles. I suggest that we get a house girl [maid], instead of me washing the plates while my wife is cooking." While a number of women informants agreed to the idea of having a housemaid, some argued that men should participate in domestic roles. To these women, using girls as housemaids is another way of exploiting the women folk.

Other informants complained that some women, especially those with college education, have gone overboard in their pursuit for gender equality. For example, Janat Nakitto, in her late forties, argued, "we do not disagree, in this era the woman must move with the times, but she has to retain the behavior of a Muganda woman; that one of respecting the man." Similarly, Tereza Kisolo, in her seventies, believed "it is necessary that a woman continues to respect her husband despite the emancipation" (interview). However, she stressed that "in the same way, the man should not mistreat his wife" (ibid.). She said that as late as the 1950s, men could tie their wives with ropes and beat them for trivial issues and because they had no voice, nothing would be done to the men. Kisolo was proud to note that since the late 1980s, women have a voice; they can report their men to village councils if they mistreat them. Although this court structure existed before, it was only a privilege to men, since men (brothers, fathers, and uncles) were the only arbitrators; their judgment was prone to bias.

During my research, major complaints were lodged against educated women, especially university graduates. A number of the men interviewed, including university graduates, vowed never to marry graduate women. They argued that these women are not only proud, but also disrespectful. One informant complained that, while gender equality may be good, it is erasing the Kiganda tradition. He noted that there are few women in the 2000s that still kneel before men. He complained that his wife knelt before him for the first few days of their marriage, and when she got used to him, she no longer kneels. He stressed that equality should not mean that women should no longer be subordinate to men. He argued that God designed women to be below men. However, a professor at Makerere University and a Muganda woman argued that kneeling before men is one of the cultural practices that construct women as submissive objects. She expressed that "as for me, I no longer allow my daughters [she has four girls] to kneel before any man, not even their father. My husband is not comfortable with it, but this is one of the ways my girls will grow up knowing that they are equal to men and that they do not have to submit to men" (anonymous, interview).

Further, educated Baganda women can no longer accept patriarchal interpretations of Biblical scriptures and cultural practices that subjugate their emancipation. Reacting to a patriarchal interpretation of the Biblical creation story, Tereza Nsamba, a member of Kirimuttu Women's Group in Kyotera (Buddu County) counter-argued that:

It is true that God first created a man and gave him all the beautiful things. However, because of the man's ignorance, he could not utilize these nice things. He suffered a lot. When God saw that the man had failed to live in the world—he did not know how to cook, he did not know how to wash—God had pity on him and He created a woman who was to help this man to survive well in the world (interview).

As women were exposed to the outside world through education and Christianity[2] the ideological myths and superstitions ceased to have a basis for living their lives. Women discovered that actually one cannot die if she beats the drum. Rather, the threat of death was on the ways through which men controlled women's access to the drum. My discussion of the women drummers as a product of women's emancipation struggle, illustrates one of the ways in which women have contested authoritative powers of the Baganda men. European education, in part, accounts for the emancipatory practices of women in relation to access to drumming and choreographic creativity as discussed later in in Chapter Five and later in this chapter, respectively. This discussion reveals struggling power relationships between men and women. While men have to accept that relations must change and are actually changing, they still have to wrestle with the fact that they can no longer dominate the women. Women can no longer accept their assigned role of being passive agents of culture.

BAAKISIMBA AT SCHOOL COMPETITIONS

Until the 1960s, European education aimed at erasing most aspects of Kiganda culture, including music and dancing. Baakisimba was one of the music and dance genres, which could not be taught in schools; the early teachers considered it sacrilegious. Instead, church music and secular European songs were taught in schools; some of which included, "Clementine," "John Brown's Body," and "My Bonnie" (Muwonge et al., 1997:13). Further, "in a few schools, there were military bands mostly used for marching purposes and for attracting more pupils. Selected pupils learnt to play bugles, flutes and drums [while] a few learnt to play the organ" (ibid.). In order to crystallize the European music in schools, in 1929, the annual Namirembe Church Music Festivals were introduced. At these festivals, school choirs sung hymns, chorales and anthems, which "boosted the standards of music in the Protestant schools . . ." (Muwonge et al., 1997: 15). These festivals were interrupted when G. M. Duncan, the initiator of these festivals, died, but resumed in 1944 and by 1955, the outstanding school choirs included, "Kings' College Budo, Gayaza [Girls'] High School, Busoga College Mwiri, Bishop Stuart College, Mbarara, Makerere College School and Bishop's School, Mukono" (Muwonge et al, 1997:16). However, dancing was not part of the performance at these festivals since it was considered heathen to perform the indigenous dances (Muwonge et al., 1997: 17).

And yet, even after independence in 1962, hopes to rehabilitate the Kiganda culture, "which for a long time had been obscured by European cultural domination . . ." (Kasozi 1979: 55), were shattered. Kasozi attributes the failure of this rehabilitation to the mode of production, which "created a ruling class that honored individuals with European modern tastes" (1979: 58). He argues that the secondary school education at the time "weakened family ties between the students and relatives, it discouraged African traditional religions, reduced the influences of [Kiganda] music and emphasized the use of foreign instead of native language" (1979: 59). During the First Conference on African Traditional Music of 1963, Dr. Zake, the then Ugandan Minister of Education lamented, "It often appears that the function of producing good music has been relegated to the less educated section of the community and this has put it somehow in danger of disappearing. The more educated people find it easier now to pick up a saxophone or a trombone rather than a harp or a xylophone" (Kakoma et al., 1964: 4). Although this conference was conducted with the aim of devising strategies of establishing a national school of traditional music, by 2004, the idea of establishing this school is only recorded in the conference report.

The early 1970s was a period of renaissance for Kiganda traditional music and dance, and particularly, baakisimba. Indeed, "'Renaissance' is the appropriate term because European missionaries and administrators, during the years of colonial rule, often denigrated, and successfully repressed, indigenous music and dance . . ." (Hanna and Hanna, 1968: 42). However, since the 1970s, and through the Uganda Schools' Music and Dance Competitions, the schools have played a big role in recapturing and yet, redefining baakisimba.[3] The Ugandan Ministry of Education organizes these inter-school competitions at sub-county, county, district, and national levels. Since the early 1990s, the inter-school music and dance competitions in primary and secondary schools, and colleges were made compulsory and absentees are punished by reducing government subsides. As a result, from January to April, the first term of the school calendar, a number of schools are involved in music and dance activities preparing for the competitions in June and July. On the other hand, the schools, especially private ones that are unable to participate in the inter-school competitions at least organize competitions within the school. Each school is divided into "houses," "colors," or classes, which form the basis for the competition. For instance, Makerere Performing Arts (MAPA), as the competition is called at Makerere College School, is an annual inter-house competition event since 1980. In addition to inter-house competitions, schools also perform music and dance on special occasions for parents and visitors and in theatrical shows. However, the schools competition contribute more to the definition of school baakisimba, and as such, my discussion will be based on these competitive contexts of baakisimba performance.

The schools' music and dance competitions account for the most changes in baakisimba drumming, dance choreography, and costumes. Schoolboy and schoolgirl dancers, trainers, as well as members of the jury participate in the creation of the "new" baakisimba. Arthur Kayizzi, a trainer of baakisimba at Makerere College School, noted that:

> Because of competition, we have changed the whole trend of baak-isimba dance and its music; in fact, it is as if we are in a revolution. We are now moving away from the traditional baakisimba and moving towards a recreated or recomposed baakisimba, although based on the one that already existed. The new ideas we add in kill the authenticity, but they foster competition (interview).

Innovation of new ways of performing baakisimba is one of the strategies participants devise so as to out-compete their rivals at these competitions. As a result, each school or house participating in the competitions recreates a "new" baakisimba. I remember, as a student in Makerere College School (from 1981–1987), our school had a distinct baakisimba style from that of either Gayaza Girls' High School, or even that of Lubiri Senior Secondary School. However, the styles of baakisimba performed outside the competition stage are different from those subjected to competition. Kayizzi, told me that, "Our performances are different when we are in competition because we have to adhere to certain rules. We are motivated by the ambition to win. Yet, outside the competitions, there is freedom; we can dress and perform, as we want without restrictions. Non-competitive performances are more of an entertainment; we do not fuss a lot."

What then are the rules to which performers of baakisimba at these schools' competitions must adhere? Shaban Kalwaza, a member of the jury, told me that the adjudicators look for "authenticity" in the accompaniment, dance techniques, uniformity in movement among the dancers and use of levels in the dance movements. The costume design is assessed in terms of materials used, fashion, neatness, and uniformity. However, important as the term "authenticity" is in the definition of school baakisimba, it is very vague; as such, the interpretation of "authenticity" is as varied as the performers, trainers, and adjudicators of the school baakisimba. In the first instance, the term "authenticity" suggests a concept with a clear origin and a known inventor as well as a state that is changeless. And yet, the origin of baak-isimba, as already discussed in Chapter Three, is only speculative.

Moreover, the structure of school baakisimba has undergone change, since the social, political, and cultural structures that created it have continually changed through time. Contrary to the suggested meaning of authenticity, all trainers and adjudicators interviewed agreed that a number of changes in baakisimba are inevitable since innovations are at the center of these schools' competitions. They contended that if all participants at these competitions were to present the same style of baakisimba, it would be impossible to determine the winner. Similarly, in her study of Malipenga ngoma of Malawi, Lisa Gilman noted that in order to win *ngoma* (music and dance) competitions "performers do something that stands out, that is admired, while remaining within the frame of what is understood to be a particular *ngoma*" (2000: 334). While innovations are at the core of school baakisimba, all the trainers and adjudicators interviewed believed in a "recomposed-authentic" baakisimba, although their agreement was atypical. For instance, while Jackson Kamuntu, a member of the jury, consented that a small white or yellow *kikooyi* (an Indian fabric) worn, as a dance skirt is appropriate costume for baakisimba, Kayizzi disagreed and argued that dressing in such a fabric is as good as being naked (interview). Ezuliya Nannyonga, a former court dancer clarified that this kind of *kikooyi* is an inner cloth for married women, meant to keep them "warm," and as such, the Baganda consider it inappropriate to expose this kind of cloth. She compared this *kikooyi* to a petticoat as underwear (interview). Further, Kayizzi criticized the costumes worn by some school dancers. He said, "I have seen a number of school dancers decorating themselves with head-bands, and the whole dressing look crowded. You look at a baakisimba dancer and you wonder; 'is this one a European or an African?' There is a lot of ornamentation that is spoiling the authentic costume of baakisimba" (interview).

While acceptable innovations in school baakisimba are relative, the majority of the trainers and adjudicators interviewed considered authentic baakisimba to be based on palace baakisimba. The view that palace baakisimba should be the basis for school baakisimba is supported by one of the theories about the origin of baakisimba, which purports that baakisimba originated from the palace before the commoners outside the palace embraced it (see Chapter Three for details). However, these trainers and adjudicators did not agree on a single definition of palace baakisimba. In a number of cases, their definition of palace baakisimba overlapped with what they considered to be village baakisimba. However, this overlap is justifiable since some trainers of baakisimba in schools have been either former court dancers, musicians, or people who were related to court musicians and dancers who taught them to dance. For instance, Evaristo Muyinda, who in the 1960s gave the first baakisimba dance and music lessons to Makerere College School students was a former court musician (Ingle 1995: 9–10); Cooke 1995: 24). Besides, Ssaalongo Christopher Kizza, a former music and dance lecturer at Kyambogo University, and a great contributor to school baakisimba, learned baakisimba from a relative who was a court musician (interview).

It should be noted, though, that there is also no clear distinction between the post-restoration palace baakisimba (palace baakisimba after 1993) and the school baakisimba of the same period since there is no specific palace baakisimba performers any more. The school baakisimba is to some extent defining palace baakisimba since the 1993, because schools are also invited to perform for the king. Moreover, some of the members of the semi-professional groups, who are invited to perform for the king, are also the trainers of baakisimba in schools. For example, Janet Nandujja, of the Planets, is a regular performer at the palace functions, and yet, she trains a number of schools in Kampala (interview). Nonetheless, the school baakisimba has some basic distinctive features; some of which are continuities from the palace baakisimba, while others are either new creations or a reinforcement of styles of baakisimba, which are performed by semi-professional groups.

One of the characteristics of school baakisimba performed during the competitions is the number of performers on stage. Because of the required number of forty-five to fifty performers on stage, the number of dancers at a single performance is quite big compared to either the palace or village baakisimba. There are usually eight to fourteen dancers, four to eight drummers, and thirty-three to thirty-eight choristers that perform baakisimba during the school's music and dance festivals. However, the biggest number of dancers at a palace performance before the abolition of Buganda kingdom was four, and yet these dancers performed one after the other (Lwewunzika, interview). It is common to have six to eight dancers when semi-professional groups perform at the palace or at a wedding ceremony in the village context.

And yet, the evaluation of a good dancers and drummers, which was informal, became formalized. The evaluation of baakisimba performances at these competitions is left to trained and hired adjudicators. In palace and village baakisimba, the general audience judged the performance by clapping and applauding the best dancers. However, the audiences at schools' competitions are not free to applaud the dancers and must keep quiet throughout the entire performance, lest they interfere with the official adjudicators' work. As a matter of fact, the organizers of these competitions assign people the responsibility of controlling the audience. For instance, during the 2002 Uganda Schools' Music and Dance Festival in Mukono District, I observed that they were five people to control the audience and one school was penalized because some members of that school, who were in the audience, made a lot of noise when their choir came on stage. The audience is alienated further when the schoolgirls and schoolboys perform on a modern raised stage with all its artistic constraints.

Because of competition, the drum accompaniment in school baakisimba has been greatly recreated. However, there are as many variations as there are the competing schools and houses. In addition to *mbuutu* and *ngalabi,* the *mpuunyi* (with similar shape as the mbuutu, but with a lower pitch) is added to enhance the deep basic beat in basic baakisimba motif (*kubiibya* motif). Sulaiti Kalungi explained that the mpuunyi is added, "Because the drummers no longer stress the basic beat as they did in the past. In baakisimba of our times [late 1940s] the *mbuutu* was beaten in the center [to produce a muted deep sound] in order to do what the *mpuunyi* is doing now" (interview). The mpuunyi stress the basic beat, which guides the speed of the dance. When the basic beat is not distinct, the dancer cannot know when to begin the cyclic footwork of the basic baakisimba motif. Furthermore, *nankasa,* a smaller and high-pitched drum, which is beaten with mallets, was also added to the *mbuutu, ngalabi,* and *mpuunyi.*[4] In school competitions, *nankasa* is beaten to signal the change from one motif to the other and directs the stage configuration.[5] Moreover, it also works as the timekeeper since the length of the performance is regulated and a penalty is given if a performing group exceeds the stipulated time. The customary all-night dancing parties are limited to minutes since baakisimba is adapted to a concert style with a number of different music and dance items to be performed by other schools. It should be noted though, that the number of drums and their combinations vary from one competing school to the other. At a number of performances, I observed that many schools presented two *mbuutu* of varying pitches, two *ngalabi,* two *nankasa,* and one *mpuunyi,* yet on other occasions, three *mbuutu,* with varying pitches, two *ngalabi,* two *nankasa* and one *mpuunyi* with varying pitches, accompanied the dance.

The innovation of baakisimba choreography is seen in terms of dance movements, dance levels, and stage design. While the palace baakisimba was performed as a fully-fledged dance, the school baakisimba is performed as part of a dance suite, which includes *nankasa* and *muwogola,* both initially independent dances that developed in the early twentieth century. School children and semi-professional ensembles perform *muwogola* differently. Within schools, it is usually performed as a climax for baakisimba performance. The following *muwogola* motif is very popular among school dancers: the chest is forward and still, and the buttocks are pushed outward. The arms are lifted and open with the palms pushing outward. The feet are shoulder-width apart and the legs are slightly bent. The dancer stands high on the balls of the feet and steps very quickly, "stubbing" her toes as she goes forward. The result is a shimmy of the buttocks.

The order of this dance suite is either *nankasa-baakisimba-muwogola,* or *baakisimba-nankasa-muwogola.* According to Shaban Kalwaza, a dance trainer, *nankasa* and *muwogola* were included in baakisimba to avoid monotony. He argued that performing baakisimba for nine minuets, as stipulated by the competition syllabus, would be very tiring to the dancers and boring to the audience (interview). In addition to *nankasa* and *muwogola,* a number of motifs are borrowed from *mbaga* dance, a Kiganda wedding dance, *maggunju,* another Kiganda royal dance, and *tamenhaibuga,* a waist dance from Busoga (eastern Uganda). The inclusion of *tamenhaibuga* movements in the school competitions is accounted for by the close similarities of the two dances. As in baakisimba dance, *tamenhaibuga* has its basic movement in the waist and the footwork; the major difference is that palace baakisimba has a round waist movement while *tamenhaibuga* has a staccato-like waist movement.

In school baakisimba, the waist is no longer the center of the dance; the chest, foot, and arms are moved equally as much as the waist. Movement of the chest and arms is a borrowing likely from the *maggunju* dance. Further, the footwork changed; it ranges from raising one foot while supporting with another alternatively, to kicking in the air, which was un-heard-of in palace baakisimba. In this case, kicking in the air is borrowing from the *mbaga* dance. While a number of new hand positions have been created in the school baakisimba, four positions are basic to the authentication of baakisimba performed at school competitions and these include: *kweyanza/kweyanjula, nsi eradde mirembe, kusaba,* and *kuwera* motifs. However, the meanings of these motifs are restructured and relate to a mere enactment of a cultural symbol if the dance is performed in the absence of the king. The school dancers mainly aim at recontextualizing a cultural symbol to depict the palace context. The festival syllabus requires that the chosen dances be performed as closely as possible to their "traditional" setting. In this case, the motifs may be interpreted as a cultural retention, devoid of their original meaning. For instance, I observed a number of schools who perform kweyanza-like motif on their knees, with the chest moving back and forth, wriggle their waists. However, Kayizzi disagreed with such innovation and argues that, "we only kneel once when thanking [the king, during the *kweyanza* motif] at the beginning of the dance. The king is not thanked many times and he is not knelt before

more than once. Dancing while kneeling down is exposing one's nakedness" (interview).

In order to fulfill the requirements of the competition, namely dancing at
different body levels, a sequence of dance motifs, collectively called *mangodooli*
were invented, although the inventor is not known. There are four types of
mangodooli dance movements: *kuseetula, kutuulira, kwambusa,* and *kutambuza.*
These innovative motifs performed mainly by school dancers were not performed in the palace. In all the motifs, the waist movement is the focus. However, the basic baakisimba drum music is maintained as explained in Chapter
Four. In *kuseetula,* which means to push along or to roll, the dancer stands in
the middle position, chest lifted and forward, and buttocks outward. When the
left foot is supporting (flat), the right leg is raised on the ball of the foot and vice
versa. With the weight on the supporting left leg, the dancer moves sideways to
the right on the first eighth beat, pushing ball-heel-ball, which gives locomotion
to the step. Meanwhile, the right leg is bent, with the ball of the foot on the
floor making a small circling pattern. This posture of the right foot allows the
right hip to lift and circle, while the buttocks are pushed up and down. The hip
lift is on the first eighth beat as well. The hands are held to the right, across the
body, undulating to the music. Yet, in *Kutuulira,* which means to "sit on," the
dancer lifts the chest forward and pushes the buttocks backwards. With slightly
bent knee and flat foot, the left leg is aligned with the body while the right leg,
with bent knee, is slightly forward and lifted on the ball of the foot. The
dancers' hands are fisted at hip level, with arms bent downward and out from
the sides of the body. While rotating her waist and hips, the dancer gradually
lowers herself until both legs are fully bent and on flat feet. One waist-and-hips
rotation is completed within a beat. *Kwambusa,* which means "to push up" or
"to raise," is the opposite of the *kutuulira* motif and usually follow *kutuulira*
motif. The dancer moves from the low position of *kutuulira* motif, with both
feet flat. The dancer then gradually lifts herself up onto the balls of her feet.
Meanwhile, the dancer maintains the hip and waist circles as she gradually lifts
and opens her hands, and completes this motif with palms facing up, until chest
level. *Kutambuza,* which means, "to dance while walking," the dancer stands in
a low position, with chest forward and buttocks pushed back. With bent knees
and flat feet, the dancer moves forward, shifting the weight alternately on the
left and right legs as she thrusts the hips sideways three times each step. She
steps on each beat of the music. The hands swing front-to-back loosely, in the
opposite direction of the weighted and stepping leg.

Furthermore, *ssenkubuge* motif (named after its inventor) is adapted as
one way of varying levels in dance. In one of the *ssenkubuge* motifs, the
dancer makes three small steps in place to one beat. A low swinging-kick

across the body forms the basis of this movement. The kick is held up for one beat, straightening the relaxed body frame in a visual pause. Then, as the leg lowers, the hip drops, adding a quivering beat to the buttock movement. The arms swing opposite the kicking leg, front-to-back, accenting the beat. *Ssenkubuge,* named after its inventor, developed during the 1980s, and became more common in schools since the 1990s. The development is attributed to the semi-professional ensembles, whose members taught the motif to school choirs. There are many types of *ssenkubuge* motif, but I will only describe one that a number of schools performed. One of the major features of this motif is the variation in dance levels, which is strictly guided by the drum music. Unlike basic baakisimba, there must be at least two *mbuutu* drums beating *ssenkubuge* motifs, although in some cases there may even be up to five *mbuutu* drums (with varying pitches) and one or two *ngalabi* drums. When I visited Ssenkubuge Nankasa Group (the ensemble of the founder of *ssenkubuge* motif), I noticed, though, that they had four *mbuutu* drums with varying pitches, three *nankasa* drums, and two *ngalabi* drums. In this *ssenkubuge* motif, the dancer makes three small steps in place to one beat. A low swinging-kick across the body forms the basis of this movement. The kick is held up for one beat, straightening the relaxed body frame in a visual pause. Then, as the leg lowers, the hip drops, adding a quivering beat to the buttocks movement. The arms swing opposite the kicking leg (as in the walking movement), front-to-back, accenting the beat (see figure 13).

Besides the innovations in the dance motifs, there is also a high level of creativity in the stage design as opposed to the straight-line formations of the palace baakisimba. As far as stage design is concerned, two important trainers of baakisimba must be mentioned. James Makubuya, a former music teacher at Makerere College School, and Moses Sserwadda, a dance lecturer at Makerere University are known for their creativity in stage configuration besides the artistry in the levels, which they neatly synchronized with corresponding music and dance movements. While the dancers in palace baakisimba performed the dance when facing the audience and in a straight-line, Makubuya and Sserwadda excelled in circular, diagonal and serpent-like formations. However, Kayizzi explained that: "when the dancers turn their backs to the audience, within the palace context, they would be, exposing their nakedness" (interview). Nonetheless, in addition to the straight-lines, circles, and semi-circles, dancers at school competitions adopt dance formations from the letters of the alphabet. Some of the commonly created letters include: V, U, X, Z, S, K, and T. In defense of these innovations, Kayizzi argued, "If I stick on the traditional formation of baakisimba and someone brings a dance which traditionally has varying formations, he/she will win the traditional

ngalabi

mbuutu 1

mbuutu 2

mbuutu 3

clapping

dance

feet:

Figure 13. Ssenkubuge motif.

dance item. As an adjudicator, I would give more marks to someone who has creative formations if he/she conforms to the basic dance techniques" (interview). With the introduction of Uganda schools' music and dance competition, baakisimba costuming got redesigned. However, in most cases, the choice and design of costume depends on the availability of funds from the school; rich schools tend to have better costumes. While many music and dance trainers have made changes in the performance of baakisimba, Makubuya made greater contributions in the area of costuming. Makubuya told me that he introduced the *bisenso*, skirts made out of raffia. In 1977, when he first presented his students of Makerere College School on the stage the Uganda National Theater, Makubuya was greatly criticized for dressing them in *bisenso* below the dancing skin (interview). However, the costume has become common practice and considered "authentic" since then. Some schools even color their *bisenso*. In the early 2000s, many school dancers wear bras, petticoats, *bikooyi*, and animal skins; it is only the *bisenso*, which are at times colored. However, some schools dress in tee shirts with school logos, *bikooyi*, *bisenso* and animal skins. Furthermore, some trainers have not only borrowed dance motifs from *mbaga* (wedding) dance to baakisimba, but also the costumes of the dance. A number of schools dress in *bijyenge*, strips of threaded cloth sown on a sheet of cloth and is dressed as a skirt), instead of *bisenso* made out of raffia. As a result, the school music and dance competitions offer a stage of formulations of "new" baakisimba music and dance styles. As such, reinvention is at the center of these competitions.

GENDERED SCHOOL BAAKISIMBA

School baakisimba illustrates situations of reaffirmation of the Baganda's gender construction, while at the same time, it contradicts it and recreates new gender roles. What, then, are the ways in which gendered meaning(s) in baakisimba are reconstructed? The performers, trainers, adjudicators, and the audience engage in producing meanings in school baakisimba. Moreover, the nature of school structure, to some extent, determines the gendering in school baakisimba; mixed-sex schools present different gender structuring from those of single-sex schools. Since my involvement in baakisimba performance, I have observed that more girls than boys get involved in music-making and dance activities. Girls are the lead singers and form the majority of the choristers. Based on my experience as a music and dance student and as a teacher at Makerere College School, boy students as well as men teachers tended to categorize music and dancing as "soft and simple" subjects. Because music and dance were considered as soft and simple subjects, more girls were encouraged to study music and dance since the teachers identified "softness" with being womanish. The few boys who joined the school choir were trained as drummers. In plate 17, the young boys are shown beating the drums while the girls are singing.

Plate 17. Primary schoolboys beating the drums while the schoolgirls sing.

While recruitment to the school choirs is open to all students in the school, some music and dance teachers tend to limit certain performance roles to specific genders. In mixed schools, it is common that girls are assigned dancing roles and boys are trained as drummers.[6] For example, when I was a student at Makerere College School, my teachers always "encouraged" me as a better dancer; I was never given the opportunity to learn the drums. While Kayizzi, like many music and dance teachers interviewed emphasized that boys tend to learn drumming faster than the girl and that girls learn how to dance faster than the boys, interviews with schoolgirls established that girls are just not given the opportunity to learn. For instance, Nnabanoba lamented that: "Whenever the [music] teacher found me, I had to run and hide because he never allowed us to beat the drums. He was never interested in seeing what I was beating. He never said to me 'let me see what you are [beating]'" (interview). My story about how I came to beat the drums may throw more light. I began to learn baakisimba dancing in 1982 while I was in Makerere College School. Although I wanted to learn how to beat the drums, my music teacher insisted that I was a better dancer. He used to say that women do not beat drums; they only dance. After one year, I decided to study music as one of the academic subjects and so I had access to the music room (all music students were expected to practice on their own). With access to this "sacred" room, where the drums were kept, I was able to "steal" the drums and beat them. After graduating from the university as a music teacher in 1991, no one could control my access to the drums. I used this opportunity to learn the drums while I taught my students. Moreover, the Local Council Women's music festivals, which were very popular from 1988 until around 1994, provided me the initial opportunities to perform as a woman in front of an audience.

Moreover, I have not observed in any mixed schools where boys dance while girls beat the drums. Explaining why boys do not dance while the girls beat the drums, Kayizzi said, "In a competition, always the best performers are the ones I choose to represent the school. Likewise, a house teacher will choose only the best performers for his or her house. That is why boys are more likely to drum than dance because they tend to learn the drumming faster than the girls" (interview). Although it is true the boys beat the drums better than the girls, it is not because the girls lack the abilities, the girls are in most cases not given the opportunity to beat the drums as the boys. However, because of the agitation for equality, an ideology that became very popular in the 1990s, a few mixed schools allow girls to beat the drums, but not when the boys are dancing. For instance, James Mugenyi, a teacher at St. Lawrence High School, explained that students are allocated to houses, which form the basis for the competitions, based on their genders. The reason for allocating houses according to genders is to "promote competitions; most big girls used to shy away from these competitions and yet, all students should participate. It is also very healthy for boys to compete with girls (interview).

In a few cases, where boys have danced with girls, still the boys were the drummers. And yet, it is mainly at primary school level that a few boys dance with girls. It is possible for these boys to dance at this level, because at this age they are not yet fully developed into the man gender. As such they are not embarrassed to perform a woman-gendered role. Plate 18 shows primary boys and girls dancing together at the Mukono Schools' Music and Dance competition on 22 August 2000.

It is justified when boys dance in all-boys' school because there are no girls to dance. But, what meanings are communicated when boys dance with girls in a mixed school? Would the boys' dancing suggest a reduced gap between men and women? Is it a probable move towards equality, where men see themselves as similar with women and can take up similar roles? Of course, one cannot make a reflexive correlation. However, from the historical point of view, where men were isolated from many of the women's activities, this performance practice suggests a redefined space between men and

Plate 18. Primary schoolboys dancing with schoolgirls.

women. As Roscoe has reported, "it was customary for women to eat apart from their husbands" (1911:438). In this case, competitions in baakisimba performance provide a terrain for negotiating gender space.

On the other hand, single-sex schools have contributed innovations in baakisimba performance practice that promote gender role reversal of drumming and dancing. The gender roles are renegotiated further when boys, in all-boys' school, take up dancing roles, originally performed by women. In all-boy's schools, boys beat the drums as well dancing. In all-girls' schools, the role of beating drums that was previously restricted to men became open to girls too (see plate 19).

This practice is more common in Church-founded schools like Gayaza Girls' High School, which do not respect mythologies related to the drum. In addition, since the Schools' Music and Dance competitions are compulsory and absenteeism is punishable by the Ministry of Education, girls' schools get the opportunity to take up drumming roles when they perform baakisimba. Moreover, Uganda having an educational system based on a non-traditional establishment that is supposed to offer equal educational opportunities to both sexes, gender restrictions to certain musical instruments are minimal compared to the village setting. Baakisimba as well as other traditional musics and dances from other Ugandan ethnic groups

Plate 19. Schoolgirls dancing and beating the drums.

became examinable, at ordinary level (since 1980) and at advanced senior secondary level (since 1990). At both levels, a student is expected to train in both Western and "Ugandan" local musical performance style. As such, there would be fewer restrictions for girls to beat instruments culturally assigned to men. While in all-girls' schools, girls beat the drums; they are yet to combine these drums with, for instance, *ndongo, ndingidi,* and *madinda,* as boys do in a number of schools.

Like in the village baakisimba, the men control the structure of school baakisimba. The majority of the adjudicators are men. In most cases, men head and form the majority of membership of the councils of the Ministry of Education that organize these competitions. As such, they determine who should adjudicate. Moreover, as already discussed, the men form the biggest majority of music and dance trainers, from whom adjudicators are chosen. Consequently, men determine what to teach the students and what is winning baakisimba.

And yet, many times the kind of costume worn does not necessarily depend on one's gender, as was the case in palace baakisimba. Sometimes boys dress in *bikooyi,* bras, and petticoats as girls, although others put on vests instead of bras. In addition, girls wear *kanzu* (long tunic, reaching to the feet), a man's wear, when beating the drum. When I asked one of the trainers at Gayaza Girls' High School, why she dresses the schoolgirl drummers in a *kanzu* and yet it is a man's wear, she said that since drumming was not a woman's role, the students put on the *kanzu* to adapt the proper character of a man (interview). Furthermore, while dressing with the *ndege* (ankle bells) was limited to male dancers in the palace, girls also tie *ndege* on their feet in the performance of baakisimba during school competitions. In fact, these bells are used as costumes as well as musical instruments. As one of the creativity, in the course of the performance, the drumming and other musical instruments are suspended, while only singing and the sounding of the bells accompany the dance. It is therefore; fair to conclude that the guidelines for evaluating the performance of baakisimba at schools competitions are the foundation to the re-invention of baakisimba.

The inclusion of *nnankasa, muwogola, mbaga, maggunju,* and *tamenhaibuga* in baakisimba of the twenty-first century suggests a redefinition of gender. The vigorous movements in these dances seem to contradict the criteria used to define baakisimba as women's dance. Is it an indication that women are now louder and less graceful? Women of the twenty-first century are certainly outwardly more assertive than before because of the changes in the cultural, social and political structures that constructed them to be calm and graceful. By interacting with other students in schools and at colleges, men and women were resocialized, opening themselves to new possible views about their own gendering. Nonetheless, one cannot claim a direct correlation between the musical and dance style and the women's changed behavior.

If baakisimba is a dance loaded with sexual connotations as discussed in Chapter Five, how has it survived in schools as a public performance in a culture where sex and gender issues are not supposed to be discussed in public? As a matter of fact, because sex is a delicate issue, a number of school have not yet offered sex education in their curriculum. Nonetheless, this dance has survived because the dance teachers of baakisimba have concealed the "preferred meanings" (Hall quoted in Brooker 1999:172).[7] Many school-teachers that I talked to, especially in schools, did not know or were shy to tell me the meanings of the intricate dance movements. Although the school dancers are not told the preferred meanings, they are still able to communicate them in their dancing. In a similar vein, John Blacking has noted that among the Venda "although many girls at domba [ritual ceremony] did not know, or could not remember, the verbal symbolism referring to the dance, they were able to perform efficiently, criticise their own and other's performances intelligently . . ." (1985:89).

One would then ask, "why are the dancers able to communicate the preferred meanings of the dance?" Like in many cultures, there are a number of 'traditions' that are passed down from one generation to another without anybody questioning their meanings. These dancers learn what their teachers teach them and because they trust their wisdom, they usually do not question the meanings of the dance. Moreover, the teachers adapt a skill of teaching that will make the student do the right thing even when no meaning is given. For instance, when my baakisimba teacher wanted his dance students to adopt the right facial expression, he would say, "I hate ugly dancers on stage." He meant that we should smile and be expressive as we wriggled our waists. During my research, I had the opportunity to meet him and when I asked him why he never explained the meanings of the dance, he said, "You were too young to be told the meaning." He noted that since the dance is so closely related to sex, when the dancers smile while wriggling their waists, they aim at enticing or arousing men in the audience. He argued that if dance students were told the meaning of the dance, they would not agree to dance (anonymous, interview). This dance has survived because the dance students, trainers, and adjudicators have reconstructed the meaning of baakisimba. Baakisimba has been translated into a competitive dance, rather than the prescribed women's dance, which communicates their gender identity.

Chapter Eight

Baakisimba and Homosexuality among the Baganda

ORIENTALISM: HOMOSEXUALITY IN BUGANDA

Although in Buganda, female-women are historically the established dancers while men are the drummers, since the 1800s, male-women began dancing in the palace too. Moreover, since the late 1980s, a big number of men have joined the women's dancing space. A number of informants, especially musicians and dancers, told me that one of the reasons why some males perform baakisimba or any other dances outside the palace, is because they are homosexuals. When I inquired about homosexuality among people outside performing groups, I was told that homosexuality did not exist in Buganda.[1] However, a few informants who could talk about the subject blamed foreigners for the introduction of homosexuality. However, through my observations and interviews during the research, it was revealed that some dancers are male homosexual. While a number of informants insisted that there was no homosexuality in Buganda, baakisimba provides a site through which this disguised gender identity is negotiated. In the first section of this chapter, I provide a background to homosexuality in Buganda, a context necessary for the discussion of male homosexual dancers later in the chapter.

In Buganda, homosexuality is regarded as taboo, a form of social deviance. Although homosexuals are not as open about their sexual identity as in the Western world, they exist in Buganda and Uganda in general. However, male homosexuality is more prominent than female homosexuality. While there are high possibilities that homosexuality could have been practiced in Buganda before foreign contact, it was after the coming of Christianity in the late nineteenth century that it was condemned.[2] J. F. Faupel noted that, "homosexuality seems to have been rife at Mutesa's [sic] court. . . .

Mutesa himself indulged in the vice and encouraged his subjects to do so. His son Ssekabaka Mwanga II was also an addict before he succeeded to the throne" (1984: 9–10). Similarly, Kaggwa wrote that:

> During Kabaka Mukabya Muteesa's reign, after the Arabs and other for-
> eigners had come to Buganda, promiscuity became more rampant. . . .
> And also those Arabs introduced another very bad behavior, that one of
> men making fellow men as their women [wives]! And yet that was not a
> behavior of the Baganda and had never been heard of in Buganda
> (1952: 172).

All the interviewees attributed the initial introduction of the "very bad behavior" to the coming of the Arabs and argued that the influx of Europeans, especially expatriates and tourists, account for the rise in homosexuality in more recent times.[3] Although the specific dates when the first Arabs came to Buganda are disputed among scholars, it is clear that they were the first people outside Africa to come to the kingdom. Some scholars estimate that Sheik Ahmed bin Ibrahim, the first Arab, came around 1844, during Ssekabaka Suuna's reign (Apter 1966: 6; Gee 1958: 139). However, John Miller Gray reported an even earlier contact and noted that during the reign of Ssemakokiro, whom he estimates to have died around 1815, Buganda had a flourishing trade of ivory for cotton, copper wires, and cowry shells in Karagwe (1947:80).[4] Notwithstanding, most scholars concur that strong relations between the Arabs and Buganda did not take root until the 1850s (see for instance, Gray 1947; Kiwanuka 1972).

Most informants, as well as scholars of Uganda martyrs (Howel 1948; Faupel 1984; Langley 1966; Cullen N.d), agreed that it was because of their refusal to have sex with Ssekabaka Mwanga II that the young pages who had become Christians were persecuted in the late 1880s. Further, Pirouet wrote that:

> Ssekabaka Mwanga II was given to the practice of sodomy, allegedly
> learnt from the Arabs, and the Christian pages often arranged to be
> missing when Ssekabaka Mwanga II wanted them, or else outrightly
> refused to gratify him. Mwafu's absence enraged the Kabaka because
> this page was still compliant: if he were now learning Christianity, Ssek-
> abaka Mwanga II was likely to lose this partner (1995: 107).

To justify that Ssekabaka Mwanga II killed the young pages because they disgraced him, one informant questioned why there were no female martyrs when it is known that some women, who lived in the palace, had converted to Christianity. He said "my grandparent told me that there were also women who were Christians; why is it that Ssekabaka Mwanga II did not kill them?" (anonymous, interview). As a matter of fact, B. M. Zimbe, a former page wrote that: "many people went to see the tragic death of the three boys and one of these was a girl who had been converted to Christianity and was called Sala Nalwanga. She went to where the boys were imprisoned and they sung together to God. The executioners questioned her if she followed the same religion as the rebels and she said yes. . . . [The three boys,] thus became the first martyrs in Buganda. . . . Sala was now set free and she afterwards married the Rev. Duta Kitakule (1939: 125–126).[5] Namirembe was also a Catholic (Faupel 1984: 89), but was not killed. Further, Princess Nalumansi contradicted the rules of the land when after baptism got married in church to a Joseph Kaddu, a Catholic. J. F. Faupel wrote, "In the eyes of the pagans these acts were crimes for the most serious nature, bound to provoke the vengeance of the gods in the form of some public calamity. They thought that the Princess and her husband should be burnt to death, to expiate the offence and to appease the outraged gods" (1984: 129).

As David Kavulu rightly pointed out, "Beyond the fact that all Ganda and mission sources claim that homosexual indulgences at Ssekabaka Mwanga II's court were introduced to Ganda society by Arabs, it is still difficult to establish the origin of the practices" (1969:18). The claim that "the Arabs introduced into Buganda a vice which was completely unknown before and for which no word existed in the language, the vice of homosexuality or sodomy" (Faupel 1984: 9) cannot stand unchallenged. Murray and Roscoe have also noted that in many African societies where there is evidence of same-sex relationships, homosexual tendencies have been denied on the basis of "no words for those who desire their own sex" (1998a: 267).

The discursive strategies that have historically been used to construct and define "the orient," as described in Edward Said's *Orientalism* (1979), inform my discussion here. According to Said,

> Orientalism is a style of thought based upon an ontological and epistemological distinction made between 'the orient' and (most of the time) 'the occident.' . . . Orientalism can be discussed and analyzed as a corporate institution for dealing with the orient—dealing with it by statements about it, authoring views of it, describing it, teaching it, selling it, ruling over it: in short, orientalism as a Western style for dominating, restricting, and having authority over the orient" (1979: 2–3).

Indeed, "without examining orientalism as a discourse one cannot possibly understand the enormously systematic discipline by which European culture was able to manage—and even—produce the orient politically, sociologically, militarily, ideologically, scientifically, and imaginatively during the post-Enlightenment period" (ibid.). Similarly, European missionaries managed to orientalize the Arabs by claiming that they introduced a vice which was not known in Buganda, hence constructing them as the "sinful ones" who infected the Baganda with their evil.

Following is my deconstruction of the European orientalization of the Arabs. First, we must question the sources of the homosexual allegation and their biases. Most reports available were authored by European missionaries who were rivals of the "'fanatical Arab Muslims'" (Kiwanuka 1972: 179) and who believed that sodomy was common among the Arabs. For instance, Père Lourdel, one of the first Catholic Missionaries, wrote that:

> If we are to accept the statements of trustworthy people, the Baganda had more normal and simple customs before the coming of the Arabs and their followers. It is they [the Arabs] who initiated these poor people . . . into their infamous practices . . . (quoted in Faupel 1984: 9).

Second, the justification that homosexuality was not known in Buganda because the Baganda had no word for it (Faupel 1984: 9) is not convincing. The Baganda use the term *bisiyaga* to refer to "sodomy" and "[o] kulya bisiyaga is to commit sodomy" (Snoxall 1967:23). The term specifically refers to male homosexuality. On the other hand, female homosexuality is referred to as *kasaawe* (anonymous communication). A number of informants argued that homosexuality must have been introduced by the Arabs since the root word of *siyaga* is of Arabic origin. Mohammed Kiggundu, an Arabic specialist and a lecturer at Makerere University, said that the root word of *bisiyaga* is *siag* in Arabic.[6] According to the *Modern Arabic-English Dictionary* by Rohi Baalbaki, *siag* means:

> Goldsmithery, goldsmithing, forming, formation, shaping, fashioning, molding, framing, working, forging, creating, originating, making, drafting, drawing up, formulating, putting down in writing, composing, couching (1997: 704).

Although the implied meaning of *siag* is not apparent from the dictionary, Kiggundu explained that, "in Arabic, anything which man does against nature as per the creation of God or *Allah* is *siag;* that is doing something that is unnatural and ungodly" (ibid.).

Although the root word of *bisiyaga* is from Arabic, this evidence is not enough to claim that Arabs introduced homosexuality even though most of the foreign items that were introduced in Buganda took on root words from the languages of the people that introduced them. For instance, *saaliti* is shirt, which was introduced by the Europeans. According to Katambula Busuulwa, who is a Luganda specialist, the word *ebisiyaga* first appeared in Luganda writing in the first translated Luganda Bible (personal communication). European missionaries translated this Bible with the assistance of the Baganda. While there is the possibility that the Baganda had no word for homosexuality, which is also true for the word heterosexuality, the European missionaries may have adapted the term *siag* (the Arabic term used to refer to homosexual practices) as a root word for the Luganda term *bisiyaga*. Further, even if the Baganda actually practiced homosexuality before the Arabs came and indeed had the term for it, how could they have admitted to the practice if the missionaries were condemning it?

Third, Kaggwa's claim that the Baganda had never heard of "sodomy" (1952: 172) overlooks the fact that public discussion of gender and sex, let alone sexuality, was a taboo among the Baganda. Moreover, if sodomy is considered a vice, how would he expect people to talk about it, let alone practice it openly except in culturally protected contexts like the palace in which the *kabaka* was only answerable to himself? And yet, even in the twenty-first-century, people are still denying the existence of homosexuality. The palace had immunity about certain behaviors, which were a taboo for the commoners to indulge in (see, for instance, Musisi 1991a: 79). Moreover, servants who were trained to conceal all his secrets surrounded the king. B. M. Zimbe, a former page, wrote that:

> There was a custom that the Kabaka of Buganda only wanted to be given young boys aged ten to fourteen years because they said that a big boy does not learn and does not know how to serve. They had a saying: 'if a tree grows crooked, it cannot be straightened later without breaking' (1939:3, quoted in Fallers 1964: 171).

Zimbe continued to say that the young pages were preferred because they were more easily tamed. Similarly, Richards reported that, "in the old days obedience was even more necessary. A careless page at the Kabaka's court might be killed for his inattention to an order" (1964a: 262). Further, John Vernon Taylor notes that although not all the four to five hundred pages "had much contact with the Kabaka, yet there is plenty of evidence that many became deeply attached to their master" (1979: 23).

Fourth, the configuration of the *kabakas'* palaces and chiefs' enclosures were possible environments for homosexual practices. Although there were many men and women in the kings' palaces, they lived in strict seclusion and were not allowed to interact freely. This kind of socialization within the palaces and the chiefs' enclosures existed long before the coming of the Arabs. As Roscoe points out, "Both the King and the chiefs exercised a certain amount of restraint over their wives, who could only visit or see other people with their husbands' consent. Wives always lived in the women's quarters, and no man could enter these [quarters] without the husband's permission" (1911: 93–94). In their study of homosexuality in Africa, Murray and Roscoe concluded that, "In several cases, age-differentiated male homosexuality occurred in settings in which women were excluded or absent. These included indigenous African court [for example, Buganda], warrior camps, and trading parties, as well as colonial mining compounds and plantations" (1998a: 268).

Moreover, as a rule, there was only one Man (the King) in the palace, and all the *bakopi* (male and females) were his "wives." During my research, I visited Mengo palace in Kyaddondo County. I was surprised when I knelt down, as required by the Kiganda culture, to greet the *bambowa* (the *kabaka's* guards) at the main entrance, only to be told that "in here, there is only one Man that you have to kneel before, and that is *ssaabasajja,* the king. However, if we go outside the palace, you may kneel before us" ("Muno mulimu omusajja omu yekka gw'olina okufukaamirira, ye Ssaabasajja. *Naye bwe tufuluma ebweru, oyinza okutufukaamirira*") (anonymous, communication). Indeed, they escorted me outside the gates of the palace, and when I knelt down to bid them farewell, they accepted my respect. They told me that they were also "women" like me. They said, "We are also wives like you; our husband is one, *ssaabasajja*" ("*ffe naffe tuli bakyala nga ggwe; baffe ali omu ye Ssaabasajja*") (ibid.).

In fact, during the seventh-coronation anniversary in 2000, I observed that majority of the Baganda men knelt before the king as a sign of their submissiveness and a show of great respect.[7] Further, both men and women referred to the king as *nnanyinimu* and *omufumbo,* titles given to a husband. Explaining the meaning of these titles, Nsimbi, wrote: "This name means that the king is the owner of the country Buganda. Buganda is related to a big family, in which [the king] is a married man, the head of the family. Sometimes, his men spoke thus: 'my husband—or our husband'" (1996: 32). The king, as the "husband," controlled both female-women and male-women's sexuality. For example, one informant said that "there was nobody who was allowed to touch any woman while in the palace [all women, male and female belonged to the king]; the king's guards had all the power to arrest and tie with ropes anybody who tried to do it" *("tewali yakirisibwanga kuk-watakwata mukazi yenna mu lubiri era abambowa baalina obuvunaanyizibwa okukwata oyo yenna eyandigezezaako okukikola ne bamusiba emigwa")* (anonymous, interview). I have already mentioned how the pages that refused Ssekabaka Mwanga II's advances ended up losing their lives.

Fifth, one must question the cultural emasculinization of *male bakopi* within the palace. Why does the Kiganda culture construct *male bakopi* as women in the palace and yet they become men outside the palace? While it is an ideological means through which the *kabaka* could dominate his male subjects, as in homosexual relations, hegemonic control is also evident. By constructing these males as women, the *kabaka* could easily control their sexuality within the palace. On the other hand, the existence of homosexual practice among the chiefs outside the palace is explained by the fact that it was among the pages that the king chose his chiefs. This palace setting strongly suggests that the Baganda had gendered homosexuality within the palace. Gendered homosexuality, as Serena Nanda defines it, is "A sex/gender ideology in which males who take the receptor role in the same-sex sexual relationship are also expected to, and do, adopt feminine behaviors" (2000: 107).

While I have argued that the Baganda may have practiced homosexuality before the Arabs came, it is also possible that Arab traders who came to Buganda, like other cultures, may have practiced homosexuality. In fact, Ssemakula Kiwanuka, a Muganda historian who suggested that homosexuality existed before the arrival of the Arabs also mentioned that:

> Equally significant was that the Arabs, unlike the Christian missionaries, did not violently oppose Baganda customs and religious practices. True enough, the customs the Christian missionaries found intolerable, such as polygamy, homosexuality and the slave trade, were, in fact, encouraged and practiced by the Arabs themselves (1972: 180).

The assumption that both the Arabs and the Baganda practiced homosexuality explains why the Arabs did not challenge the very practice they were involved in themselves. While it is not the main focus of this book to trace when and who introduced homosexuality in Buganda, it is important to note that it is after the coming of the foreigners outside Africa that homosexuality was openly recorded in Buganda's history. However, I strongly contend that although the Baganda may have been influenced by the contact with other non-African cultures, there is no concrete evidence that Arabs introduced homosexuality in Buganda. It is more likely that the Baganda practiced homosexuality long before any foreign influence.

MALE DANCERS: COCKS LAYING EGGS?

If baakisimba is a women's dance, what does it mean for males outside the palace to perform a dance that participates in defining a woman gender?[8] What does it mean for men to perform a dance that signifies women's sexuality, submissiveness, productivity, and reproductivity? Are these dancers, as several performers called them, "cocks laying eggs"? There were mixed views about men dancers among the Baganda interviewed. The majority of the informants referred to these dancers, especially the young men, as "cocks laying eggs." They compared men's dancing to cocks laying eggs, an activity, which according to nature is impossible. This metaphor relates to the Baganda's proverb, which goes: "Amaanyi gampweddeko: ng'omusajja azaala. 'My strength is finished' (says the lazy man). (And they answer him ironically) like that of a man who brings forth. [Meaning] That might happen to a woman. But not to a man" (Walser 1982: 40, no. 0432). This metaphor of cocks laying eggs suggests the abnormality of male dancers. In terms of gender constructed outside the palace, these dancers are social outcasts since they subvert their "natural" gender as men and reproduce themselves as womanly-males, the "cocks that lay eggs."

On the other hand, some informants interpreted the male's dancing as a form of empowerment because men are able to perform the women's role effectively. It was an affirmation of men's power as people with ability beyond what "nature" prescribes for them. One female informant exclaimed, "There is nothing that a man cannot do! After all, he has to be in control of everything" *("omusajja ye talina kimulema! Ate era, y'alina kusajjalata busajjalaasi mubuli kintu")* (interview). Similarly, Margaret Mead has also observed that, "no art is recognized as an art until men do it, from cooking to medicine to dance" (quoted in Hanna 1988:147). It is ironical because while dancing is regarded as empowering men, drumming demeans the woman. As such, because dancing is looked at as an empowerment these males do not revoke their gender; they are considered even more powerful. Why is comparable behavior admired in men and denigrated in women? Why are women judged so differently when they beat drums, supposedly a men's role, and yet when men perform a women's dance, they are venerated as being powerful? This section interrogates the role of male-women and men dancers, and how their participation in baakisimba redefines gender in Buganda. I examine the ways in which baakisimba creates a space for constructing alternative identities.

Although males outside the palace began dancing formalized baakisimba at wedding parties in the 1940s, it was after the abolition of Kingship and especially from the 1980s that more womanly-males "encroached" on the women's dancing space. A number of reasons account for this drastic change. First, as the dance became a commercial enterprise, men were attracted to baakisimba for monetary reasons. Moreover, men dancers were paid more than the women dancers. Sulaimani Mukwaya explained that: "because men dancers were few and rare, the audience was always happy to see them dance and considered the men dancers powerful" (interview). In this case, whereas baakisimba provides a terrain of gender struggle, it offers opportunities for social and economic advancement.

Second, the informants who rejected these dancers argue that some males, especially the young dancers, perform the dance because they want to attract fellow males. One informant said, "You know our country got spoiled a long time ago. Some men dancers practice homosexuality" (anonymous, interview). Informants enumerated six womanly-male dancers that allegedly homosexuals and three other dancers were already dead. They stressed, however, that not all young male dancers were homosexuals. I had a closer observation of three of the alleged male homosexual dancers both on stage and off stage, in the dressing rooms together with women dancers. I had the opportunity to interview one of them at his home and later in the chapter; I present the most salient issues of our discussion. Moreover, my informants' views about these male dancers while on stage and off stage in their "normal" lives informs my discussion. In order to protect their identities, I do not mention their names or include their pictures for ethical reasons.

During one of the wedding ceremonies that I attended, there were five women dancers and a male dancer. However, it was not easy for one to identify the gender of this dancer unless one paid closer attention. In front of me were seated a man and a woman, who argued throughout the dance performance whether this dancer was a man or a woman.[9] These people drew my attention to a closer look at all dancers so as to be certain of their sex, since I realized it was not necessarily that all dancers were females and, therefore women since they were performing outside the palace contexts. Indeed, if I had not known this dancer before the performance, I would have mistaken him for a female. But was this dancer a man or a woman? The way this dancer appeared on stage challenged the Baganda's categorization of men and women. Given the fact that this dancer was performing outside the palace, where all males are supposed to be men, one expected this dancer to maintain an identity of a man. Based on his physical appearance, dancing style, and costume, this dancer constructed an alternative identity. While in Buganda "men unlike women follow a rule of simplicity in their appearance [;] they lay completely little stress on bodily ornamentation and other accessories" (Nanono 1977: 3), this dancer had treated hair, painted nails, pierced ear with one earring, a ring on the forefinger, and a bracelet. Moreover, the dancer had a bleached face and seemed to have used a cream that left no trace of a beard.[10] The major distinction from the other dancers this dancer had was the masculine body structure and lack of protruding breasts.

Beyond the dance motifs, which project the womanliness among the Baganda, the dance costume presented this dancer as a woman rather than a man. Like women dancers, he was dressed in a petticoat and a bra. On top of the petticoat, he put on *kikooyi* (pl. *bikooyi),* a sheet of cloth wrapped as a skirt that reached down to the ankles. On top of the *kikooyi,* he tied on a *kigyenge* (dancing skirt made of strips of thread) and the *kaliba* (animal's skin with fur) around the waist. All the informants I interviewed agreed that although male-women's dance costumes have changed over time, they have always been distinct from that of women. Peter Ggayira explained that male dancers used to put on trousers when dancing. He said that even when they changed to *bikooyi,* they did not put on long ones down to the ankles; theirs stopped at the knees, a distinction from the women's dressing (interview). Further, Tereza Kisolo said that in the 1950s dancers used to perform bare chest, and with a *kanzu* (men's robe of Arabic origin) tied around their waists. However, I have also seen male dancers dressed in vests, instead of bras or bare chests. What does it mean when a male outside the palace adapts a dance and its costumes that project the conceived identity of Baganda women?

In this case, my discussion points to what Murray and Roscoe have called "gender-based homosexuality" (1998b: 8). Gender-based homosexuals typically appear and behave like stereotypes of women, conforming to the behaviors and social roles of women. These homosexuals' "behavior is often an exaggeration of that of women, and they fulfill some but not all the social roles of women (for example, women's productive work but not their reproductive roles)" (ibid.). In this case, baakisimba creates possible avenues through which males outside the palace define themselves as women.

MALE-WOMEN DANCING: HOMOSEXUALITY IN THE PALACE?

Like the origin of baakisimba, it is not certain when male-women began performing baakisimba in the palace. Sulaiti Kalungi speculated that male-women began to perform the dance in the palace during Ssekabaka Suuna II's reign (interview). Although they could not name specific dancers, the informants at Ssekabaka Suuna II's tombs confirmed that there were male-women dancers during the Kabaka's reign (anonymous, interview). Further, there is evidence that male-women danced in Ssekabaka Muteesa I's palace. As already mentioned in Chapter Four, during Ssekabaka Muteesa I's reign, a number of raids to Busoga brought in, among other things, many musicians and dancers. And since among the Busoga there were no restrictions that limited men's participation in dancing, males could also dance, when they came to Buganda, they continued with their practice. It was during Ssekabaka Muteesa I's reign that the biggest number of male-women dancers was recorded.[11] Zimbe wrote that:

> Kabaka [Ssekabaka Muteesa I] chose boys who were the best dancers and one of them was very black whom they called *Omuddugavu Kagongolo,* but was very handsome and his Lusoga name was Bifakumbuga or Bibino, meaning 'what is up in the chief's enclosure.' Kabaka liked this boy very much and changed his name saying, he should be called Balikubuga. . . . To prove that he was favourite, Kabaka used to send him some of the royal food (akatuuso), food and meat which was specially cooked for him (1939, translated by Kalibala n.d.:43).

When performing baakisimba in the palace, the male-women dancers adopted, in most cases, similar movements, costumes, and formations as those of the female-women dancers. Like the female-women dancers, the male-women dancers emphasized the waist wriggling as the core of their dance motifs. While they adopted a different movement in *kweyanza/ kweyanjula* motif, the movement they adopted communicated the same message of submission. Instead of kneeling, as the female-women dancers, the male-women dancers prostrated. When the dancer prostrated before the king, he expressed submissiveness and the commitment to offer the best of his dancing to the king. Lugira has written that, "Official dances for the king symbolized not only pleasure and honor rendered to the monarch, but also exhibited submission to the king through prostrations which often took place in the course of the dance (1972: 140).

The male-women dancers' costume differed only slightly from that of the female-women dancers. Lwewunzika, a former male-woman dancer, told me that with bare chest, the male-women dancers wore a sheet of bark cloth below their waists. Like the female-women, they also tied a skirt, made out of banana leaves on top of a sash, made out of bark cloth, around their waists. In 1940, the costume was changed; the *bikooyi,* an Indian fabric, and cotton linen, which were initially introduced by the Arabs, replaced bark cloth. However, the fashion was maintained. The bare-chest male-women dancers wore long skirts that covered the ankles, while the female-women wore *bikooyi,* which also covered their ankles. Instead of the *mpina,* both dancers wore dance skins from goats or, serval cat. In addition, both dancers had the *kasongezo,* a strip of white linen cloth that was worn under the skirt before tying on the sash and a dance skin. Explaining why they used the *kasongezo,* Lwewunzika said that it was intended to replace the waist beads, which would make the dancer uncomfortable had she worn the real beads. Lwewunzika said that it was exciting to men for women to wear beads and so, since dancing was meant to make the audience "happy," they had to wear the *kasongezo.* He mentioned that the *kasongezo* had to be kept as spackling white so that even someone far in the audience would see it. Although petticoats were later introduced to cover the exposed bellies of the women "even us men began dressing in petticoats so as to be uniform with the [female-] women" (Lwewunzika, interview). Much as this exaggerated costume aimed at revealing the dancers' waist movement, it also projected the constructed women's beauty.

While there was an instituted code of dressing within the court, these male-women dancers explored an alternative space. Outside the dance space, "The death sentence was imposed on courtiers or pages who accidentally exposed limbs in a fashion thought indecent. . . ." (Richards 1964b: 298). In this case, the male-women had to dress in a similar fashion to that of female-women dancers since their role during the dance performance was to make the king happy. As such, rules could be bent in order to give pleasure to the king.

Were male-women "laying eggs" in the palace when they danced before the king? Although they were gendered as women, sexually they were males. What does it mean for these males to perform a dance that defined female sexuality in an environment where homosexuality is said to have flourished? When the male-women performed baakisimba in the palace, they were performing their woman gender, their identity as sexual objects. In this case, baakisimba legitimizes the power of the king to manipulate the male's sexuality and the male-women gender identity and roles. One is tempted to imagine that male-women danced in the palace in order to satisfy the sexual desires of the Baganda kings.

BAAKISIMBA: SPACE FOR MALE HOMOSEXUAL DANCERS

While homosexual orientations are publicly dismissed among the majority of the Baganda, baakisimba performance presents a possibility where male homosexuals acquire for themselves a space that is somehow "concealed" and relatively "safe." By becoming a dancer, a male homosexual occupies a space, which is constrained in ordinary discourse. While they are highly discriminated against, through performance, male homosexuals are able to negotiate and manipulate their identity in a restrictive society. Similarly, Hanna has noted that one option, among many, for male homosexuals in the United States to escape stigmatization "was to go into dance, a metonym and metaphor of existence, for life is movement." In this section, I present my encounter with a male homosexual dancer. Although this dancer did not explicitly declare his homosexual orientation, my observations, and interviews with him, and opinions from people around him as co-performers, members of the audience and the neighbors where he lived, inform my discussion.

This dancer, whom I will call "Julie-Tom," is of medium height, medium body statue, and light complexion (from bleaching). Julie-Tom always wore a treated French-cut hairdo and had a completely shaved beard with an obvious use of a smoothening cream. Julie-Tom usually had a left earring and rings on his two baby fingers, and had all "his" fingernails painted. However, he maintained man gendered-clothing, trousers and shirts. And yet, when performing baakisimba, he dressed like the women dancers with facial makeup. In Buganda, men mainly wear trousers and rarely do women wear trousers, although in cities and educational institutions college girls wear trousers. Based on biological traits, the Baganda would consider Julie-Tom a man; however, with this makeup and hairdo, Julie-Tom does not fit the constructed appearance of Baganda men. "He" is not a woman, since it is clear that he is a male and all males outside the palace ought to be men.

I first met Julie-Tom at a wedding ceremony where he was a dancer. I happened to know one of the women dancers with whom Julie-Tom performed, who invited me to their dressing room. I found Julie-Tom folding a piece of cloth to put beneath the *kikooyi* to create big buttocks like the women dancers. Besides Julie-Tom, other women dancers were folding clothes for their buttocks too. When I asked Julie-Tom why he had to put an extra cloth beneath the *kikooyi,* Julie-Tom told me that dancers with big buttocks dance better. However, one of the women dancers interjected and said, "he is lying; a man dancer does not need it" (*"wamma oyo alimba, omusajja omuzinyi tekyetaagisa"*) (anonymous communication). Nonetheless, Julie-Tom was not disturbed; he went ahead with his dressing. He asked for a mirror to make sure that his hair was neat for the stage. If I had not seen Julie-Tom before (behind the stage), seeing him on stage from a distance, I would not have known that he was not a woman. I was surprised that I never heard anybody among the audience questioning his identity probably because Julie-Tom was dancing well like his fellow women dancers. In fact, a number of people from the audience applauded him as they did the other dancers.

I had the opportunity to speak to some women dancers after the performance. When I commented about Julie-Tom's skill as a dancer, I provoked one woman dancer who replied bluntly:

> Moreover, that one practices homosexuality. Many dancers of these days have spoiled themselves; they do womanish things. But that one in particular, practices homosexuality and he is also a prostitute. Moreover, he always imitates women's behaviors; for instance, the way he speaks, rolling his eyes and growing long nails! But I think this world is becoming insane. It is surprising to see a male desiring a fellow male and he leaves the females. Indeed, I am surprised by that kind of behavior.
>
> *Oyo ndaba mulyi wabisiyaga. Abazinyi b'ennaku zino bangi beeyonoonye. Beekola eby'ekikazikazi. Naye ate oyo aliira ddala ebisiyaga ne yeetunda n'okwetunda. Ate n'ekikulu ayagala nnyo ekwekola eby'ekikazi. Yeekola okwegingaginga enjogera, okumoolamoola amaaso, n'okukuza enjala empanvu. Naye kweggamba ensi eno ndowooza eyonoonese bwonoonesi! Kyewuunyisa okulaba ng'omusajja yegomba musajja munne n'alekawo omukazi wali. Kale nze ekintu ekyo nkyewuunya!* (anonymous, communication).

The same view about Julie-Tom's identity was confirmed by the main drummer of the group who told me that they had been trying to counsel him. This drummer said that, "in fact, Julie-Tom was worse." These comments prompted me to find out more about Julie-Tom. I made an appointment to interview Julie-Tom, and we met two weeks later.

Unfortunately, when I went to look for Julie-Tom on the appointed date, I could not find his place immediately because I had misunderstood the directions. However, I remembered that Julie-Tom had told me that most of his neighbors knew him and that I only needed to ask for a man who had a hair salon. I met three women and a man at a shop quite close to Julie-Tom's beauty salon. When I asked them for the directions, one of the women answered back with a disgusted expression: "you mean this one who behaves like a woman? The one who does womanish things?" (*"ogamba ono eyeeyisa ng'omukazi? Ono eyeekola eby'ekikazi?"*). I dodged the question and insisted that I was looking for the man who owned a hair salon. They all looked at me, wondering what I wanted from this "Julie-Tom man." From their facial expression, they seemed like saying, "Do not waste your time; he is not a man. He is lying you." I introduced myself, "I am Nnaalongo Nannyonga," with the hope that once I tell them I am nnaalongo, a mother of twins, they would not think of me as a conned woman. Fortunately, before they could ask me anymore questions, Julie-Tom emerged and we left. He decided that we go to his home, knowing that his customers at the salon would interrupt us. I did not feel comfortable walking with him to his home, because it seemed as if we were on a big stage screen for everyone to see. I could read people's faces as saying "what does she want from him?"

Entering Julie-Tom's house, it became immediately clear to me that Julie-Tom did not behave like the majority of the men I knew. His single-roomed home was too neat and decorated to be a home for a single man who was not married to a woman. He had very white hand-made tablecloths covered decoratively around the room. He had three flowerpots; one on the small-sized fridge, another on the coffee table and the other on cupboard, which was also covered with a tablecloth. Everything in his room seemed to be organized in a certain order. The only pictures that I saw hanging on the wall were posters of wrestling men. Although I was convinced at this point that Julie-Tom was homosexual, I could not confront him with direct questions that would make him suspicious and lose the confidence to talk to me, not to mention throwing me out of his house. Here, I present some of the most salient issues of our interview as well as issues raised by other people who knew Julie-Tom. I discuss issues mainly related to the ways in which baakisimba, and dance in general, forms a liberating space for Julie-Tom. However, this space that Julie-Tom and other male homosexuals occupy is not uncontested. Although no one confronts Julie-Tom directly, a hidden transcript of disapproval is performed behind his back (Scott 1990). Despite of all this, he still survives because the dance space is one of the few sites where he can enact his hidden transcript. Therefore, I also present issues that relate to the contested space that Julie-Tom shares with women dancers.

Although Julie-Tom began to learn baakisimba when he was a child, he never belonged to a semi-professional group until he was in his mid twenties. Julie-Tom, who is now in his mid-thirties, believes that his dancing is inherited, although none of his family members that he knows of is a musician or a dancer. Julie-Tom was inspired to dance when he saw a man dancing at a wedding ceremony one day. Since he became a dancer, Julie-Tom performed with a number of dancing ensembles at wedding ceremonies, in hotels for tourists, and as part of touring ensembles in countries surrounding Uganda.

How does dancing facilitate the definition of Julie-Tom, the identity he desires to be? Although Julie-Tom admitted that men were not meant to be dancers, he does not see anything wrong with a man dancing. In a small voice with a lot of gestured expressions, he said, "It is true, men were not meant to be dancers. In fact, my parents too never wanted me to dance, but when I became of age, they could not control me any longer" (*"Kyo kituufu ffe abasajja tetwali bazinyi era n'abazzadde bange tebaayagala nnyo nnyingire byamazina bino. Naye bwe nakula nga tebakyasobola kunkugira"*). He said that it is mainly his socialization as a child that drew him to dancing. He contended, "Dancing was meant to be a women's role, but I can also dance. As a child, I performed many roles culturally assigned to women; in our home, we never had roles restricted to boys or girls. I also had a schedule to cook during the week." (*"Amazina gwali mulimu gwa bakazi naye nange ngusobola. Nze wennakulira nakola nnyo emirimu gy'ekikazi. Ewaffe awaka tewaaliwo nti guno mulimu gwa musajja nti guno gwa mukazi. Nange nabeerangako n'ekiyungu buli wiiki"*). Although Baganda girls and boys are socialized differently, Julie-Tom is one of the few exceptions. Few parents train their boy children in women's chores like cooking.

Besides dancing, Julie-Tom participates in activities that are considered to be for women. Julie-Tom owns a beauty salon.[12] Julie-Tom's job becomes another controversial issue regarding his identity in a society where specific jobs still define people's gender identities. In addition to the salon where he specializes in treating women's hair, Julie-Tom said, "for me I know very much how to make tablecloths and these ones you see in my home, it is me who made them" (*Nze manyi nnyo okuluka ebitambaala era nabino ebiri mu nnyumba nze nabiruka"*). Julie-Tom believes that although he is a male, there are some things that men do that he cannot do, and even though he is not a woman, there are some things "traditionally" done by women that he is comfortable doing. Relating, with disgust, to the assignment of specific gender roles, Julie-Tom said:

> The idea of saying that a man does not do this and that, a woman does this; I see it as taking away our freedom. Although I was created as a man, there are some roles for men that I cannot do. Now why shouldn't I do what I am able to do instead of forcing myself onto assigned roles of men that I cannot perform well? For me I can only dance, I tried to learn how to drum, but I failed it.

> *Ekyokugamba nti omusajja takola kino, omukazi akola kino nze ndaba byakutumala mirembe gyaffe. Kubanga nze yadde natonndebwa nga ndi musajja naye waliwo emirimu egy'ekisajja gye sisobola. Kati lwaki sikola*

ekyo kye nsobola okusinga okwepaatika ku by'abasajja. Nze nsobola kuzina,
engoma, nagigezaako naye yannema.

From this stance, when Julie-Tom dances, he is not only doing it for pleasure, but he is actually contesting the very structures that he believes constrained his freedom. Similar to Nnabanoba, the *nakawanga* drummer (discussed in Chapter Five), for Julie-Tom to dance is to be himself. The dance affords him the opportunity to do those things he feels he can do best, which the Baganda society restricts "him" from doing. As a dancer, like the women dancers, Julie-Tom shares in the power to control and manipulate the sexual desires of his audience. When dancing, Julie-Tom is very good; he attracts both men and women. In this case Julie-Tom is even more powerful, since he controls both men and women. While some women look at him as a potential sexual partner, fellow male homosexuals desire him too. This dual identity allows Julie-Tom to disguise his true identity. He told me, that on a number of occasions women and men have confronted him after performances, with suggestive invitations. He said:

> When I begin dancing, because of my appearance and the way I dance, people admire me. Sometimes one of the members of the audience would ask me 'where do you live? You dance so well!' Then, I direct him or her and he or she comes to visit me. My dear, these people become my real friends!

> *Kati kweggamba bwemba ntandise okuzina, okusinziira ku ndabika yange era ne kye nkola, abantu banneegomba. Oluusi oli akubuuza nti 'yii obeera ludda wa, ng'ozina bulungi?' N'omulagirirra. Oba oli awo ng'omulaba azze akunoonya. Munange abantu bafuukira ddala mikwano gyange!*

When I asked him about his socialization, he told me that it has been easier for him to get along well with men as opposed to women. He said, "My dear, I have to be cautious about [AIDS]" (*"Munange nina okwegendereza siri-imu"*). In fact, he told me that the majority of his fans and friends are men and he feels safe that way. Further, he stressed that it was very risky to trust women.

It was apparent, however, that Julie-Tom was occupying a contested space. While dancing offered him a possibility to realize who he wanted to be, the women dancers are in competition with him for the same space. As the men drummers control the drumming arena, the women dancers desire to control the domain of dance. He complained, "Some women dancers do not like me very much, because of the way I dance. When they see that I get more audience than they do, it hurts them. You know, people are surprised that I am soft and I can dance" *("Abakyala abazinyi abamu tebanjagala. Engeri gyenzinamu, bwe balaba nga nfuna odiyensi okubasinga kibaluma. Omanyi abantu bakyewuunya nnyo okulaba ng'omusajja ngonda, ne nzina!").* I then asked him whether women dancers envy him because he is a male dancing or because he is just a good dancer. He answered:

> Some people in the kind of audiences we perform for enjoy seeing men dancing. So, when the women dancers see me dancing so well, with skills that attract the audience to give me money tips, it does not make them feel good.

> *Odiyensi zetubeeramu abantu abamu banyumirwa nnyo abasajja nga bazina. Kati abakyala abazinyi bwe balaba nga ggwe omusajja ozinye bulingi, n'owoomesa ekintu kyo ne bakufuuwa, abakyala abo muli kiba tekibayisa bulungi.*

One of the drummers with whom Julie-Tom performs confirmed what Julie-Tom told me. This drummer said that there are also members of the audience who are homosexual and who enjoy seeing men dancing. The drummer confided that, "although they never come out in the open, they [male homosexuals] are there and they enjoy such dancing as that of [Julie-Tom]" *("yadde tebavaayo mulujjudde, naye gye bali era banyumirwa nnyo amazina ng'ago oyo")* (anonymous, interview). In this case, dancing contexts lay the grounds for solidarity among homosexuals in a society where they are considered outcasts.

While Julie-Tom and other male homosexuals dancers find a voice in performing baakisimba and other Kiganda women dances (*nankasa* and *mbaga*), this voice is not unchallenged. Homosexual dancers struggle against homophobia and discrimination on an everyday basis. Nonetheless, dancing provides a site through which both male homosexual dancers and homosexual members of the audience can identify themselves. When male homosexuals perform baakisimba dance, they confirm that "on the fringe of society and receptive to the unconventional, the art world offers gay men an opportunity to express an aesthetic sensibility that is emotional and erotic, an insulation from a reflecting society, an avenue of courtship and an arena in which to deal with homosexual concerns" (Hanna 1988:136). By becoming a baakisimba dancer, the male homosexual dancer refocuses his non-homosexual audience away from his sexual orientation to the justification of his dancing as an art. At the same time, he is able to identify with the homosexual audience with whom he shares his emotional and erotic feelings. On the other hand, Julie-Tom's dancing is condemned in some circles. One of the women dancers who performed with Julie-Tom complained, "On my side, I condemn Julie-Tom's behavior. Because as a man, he should remain a man. For a man to behave in an enticing way, like a woman; to me, it does not look good" (*"Nze ku lwange [Julie-Tom] muvumirira. Kubanga ye ng'omusajja yandisigaddeyo ng'omusajja. Naye omusajja okweligomba ddala ng'omukazi, nze ku lwange tekindabikira bulungi"*) (anonymous, interview).

Another woman dancer was particularly unhappy with Julie-Tom's cross dressing in and outside dance contexts. Julie-Tom's earrings, treated hair and his bleached face specifically disturbed her. However, she was not disturbed by Julie-Tom's dancing. She said Julie-Tom was free to dance as long as he did not have to recreate "himself" as a woman. Defending why he treats his hair, and uses makeup, Julie-Tom said, "How can you attract people to come to your salon if you are looking horrible? I also have to do some makeup, so that I do not send away my customers. And another thing, now that I am a dancer, I must also look nice" (*"Kati ggwe oyinza otya okusikiriza abantu okujja mu saluuni yo ng'ate ggwe olabika bubi. Nange neekolako nneme kugoba bakasitoma. Ate n'ekirala, kati nze nga bwendi omuzinyi, nina okulabika obulungi"*). The woman informant said, however, "Julie-Tom has now improved; we just had to quarrel with him. To make him stop dressing in long *kikooyi* (dance costume) as women dancers do, was not easy at all. He would say, 'my legs are embarrassing!'" (*"Julie-Tom kati akendezzaako; twali tulina kumuvuma buvumi. Ate okumugya ku kikooyi ekiwanvu eky'abakyala zaali mpaka ng'agamba nti 'nze obugulu buswala!'"*) (anonymous, interview). Julie-Tom explained that this change in the men's costume was made after the restoration of Buganda kingdom in 1993. He said:

> In the past, we used to put on bras [like that of women], but since the restoration of kingship, men were told to dress like men. That is why men dress in vests [instead of the women's bras], short *bikooyi* or short skirts.

> *Edda twayambalanga obuleega, naye kati engeri obwakabaka bwe bwadda, kati abasajja batugamba twambale ng'abasajja. Kati abasajja kyetuva twambala vesiti n'ebikooyi oba sikaati ennyimpi.*

However, Julie-Tom contested this change and argued, "Short *kikooyi* or a short skirt makes me feel like I am naked and embarrasses me among my friends. I want to put on a long one that covers up to ankles" (*"Ekikooyi ekimpi oba sikaati, muli nze mba mpulira nga ninga akunama mu bannange. Njagala kwesiba kiwanvu mbikke bwenti obukongovule"*). As I discussed in Chapter Five, the Kiganda culture requires that women cover the ankles. The Baganda consider it inappropriate for a woman to show parts of her body. In a similar vein, Julie-Tom sees it as embarrassing for "him" to expose his legs while dancing, although it is required of men to cover their bodies only down to the knees.

Besides using the same costume, Julie-Tom competes with women in terms of the remuneration for dancing. Like other men dancers, Julie-Tom is at times paid more than the women dancers. He said that depending on the nature of the audience and performance contexts, men dancers get more money than the women dancers, especially if the host particularly requested a man dancer. Likewise, Janat Nakitto confirmed that men dancers tend to get paid more money than women dancers. She said "women give a lot of money tips to men dancers. Moreover, these days, men dancers are very lucky; fellow men also give them money tips too! It is common that you may leave the dancing stage when a male dancer has far more money than you" (*"abakyala bafuuwa nnyo abasajja abazinyi. Ate n'ekirala, abasajja balina omukisa, ennaku zino basajja bannaabwe babafuuwa nnyo. Muyinza okuva mu mazina ng'omusajja okusingira wala nnyo mu ssente!"*) (interview). As such, baakisimba offers a dialogic space where gender is performed, contested, and crystallized. Through performance contexts, dance choreography, costuming, and interaction between the audience, drummers and dancers, gender roles, relations, and identities among the Baganda take shape. Baakisimba offers a rare "stage" for performing alternative gender in Buganda.

Chapter Nine

Recapitulation

Reflecting on my school days, I questioned: "Why is it that my baakisimba music and dance teachers did not allow me to beat the drums and claimed that since I was a woman I should dance, instead? Why was I branded *nnalukalala* and *nnakawanga,* all denoting manly-female, when I beat the drum before a public audience? Why, after praising how great I was at performing baakisimba dance, did a colleague at the university of Pittsburgh, USA, from a completely different culture, ask for any sexual connotations of the dance? I recalled the religious sister performing the dance before the clergy during one of their commissioning celebrations. Then, how can baakisimba have sexual connotations if celibate sisters perform it in church? No, it cannot be true that baakisimba is a sexual dance; I believed teachers should be at least the custodians of moral standards after the monarch was abolished. How is it that school children are also allowed to perform the dance during music and dance competitions? These, and many other questions, discussed in this book, provoked the study of the relationships between baakisimba and gender identities, roles, and relations of the Baganda. My research revealed that baakisimba, a set of drums, as well as a genre of music and dance, has historically reciprocal connections with gender construction among the Baganda. My research has established that while baakisimba partakes in defining gender, gender takes part in structuring baakisimba. However, the structures of baakisimba do not simply produce gender; instead, baakisimba is at the center of Baganda's understanding of gender. It is the meanings that the Baganda construct from the performance of baakisimba that crystallize and contest gender definitions in Buganda. For instance, the Baganda's definition of the *mbuutu* as a woman drum and the *ngalabi* as the man drum exemplifies the constructed ideology of women as the subordinate characters, and men as the dominant actors in the performance of power relations between men and women.

This study has revealed that baakisimba, as a part of the Baganda's lives, intersects with social, political, and cultural structures that historically constitute the Baganda's world. Because of the complexity of gender construction in Buganda, as a biocultural and sociocultural construct, within historically shifting political, cultural, and social contexts, my academic adventures led me beyond gendered spaces. I also ventured into politics and history of, and colonialism and Christianity in Buganda, all sites that have participated in shaping and deconstructing baakisimba. In order to understand how the Baganda's historical, political, Christian, and cultural ideologies are at the core of defining gender and baakisimba, I had to appropriate an inter-disciplinary approach. Moreover, as an indigenous researcher, who had performed and taught baakisimba, I had to move away from knowing to understanding baakisimba and its connection with the Baganda, and particularly, their gender constructions. Likewise, Timothy J. Cooley has rightly stressed, "the shift in emphasis from classification, description, and explanation of music structures [as well as dance structures] toward attempts to understand music [and dance] as culture necessitates new fieldwork theories, methodologies, and epistemologies . . ." (1997:11). As such, and prompted by the research data, this study has "crossed boundaries," to use Kay Kaufman Shelemay's metaphorical term (1996). I have borrowed ideas, theories, and methodologies mainly from anthropology, ethnochoreography (study of non-Western dance), gender studies, history, cultural studies, and political science.

However, my major contribution has been particularly to ethnomusicology, gender studies, ethnochoreography, African studies, and cultural studies. I add my voice to that of a number of ethnomusicologists who have contributed to the ethnography of music and dance (see for instance essays edited by Barz and Cooley 1997). I have reemphasized the need to redefine the "field" in ethnomusicology so as to fully accommodate both scholars studying their own cultures and those studying other people's cultures. In my opinion, the field should be a dialogic place where ethnomusicologists learn about others and themselves and then communicate this knowledge to other people. I have advocated for the integration of both formal and informal researches in order to capture data, which may be important, but not collected in formal research settings. Further, as pointed out in Chapter Two, I discussed how being a member of the culture I studied did not guarantee my access to all knowledge about the Baganda. It was by working with non-indigenous scholars, Jean-Jacques Nattiez and Gerhard Kubik that I was able to collect certain data in a neo-colonial Buganda. On the other hand, knowledge of Luganda language, Kiganda culture, and being a performer of baakisimba were advantages I had over the non-indigenous scholars. Therefore, I have suggested a complete erasure of privileging the so-called "outsider" research over the "insider" research and vice versa; both types of research compliment each other in unique ways. I advocate for collaborative relationships between "indigenous" scholars and "foreign" scholars. However, when indigenous scholars work with foreign researchers, the indigenous scholars should be considered collaborators or co-researchers, but not research assistants or research coordinators, positions only slightly higher than being informants. This book has illustrated that the abilities of indigenous researchers can go beyond mere translation of data as assistants, but make critical reviews of their cultures to compliment the analyses done by foreign scholars. However, researchers must be careful not to allow informal experience to overshadow in-depth research experiences of their culture. They should aim at moving away from knowing to understanding their culture.

Fieldwork is a process of negotiating identities in the field. Ethnomusicologists carry identities in the field as people belonging to a particular race, ethnic group, class, educational background, and gender. They acquire new identities in the process of interacting with informants, teachers, friends, and relatives, who share their experiences and culture with them. I have emphasized that writing culture should be a collaborative venture between the researcher and the people being researched; the people being studied should participate in the analyses of their culture. Therefore, as I have illustrated in this work, the analyses and the final presentation of the research data should involve the interaction of the views of the people whose culture is being studied with those of the scholar. It was important to present the voices of my informants extensively, since in a number of cases we analyzed the data together. As a result, in a number of instances, I have allowed the informants to speak directly to the readers in Luganda language. While I have tried to make translations, I must confess, that I could not capture some intricate nuances of the Luganda. Presenting the direct voice of the informants addresses although, to a minimal extent, the issue of "crisis of representation," where "interpreters constantly construct themselves through the others they study (Clifford 1986:10). As such, the provision of the direct voice from the informants provides a possibility for those who may know Luganda to make their own interpretations.

This study foregrounds the conceptualization of gender as a construction, and a cultural and time specific phenomenon. The complexity of the non-conventional terms, I have used to explain the gender conceptualization of the Baganda (I apologize), only point to a small percentage of the whole story about the contradictions of gendering in Baganda. I hope that my initial proposal on the gendered language will stimulate further studies to ease the problems non-linguists face in communicating about gender constructions of non-conventional culture. Despite my attempt to theorize gender, because of the nature of the study namely, the interaction of gender and baakisimba, I could not address all the dimensions of gender in Buganda. I believe that the historical evidence I have given to support my thesis will contribute to the general history of gender construction in Buganda. It is my hope that this study will not only be a contribution to the sparse literature on gender in Africa, but will stimulate further research on the subject.

Studying baakisimba as an integration of music and dance has been a major contribution to ethnochoreography as well as ethnomusicology. While most studies of African music and dance have either focused on description of structures of dance music or dance alone, I have examined how the integration of music and dance articulate with the society from which they emerge. I hope that my initial step in a creating a notation with borrowings from Benesh notation system will stimulate further creativity in the transcription of non-Western dance. Of course, I still contend that one can only capture what actually happens in baakisimba performance, like in any other dance, by participating first as a performer, and then as a member of the audience. While visual recordings may offer an alternative, they mainly portray what the operator of the video decides to capture, leave alone the limitation that the video can only capture a specific space at a time. By suggesting further input in the transcription, my focus is mainly to facilitate analytical discussions. It is my intention that the study of baakisimba and gender of the Baganda will stimulate further research on other dance musics of the Baganda as well as other cultures. This method of music and dance analysis has great potential for scholars of ethnomusicology in Africa and beyond as a model for examining music and dance in relation to the people that create it.

The study of baakisimba and gender in Buganda has confirmed that aspects of a culture are connected in non-reductionist ways; culture is not simply reflective. Because of the historical contingence of culture, the connection between elements of culture is not stable; it is a process, never completed, always in process. Consequently, the meaning of culture, and in this case baakisimba, is very fluid. The context in which baakisimba is performed is very important to understanding how baakisimba articulates with gender. I analyzed the different meanings that emerge when baakisimba is performed in the palace, schools, churches, at beer parties, and during ceremonial festivities. In these gendered sites, men have, to a greater extent, tended to control the style of dancing and drumming. Even when baakisimba has been redefined, in many cases, its meanings conflict with the contexts in which it is performed. For instance, I pointed out how church choirmasters, as well as the religious, disagree on what constitutes "liturgical" baakisimba dance. As a result, baakisimba performance in the church has focused mainly on the music and isolated the dancing. However, even when the sisters redressed the dance in their habits, the wriggling waist still conflict with liturgical correctness of the performance of baakisimba in church. In school contexts, the trainers conceal the "traditional" meanings (especially those relating to marriage and sexuality) in order to keep the genre in schools since it is one of the dances performed at the music and dance competitions. While negotiating the "proper" baakisimba befitting the church and school contexts, trainers have selected some dance styles and costumes, while eliminating others. These aesthetic negotiations represent struggles over the meanings of baakisimba.

I have argued that baakisimba defines gender through gendered performance practice, shapes of the drums, drum sounds, dance movements, costumes, and the interaction of drummers, dancers, adjudicators, and the audience during baakisimba performances. The performance practice that assigns men drumming roles and restricts women to dancing outside the palace helps to crystallize the prescribed roles of the two genders. Since the Baganda consider the drum to symbolize power, the restriction, in this case, suggests men's association with power. Further, when the male-women perform baakisimba, a female-women's dance in the palace, they reaffirm their situational male-women role.

There are a number of ways in which gender shapes baakisimba. For instance, while performing before the king, the man among men, the dancers shuffled, yet outside the palace contexts, they were free to lift their feet as much as they liked. In this case, the man gender of the *kabaka* dictated the acceptable dance style. Furthermore, men generally control the teaching of drumming as well as dancing. My research has shown that as drum teachers, men usually teach better skills to fellow men than women. This unbalanced training process—as opposed to the biological construction that women are weaker then men—for the most part, accounts for the distinct styles of beating the drums between men and women.

My analyses offer evidence that men have restricted women from beating the drums as a means to control women's power. The Baganda men have managed to control women's access to the drums through ideological narratives (myths and customs) and other discursive practices including a discourse of honoring and preserving women's beauty. Discursive practices privileging man dominance were shaped by a particular historical relationship between the institutions of kingship, colonialism, and Christianity.

When the structures that created these hegemonic relations broke down, new counter-hegemonic possibilities could be negotiated. Men could no longer control women's access to drumming in the public space. In Chapter Five, I noted that after the abolition of the Buganda kingdom, the chief custodian of the Kiganda customs, women got more access to the public sphere. As more women become educated, coupled with a discourse of emancipation in schools, churches, and local clubs, women began redefining their spaces. The voice of Rehema Nnabanoba, a fluent woman drummer, speaks loudly as an illustration of women's active participation in cultural transformation. Nnabanoba, like other assigned manly-females, is a voice of resistance to men's domination in Buganda.

Throughout the book, baakisimba presents itself as a multivocal site through which gender is negotiated. While baakisimba presents women as sexual and submissive objects, it presents them as powerful characters through the manipulation of their sexual bodies. Further, baakisimba, being a women's dance, enables male homosexuals to assert their identities in the restrictive and conservative Kiganda culture. Baakisimba forms one of the few spaces where homosexuals have survived with little challenge. Baakisimba, therefore, provides a space where the Baganda can perform their hidden and usually dismissed identities.

The present sensitivity to "gender equity" is critical not only for the achievement of economic development and to genuine democracy, but also as a matter of social justice and social transformation aimed at redistributing resources and social values more equally between men and women (Fiedler 1999). The need for gender-sensitive structural and cultural changes as one of the steps to this equity calls for an examination of how gender inequities are manifest in the past and present Buganda. Therefore, the study of baakisimba, as one of the performance sites through which gender constructions are crystallized, has not only enabled us to access the unique structural organization of baakisimba dance and music, but also provided an understanding of how performed arts can be used to communicate social relations in general, and Kiganda gender constructions, in particular. This study has provided data on the ways in which performed arts are appropriated to marginalize subordinate people, particularly women and yet, the discourse of baakisimba has shown how performed arts can be used as spaces for social and cultural change to take place. From the discussion thus far, I am tempted to suggest a deductive proposal. Since there is a reciprocal relationship between baakisimba and Kiganda gender, a lead in balancing space in music and dance performance may contribute to narrowing down the gap between genders outside the performance stage.

Notes

NOTES TO CHAPTER ONE

1. Unlike in the West where drums are "played," the Baganda "beat the drums" ("okukuba engoma"). As Muzzanganda A. Lugira has noted, "Okukuba: literally means to beat, to win, use energy and force . . ." (1970: 17). The Baganda consider the act of producing sound from the drum "as a practice of exerting energy mentally and physically beating . . . with force" (ibid.). Throughout this book I write to "beat" as opposed to "play" the drum.

2. Gender roles are the social skills, abilities, and ways of behavior thought appropriate for specific gender as defined by a particular culture. One takes up the identity of a specified gender after satisfactorily accomplishing the roles a culture assigns it. Failure in any of the prescribed roles disqualifies that person as belonging to that gender. By gender relations I refer to the political, social, and power relations between and within genders.

3. When the term "choreography" was first used in the eighteenth century, it referred to writing down a dance, which is now called dance notation. Later, it came to mean the art of composing a dance (Beaumont 1970: 8). In this book, I use choreography to refer to the overall composition or constitution of baakisimba dance.

4. By formalized baakisimba, I refer to performances that are formally choreographed and not spontaneous dancing.

5. *Ngoma* (pl. and sing.) is a generic term for all the various types of drums of the Baganda. The Kiganda drums can be divided into two broad categories: the *ngoma ez'emikolo* (ritual drums) and the *ngoma ez'ekinyumu* (festival drums). Baakisimba drum music falls under the category of both the *ngoma z'ekinyumu* and the *ngoma z'emikolo*, because baakisimba is performed at both secular and sacred functions.

6. I use the metaphor of the "forbidden fruit" to highlight a similar analogy in the Holy Bible where Adam and Eve ate the forbidden fruit, which led to

the end of their joy and freedom in the Garden of Eden. In a similar vein, the Ganda culture (through its myths and language) promised women death if they dared to beat the drums. As Adam and Eve met their "death," women too were promised death if they beat the drums.

7. It is important, however, to subject the women's political participation to critical review. Sylvia Tamale (1999) gives an initial and detailed review of women's participation in Ugandan politics.

8. It is important to note that there has been a perpetual confusion about the term "Uganda" and a number of times caused political conflicts. According to Chave Margret Fallers that: "'Uganda' is actually the Kiswahili word for the [region] of the [Ba] Ganda and should mean the same as 'Buganda.' . . . However, in the early days 'Uganda' came to be used, first for the territory, roughly defined, in which the East African Company worked, with Buganda as the center, and later for the Protectorate. The confusion was never completely cleared" (1968:16).

9. The map presented indicates county boundaries before the abolition of Buganda kingdom in 1967. I have used this map because it is more relevant when one refers to Buganda as a kingdom. Moreover, it is hard to keep up with the ever-changing boundaries of new districts and towns, which in many cases overlap with the boundaries of the historic Buganda, which is basic to the present discussion.

10. Reference is made to "his" house and not "her" house, because among the Baganda, the man is the head of a home although most burdens of running the home fall on women.

11. See for instance, Roscoe (1911); Kaggwa (1934); Kiwanuka (1972); Ray (1991); and Nsimbi (1996).

12. A clan is a family-group, which has the same ancestry and totems, mainly animals and plants, honored by all its members. John Milner Gray reported that, "At least five (the Civet Cat, Lugave, Reedbuck, Colobus Monkey, and Bird) clans claim to have been settled in the land before [Kintu] came" (1935: 265).

13. For other versions and more detailed narration, see Le Veux (1994: 49–58); Kaggwa (1951:1–8); Johnston (1902: 700–705); Roscoe (1911); and Mulira (1959, 1965, 1970).

14. In most publications, this author's name has been misspelled. The correct spelling should have been "Kagwa," instead of Kaggwa. I maintain the spelling of his name only in his quotations. Further, most of Kagwa's publications have a number of spelling mistakes, which I have maintained in my quotations.

15. I use the term "traditional" in reference to those practices whose origins are believed to pre-date the influence of Arabic, European and other foreign people in Buganda.

16. Before Buganda was established, the region, then called Muwawa, constituted only three counties: Kyaddondo, Mawokota, and Busiro (Kizito 1915b: 62); Kabuga (1963: 208); Kasirye (1971). The people who inhabited this area were called Balasangeye ("those who shoot black and white colobus monkeys"), "because they most often hunted animals for food" ("kubanga nabo bali basinga kuyigga busolo bulibwa") (Kizito 1915b: 62).

17. Similar stories were authored by Kaggwa (1912a, 1934); Gray (1935); and Kiwanuka (1972).

18. See Kaggwa (1912a, 1912b, 1952); Roscoe (1911); Cox (1950); Kiwanuka (1972: 93).

19. See Kizito (1915a); Gray (1935: 265); Nsimbi (1996: 27–36); Kasirye (1971: 1) Kiwanuka (1972: 31, 94, 96).

20. See also M.B. Nsimbi (1996: 149).

21. I am grateful to Nakanyike Musisi (1991a), whose struggle to recreate gender history inspired me to join her in this venture to rediscover the concealed history.

22. Ssekabaka is a title given to a deceased king as a way of appeasing his spirit. It is believed that a dead king is even more powerful than the living one.

23. "Eating the kingship," means to become king. The Baganda say "alidde obwakabaka" ("he has eaten kingship").

24. Similar characteristics of gender role assignment also exist among the Hausa of Nigeria. Barbara Callaway notes that the "Perceptions of a woman's life cycle stress her current status in relation to men and her reproductive status as well as her approximate age" (1997: 133).

25. By third gender, I refer to people who are culturally defined as men or women, but present themselves more like the opposite gender, either in terms of gender roles or sexual orientation, or both.

26. However, baakisimba, in restricted contexts, especially in church, has been performed independently of dance.

27. Jennifer Daryl Slack discusses the different ways in which "articulation" is conceptualized among cultural theorists. To some, it is a theory (the way in which this book uses it); to others; it is a methodological framework, while others consider it as a strategy, a way of 'conceptualizing' the object of one's analysis (1996: 112).

28. Similarly, Richard Middleton has argued that music is a result of "elements from a variety of sources, each with a variety of histories and connotations, and these assemblages can, in appropriate circumstances, be prised open and the elements rearticulated in different contexts" (Middleton 2000: 137).

29. The Baganda use the term "Arabs" to refer to traders who came from the East African coast to the kingdom in the 1800s. This categorization included people from the Far East as well as the Coastal Swahili.

NOTES TO CHAPTER TWO

1. See for instance, Kubik (1960, 1969); and Cooke (1970, 1992).
2. I need not dwell on the issue of objectivity in ethnography; it has been examined extensively by many scholars (see for instance, Burnin 1995; Agawu 1995). However, I contend that objectivity in ethnography is a mere myth.
3. In fact, the study of music and gender is a new direction for ethnomusicologists. Susan C. Cook and Judy S. Tsou have noted that "A recognition of gender as a category of analysis has come slowly and often with difficulty to the academic disciplines of music. Similarly, Gerhard Kubik who studied Kiganda music in the 1960s, agrees that he never paid particular attention to gender issues, as they were not issues of the time.
4. As I discuss in more detail in Chapter Five, a *nnaalongo*, mother of twins is venerated in Buganda; she is considered to have supernatural power that enabled her to produce two children at a go.
5. Carol Babaraki reminded me of how gender identities impact on the ethnography of culture (1997:122).
6. Personal communication, 15th Feb 2000, Makerere University, Uganda.
7. However, I do not provide records for anonymous interviews for obvious reasons.

NOTES TO CHAPTER THREE

1. For more proverbs relating to dancing and beer, see Walser (1982: 174, 177, 1926 and 1959, respectively).
2. All the dance students in colleges and schools that I interviewed contended that baakisimba is a dance of the palace. However, as I discuss in Chapter Six, these students do not have a homogenous definition of palace baakisimba.
3. However, Kasujja also agreed that the *bakopi* (commoners) also performed baakisimba at beer parties, although they were never in full costume as the performers of palace.
4. Kalyango, the elder at Kintu's tomb, held a similar view.
5. Benesh notation was developed in England in the 1940s by Joan and Rudolf Benesh to transcribe ballet choreography (Royce 1977: 48). Julia McGuinness-Scott's book on Benesh notation guides my notation (1983).
6. It is not only among the Baganda that drums are gendered. Among the Lugbara of Uganda, the three double-headed drums performed in funeral dances are "the daughter (treble), mother, and grandmother (bass). They play together, the mother supplying the main beat, the grandmother the steady bass supporting beat, and the daughter the high chattering that the Lugbara say makes the music exciting" (Middleton 1985: 174).
7. As a matter of fact, all the groups that I interviewed emphasized that the *ngalabi* must have a higher pitch than the *mbuutu*. On a number of occasions, I

noticed that the *ngalabi* beater would leave the performance stage to tune the *ngalabi* whenever it lost its high pitch. I observed on two occasions when fire was burnt in front of the ngalabi.

8. I refer to these dancers as "women" dancers, instead of the more conventional categorization of "female" dancer. I do so because the Baganda assign these individuals the dancing role because they are women, and not because they are females. This assigned role justifies why for a long time male-women did not participate in formal baakisimba dance outside the palace because outside the palace, they are considered men.

9. This was Julius Kyakuwa's contribution to my paper presentation during the Gender and Development Lunch-Time Seminar, December 14, 1999.

10. Other views about men's dancing are discussed in greater details in Chapter Eight.

NOTES TO CHAPTER FOUR

1. Phares Mitibwa reported that the chiefs who negotiated the Agreement were allocated several miles of land as a reward (1992: 5).

2. Marriage among the royal family and within paternal and maternal clans was generally not acceptable among the Baganda.

3. My use of the term "female-husband" is different from the way many scholars have used the same term (Obbo 1976; O'Brien 1977; Krige 1974; and Amadiume 1987). While in my case, female-husband refers to a female who marries a male (which also includes paying bride price); these scholars use the term to refer to a woman who pays bride price to acquire a husband's right to another woman. Edward E. Evans-Pritchard refers to the same relationship as woman husband (1951).

4. As a matter of fact, one informant could not release any information to me because I did not address her properly. When I first met her, I did not know that he was a princess. I address him as *nnyabo*, madam. He kept on postponed our appointment four times for over six months until I gave up. Later, her neighbors told me that he was a princess.

5. See also Roscoe (1911: 234, 244–246, 269, 447); Kaggwa (1934: 95); and Fallers (1964:112, 201, 208).

6. Similarly, El-Tounsy reported that among the Dar fur of Sudan, the king's mother "held the highest rank in the kingdom next to the king, even though her position was not combined with power" (quoted in Irstam 1970: 170).

7. According to Klaus Wachsmann, "ttimba is a big drum made of wood, with a snake carved out of the surface of the drum body" (1953: 367).

8. There is inadequate information available about baakisimba performance from Kabaka Kintu's time until Muteesa I's reign in the mid-nineteenth century. Therefore, my discussion mainly focuses on the dance and its

music from the nineteenth century, although I include some information on baakisimba of earlier periods whenever possible.

9. Apart from the baakisimba festivities that Ssekabaka Kyabaggu hosted, according to Apollo Kaggwa, it is during his reign that the *ntenga* (drum-chime) was introduced in the palace (1912b: 48).

10. These regions include Bunyoro (western Uganda), Ankole (western Uganda), Toro (western Uganda), and Busoga (eastern Uganda).

11. Busoga, a region that harbors the source of the Nile River, is in the eastern part of Uganda. The people are called Basoga and their language is Lusoga.

12. The movement of the *maggunju* dance concentrates in the chest movement and jumping up in the air. In fact, women never performed the dance. It is mainly after the abolition of Buganda kingdom and the performance of the dance in schools that women began to perform the dance.

13. It is somehow possible to confuse the two dances. I opted not to learn *tamenhaibuga* so that I would be able to perform baakisimba fairly well. Although a number of dancers try to perform both dances, few can present satisfactory performance of both dances.

14. Marriage themes include sex, procreation, food production, and other house chores among others.

15. As A. I. Richards reported, when Ssekabaka Muteesa II was first exiled to England in 1953, the palace drums were silent and "thundered continuously on the day of his return [in 1955]" (1964a: 279). She notes further, in a footnote that, "some commoners also refused to beat their drums since 'the country was mourning for the Kabaka'" (1964a: 291, fn. 49).

16. According to Ganda customs, the Baganda were not supposed to beat drums in the absence of the king, especially in a situation where Buganda was at war; in this case, they were at war with the colonial government.

17. In Chapter Five, I explore further aspects of the male authority and control over baakisimba as the trainers, patrons, and heads of ensembles.

18. The commodification of women within the palace did not only involve the king giving women to drummers, but his people would also offer him gifts of women. Women were gifts to Kings and chiefs, and also payments as fines for a male-woman's misconduct. Roscoe reports, "It was customary for a person to present the King with one or two girls when asking a favour. Again, if a male-woman was in disgrace, he made the King a present of women, in order to obtain his forgiveness" (1911: 86). In fact, Speke, who visited Ssekabaka Muteesa I's palace in the mid-nineteenth century, reported that the Kabaka had about 300 to 400 female-women (1863:234).

19. I was told that the king always moves in front of every one and no one is supposed to walk ahead of him. It is taken to be an honor since he is supposed to be the head of all people in Buganda.

20. Live TV recording broadcast by WBS TV station on the 27th of August 1999 (their wedding day). Of course, I cannot compare the present Nnabagereka to the wives of the past kings. At least she has the opportunity to attend functions with the king, although the king does not show close attachment to her in public.

21. Walumbe is Nnambi's brother in the legend of Kintu and Nnambi (see Chapter Two). Because Walumbe killed many of Kintu and Nnambi's children, the Baganda began to venerate him and turned him into a god.

22. The plural of *Omulongo wa kabaka* is *abalongo ba kabaka*. *Omulongo wa kabaka* is a stump of umbilical cord taken form the navel.

23. I saw them at Kyebando, Kyabaggu's tombs; at Wamala, Suuna's tombs; and at Kasengejje, Prince Walugembe's tombs.

24. In this plate, the performers were Music, Dance and Drama Department students of Makerere University. The photograph was taken during the convocation ceremony at Makerere University on 17 January 2003. For security, taking photographs at the palace functions is restricted to the official press only. As such, while I attended a number of palace functions, I was not able to take photographs. However, the motif illustrated by the University students, although performed in a different context, is the same as that one performed in the palace. For the rest of the book, I have used pictures taken outside the palace contexts for the same reasons.

25. In this plate, Kanyanya Muyinda Ensemble was performing for the French Ambassador to Uganda in the summer of 1996.

26. This photograph was taken in the summer of 1996.

27. I was not able to find out why a set of four songs is sung.

28. Ironically, after these twin songs, the religious leaders including representatives from the Protestant, Catholic, Orthodox and Seventh-day Adventists churches and Moslems prayed for the king one after the other. Moreover, the performers of the twin songs were positioned just next of the seats of the religious. The question is: to who was the king and the kingdom dedicated? This concept of syncretism is very common not only among the Baganda, but also in many African cultures.

29. Since writing in Buganda was only introduced in the late nineteenth century, historical songs have remained an important source of Buganda's history.

NOTES TO CHAPTER FIVE

1. Among the Baganda, one is socialized to use the right hand when eating; children are punished for eating with the left hand.

2. Many informants testified to this practice. Even when scientific evidence claims that the man determines the child's sex, among the Baganda, it is

believed the woman determines the sex of the child and she is stigmatized for not having boys.

3. Females are only a "supporting hand" to the right hand. Female babies are only good if male babies already exist; only sons can become heirs to their fathers. Being a patrilineal society, sons represent the continuity of the lineage and therefore, are considered more important. A woman is said to have secured her marriage if she gives birth to a baby boy.

4. *mbirigo* is a game played with short sticks and the player aims at throwing them far away. On the other hand, *ggoggolo* is a game were boys slide down the slope on a sled made of plantain stem.

5. See also Kankwenzire (1996) and Tamale (1996).

6. I have used the word "marry" for lack of a proper English word. I use the word following the Kiganda saying, "a man pays for a woman and takes her while a woman is bought and taken [by the man]" *("omusajja asasula omukazi n'amutwala ate omukazi agulwa n'atwalibwa").*

7. In Chapter Five, I discuss how baakisimba dance movements help to establish women's subordinate position through the "kneeling" dance motif.

8. Of course, once married, she is expected to contribute a great deal to the man's family. There is even a ritual called "okugya omugole mu kisenge" (getting the bride from the bedroom, ending the honey-moon period), where the mother in-law gives the bride a knife and hoe. As such, the bride is informed that her honeymoon is over; she should start her role of providing food to the husband's clan.

9. In Zaire, as Bernadette Mbuy Beya reports, the major purpose for marriage is procreation (1992: 158).

10. Goats are restrained by tying a rope around their necks. However, goats without horns easily lose their ropes; horns help hold the ropes.

11. One informant narrated to me how he divorced his wife because she could not have a child.

12. However, Molara Ogundipe-Leslie reminds us that men's dominance does not only occur in patrilineal societies like in Buganda, but also in matrilineal African societies. She noted that "Even in matrilineal societies, women were still subordinate to men, considered as second in place to men; the only difference being that inheritance and authority pass through the women to the male of the line" (1994: 34).

13. For details on Kadongo-kamu music, see Sylvia Nannyonga-Tamusuza (2002).

14. See also Warren L. D'Azevedo for an example from Sierra Leone (1994: 355).

15. Similarly, Layne Redmond has observed that: "banning women's drumming from religious life was central to the disempowerment of women in Western culture" (1997: 2).

16. Since the mid 1980s, the agitation for gender equality has been high. The Ugandan government affirmative policy opened many spaces to women's

participation formerly limited to men. Among the activities were music, dance, and drama, acted as powerful agents for change, the music and dance festivals organized from village to national levels were important vehicles for sensitizing the men the need for delimiting women's space. These festivals required women to beat drums if the dance they presented for competitions needed drum accompaniment.

17. For details see Nannyonga-Tamusuza and Jean-Jacque Nattiez (2003).
18. The Baganda have many different types of bananas. Some are eaten while ripe, others are used to make local beer. Another type is cooked while green. To cook these bananas, you peel and wrap them in banana leaves and then steam them. When they are tender, they are kneaded before they are steamed again.
19. See also Betty E. Manyolo 1960; Sarah Ntiro 1961.
20. This was my personal experience as a growing child and also was emphasized when my aunt was preparing me for marriage in 1996. Refer also to Roscoe (1911: 104). However, because of the changes in the social structure a number of women no longer kneel before their husbands. I have discussed in some detailed conflicts about this issue in Chapter 71.
21. For unmarried women, a letter from the local council chairman of the village, indicating that she lives in that village and is a good citizenship, is mandatory.
22. Following is the translation of my husband's letter.

> P. O. Box 22880
> Kampala,
> Uganda
>
> 15/12/99
>
> Madam Madiina Nakintu
> Bazannya N'Engo Cultural Group
> Kasangati
>
> Dear Madam Nakintu,
>
> How are you these days? Thank you for all that you are doing. Madam, I have written with humility to request you to give my wife Nnaalongo Sylvia Tamusuza the opportunity to learn how to dance with your group, Bazannya N'Engo Cultural group. I will be grateful if you give her that opportunity. Thank you very much and May God protect you.
>
> Yours respectfully,
> Ssaalongo Justinian Tamusuza

NOTES TO CHAPTER SIX

1. The first Christian missionaries, who were Protestants, Shergold Smith and C. T. Wilson (Protestants), arrived in Buganda in 1877 (Kagwa and Duta 1947: 112). Although the Protestant religion mainly refers to the Anglican faith from England, generally all Christian religions that were not of the Catholic faith come to be known as Protestant. This generalization still existed among the informants I interviewed in 1999–2000 and 2002. Lois Pirouet reports that the Seventh-Day Adventists came in 1926 and other Protestant denominations came after independence in 1962 (1995: 38).

2. I do not claim the Baganda no longer believe in superstitions; however, it is true that the level of their beliefs in them receded with the introduction of Christianity, especially among the converts.

3. In Buganda, the paternal aunt carries the overall responsibility to prepare her brother's daughter for marriage. She is the final person to approve the potential suitor; she actually introduces him to all the relatives on behave of her niece, the bride-to be. It is believed that if the aunt does not consent, the girl would not have a successful marriage.

4. It is not the concern of this discussion to examine whether these priests, brothers, and sisters keep their vows; what is at issue is that they denounce in public their Kiganda genders.

5. Moreover, since the Baganda looked upon the palace for cultural initiatives, Ssekabaka Muteesa II played a role in promoting European musical instruments. For instance, Peter Cooke reported that: "by the 1960s the Kabaka [Muteesa II] had established his own Western-style military band which played for parades of his private police regiment" (1996: 440).

6. Catherine Gray discusses the details of the music structures of the Catholic Church songs (1995).

7. However, the missionaries under estimated the power of these drums, especially those, which had direct connections with the worship of the Baganda's gods.

8. A similar situation happened in Zaire. Pamela A. R. Blakely and Thomas Blakely have recorded that after Vatican II, "local drums, rattles, rhythms, melodies, ululation, metaphors, and verbal art (especially proverbs) also are integrated into the mass and other ritual" (1994: 401).

9. The influence of Christianity on music and dance did not only occur in Buganda, but also in other parts of the world where Christianity exists. Christy Adair noted that one of the factors affecting dance production and training in Western society is the negative attitudes of Christianity towards dancing. She noted, "These attitudes hold the body and sexuality to be indecent which in turn affects any expression through the body and hence dance" (1992:14). "Of course, the choice of traditional tunes [as well as dances] was important, because the associations as well as the character of the original song must be appropriate to its new purpose" (Kakoma 1964:

35). However, one must remember that, "many of the present Western hymns tune were originally folksongs and art songs" (Kakoma 1964: 34).

10. Kyagambiddwa uses the term "oratorio" differently from the Western sense of the term. Instead he uses the term because the composition depicts a sacred story, with a clear plot and the use of specific characters, which are some of the characteristics of an oratorio.

11. The greatest restriction for women in the Catholic Church is to become a priest. Similarly, in her discussion of women's participation in Christian churches in Africa, R. Modupe Owanikin has argued that: "The common argument against women playing a leadership role in the church is that women are divinely decreed to be subordinate to men, and thus there was no basis for their ruling over men in whatever capacity" (1992: 209–210).

NOTES TO CHAPTER SEVEN

1. See also Tamale 1999:12; Lugumba and Ssekamwa 1973:83).

2. A similar situation also happened in Tunisia. Jones has also reported that in Tunisia, girls had access to music training when the subject was included in the school curricula of the public schools (1987:78).

3. It should be noted, however, that baakisimba is only one of the items performed at these competitions. Other items competed for include; Ugandan "folk" songs, Western choral singing, Ugandan traditional folk dance, Western sight singing, creative dance, Ugandan instrumental composition, and original vocal composition.

4. *Nankasa* is a name of a drum as well as a dance genre. The *nankasa* dance is very vigorous, while baakisimba is supposed to be more graceful.

5. However, outside the school contexts, when the *nankasa* drum is beaten with *mbuutu, ngalabi,* and *mpuunyi* the dance ceases to be baakisimba, instead, it becomes *nankasa.*

6. Some of the girls' schools I observed beating the drums during the Schools' Music and Dance Competitions include: Gayaza Girls' High School, Namiryango St. Theresa Girls' Primary School, St Kizito Girls' High School, Bethany, Naggalama St. Agnes Girls' Primary School. However, in some mixed schools, when girls beat the drum, they only beat the basic beat, which is considered to be simple.

7. As Stuart Hall has argued, although there can never be only one single meaning attached to any discourse, most often there is a preferred meaning or reading. Preferred meaning is "the 'intended' meaning which the producers of the message wish its listeners or viewers to accept and act on" (quoted in Brooker 1999:172).

NOTES TO CHAPTER EIGHT

1. In the context of this study, I define homosexuality as a sexual orientation toward a person of the same sex.
2. Historical studies of Buganda do not mention homosexuality until after the Christians condemned it in the late nineteenth century.
3. Stephen O. Murray and Will Roscoe have also noted that "Today, especially where Western influences (notably Christianity and Marxism) have been strong, the belief that homosexuality is a decadent, bourgeois, Western import has became common" (1998a: xv).
4. Karagwe was one of the important interior trading centers of the Arabs in Tanzania.
5. See also Faupel 1984: 73–76.
6. I am grateful to Mohammed Kiggundu who gave me the term, translated it and explained the hidden meaning of *siag*, which is not apparent from the dictionary. Mohammed Kiggundu, communication by e-mail, 8 January 2001.
7. However, the religious leaders did not kneel before the king.
8. Gender shifts among performers are not uncommon in theatrical performances historically. Hanna has noted that exclusively women played roles in Japanese kabuki until they were taken over by men. Men play both male and female roles in the dance (1988: 67).
9. One woman dancer told me that on several occasions the audience had argued whether the man in her group was a man or a woman. This man dancer too used to put on makeup and also kept his nails long, which created an alternative identification.
10. One informant told me he had seen a number of such dancers who use make up in their faces and grow their nails, a behavior associated with women. Yet, another informant told me that in her village there was a male dancer who would construct breasts from pieces of cloth. This dancer also wore a *gomesi* (a women's "traditional" dress) and would always chew gum imitating the behavior of some women (anonymous, interview).
11. Prominent among the dancers of Ssekabaka Muteesa II is Consitantino Lwewunzika, who was one of the main informants for this study.
12. Hairdressing in Buganda and Uganda in general, tends to be a women's job. Most men who are involved in hair styling are mainly barbers dealing with haircuts, rather than treating women's hair.

Glossary

badongo	musicians or dancers
Baganda	people of the Buganda region in southern Uganda
bagoma	drummers
bakopi	peasants, commoners or ordinary people
balaguzi	oracles
balangira	princes
bambejja	princesses
basamize	mediums
bazinyi	dancers
bikooyi	sheets of Indian fabric worn by women in Buganda
bisanja	work contracts in the palace (plu)
bisenso	straw dance skirts
bisiyaga	homosexual practice
bisoko	musical or dance motifs/ variations
boodingi	women's dress with gathered sleeves
Buganda	oldest kingdom in Uganda
Bulaaza	reverend brother
buliba	dance skins

busuuti	women's dress with gathered sleeves
conversational interviews	informal interviews in taxis, market places, and on the street geared towards collecting research data
faaza	reverend father
female-men	females with man gender (princesses in Buganda)
female-women	females with woman gender (outside the palace)
gendered homosexuality	males in same-sex sexual relationship adopting feminine behaviors
gender identity	being a man or a woman based on the responsibilities and roles society assigns someone
gender relations	interaction between and within genders
gender roles	assigned expectations dependant on one's being a man or a woman
gomesi	women's dress with gathered sleeves
Kabaka	king
kaliba	dance skin
kalira	umbilical cord
kanzu	men's long robe of Arabic origin
kasaawe	female homosexuality
kasiki	eve of the wedding
Kiganda	that which belongs to the Baganda
kikazikazi	womanish male
kikooyi	a sheet of Indian fabric worn by women in Buganda
kisanja	job contract at the palace (sing.)
kisenso	dance skirt made out of straw

kisoko	musical or dance motif/ variation
kubiibya	to dance
kusamira	worship of ancestral spirits and gods
kwalula	to initiate children into a clan
kyakulassajja	a manly-female with characteristics, which the Baganda assign to men
lubiri	palace
Luganda	language of the Baganda
madinda	twelve-key xylophone of the Baganda
maggunju	ceremonial palace dance
male-men	males that belong to the royal family
male-women	males within the palace that belong outside the royal family
masabo	ancestral shrines
masiro	king's tombs, palaces of deceased kings
matooke	different kinds of bananas
mazina	dance(s)
mbaga	wedding dance and ceremony
mbuutu	a large conical double-membrane hand drum (female drum)
mibala	praise drums or clan drum beats
mpina	dancing skirt made out of banana leaves
mpuunyi	drum which provides the basic beat
mubala	praise drum beat
Muganda	a person belonging to a Kiganda clan
mugoma	drummer
mujaguzo	most important ceremonial drums of the king
mukopi	peasant, ordinary person

mukyala	lady of the house or someone's wife
mulaguzi	oracle
mulangira	prince
mumbejja	princess
musamize	medium
muzinyi	dancer
muwogola	fast and vigorous dance usually performed at the climax of baakisimba in schools
muzaana	female servant in the king's palace
mwami	a village chief or someone's husband
mwenge bigere	local beer made of banana juice (sometimes squeezed by feet) fermented with sorghum
nakinsige	brown grass-finch clan
nankasa	a small drum and moderately fast dance
ndere	horizontal notched flute of the Baganda
ndingidi	one-stringed tube fiddle of the Baganda
ndongo	bowl lyre
ngabi	antelope clan
ngalabi	long slender single-membrane hand drum with an open bottom end (male drum)
ngeye	white and black colobus monkey
ngoma	generic term for all kinds of drums
ngoma z'emikolo	ritual drums
ngoma ez'ekinyumu	festival drums
nnaabagereka	the king's first wife
nnaalinnya	queen sister
nnaalongo	mother of twins
nnabyewanga	pretentious woman

nnakyeyombekedde	a woman house-owner without a husband
nnamasole	queen mother
nnalukalala	intrepid woman
nnaluwali	aggressive woman
nnyabo	madam
nsaasi	a pair of gourd rattles
ntamiivu	a set of drums accompanied by xylophone
siisita	reverend sister
ssaalongo	father of twins
ssebo	sir
ssenkubuge	drum and dance type invented by Ssenkubuge
tamenaibuga	dance from Busoga

Appendix Two
Dynastic Chronology of Buganda Kings

King	Dates of Reign
Kato Kintu	1314- 1344
Chwa Nnabakka I	1344–1374?
Kimera	1374–1404
Ttembo	1404–1434
Kiggala Mukaabya Kkungubu	1434–1464
Kiyimba	1464–1494
Kayima	1494–1524
Nakibinge	1494–1524
Mulondo	1524–1539
Jjemba	1539–1544
Suuna I	1554–1584
Ssekamaanya	1554–1599
Kimbugwe	1599–1614
Kateregga	1614–1644
Mutebi I	1644–1654
Jjuuko	1654–1664
Kayemba	1664–1674
Tebandeke	1674–1689
Ndawula	1689–1704
Kagulu Tebuucwereke	1704–1714
Kikulwe	1714–1724

Mawanda	1724–1734
Mwanga I	1734–1744
Namugala	1744–1754
Kyabaggu	1754–1764
Jjunju	1764–1779
Ssemakookiro	1779–1794
Kamaanya	1794–1824
Suuna II	1824–1856
Muteesa I	1856–1884
Mwanga II	1884–1897
Kiweewa	1886–1887
Kalema	1887–1888
Daudi Chwa II	1897–1939
Edward Muteesa II	1939–1969
Ronald Muwenda Mutebi II	1993-

Invitation to Kabaka Muwenda Mutebi II's Seventh Coronation Anniversary

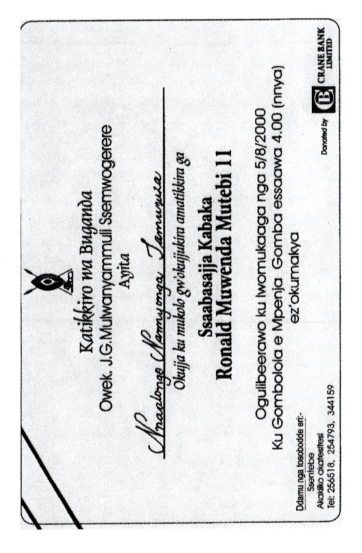

Katikkiro wa Buganda
Owek. J.G. Mulwanyammuli Ssemwogerere
Ayita

Namyonga Jamunuza

Okujja ku mukolo gw'okujjukira amatikkira ga

**Ssaabasajja Kabaka
Ronald Muwenda Mutebi I I**

Ogulibeerawo ku Iwomukaaga nga 5/8/2000
Ku Gomboloja e Mpenja Gomba essaawa 4.00 (nnya)
ez'okumakya

Ddamu nga tosobodde eri:-
Ssentebe
Akakiiko akatesitsesi
Tel: 266518, 254793, 344159

Donated by

CB CRANE BANK
LIMITED

Appendix Four
Events Attended

Date	Event	Performer(s)	Location
21 November, 1999	Organized performance	Sulaiti Kalungi Badongo Group	Makerere University, Music Department, Kyaddondo
4 December, 1999	Wedding in an urban setting	Sulaiti Kalungi Badongo Group; Disco music;St. Peter's Primary School Band	Namboole, Kyaddondo
5 December, 1999	Wedding in a rural setting	Sulaiti Kalungi; Disco music	Butambala, Butambala (county)
7 December, 1999	Training session	Hajati Nakintu (dance teacher); Peter Lubwaama (drum teacher); Sylvia Tamusuza (student)	Kasangati, Kyaddondo
9 December, 1999	Training session	Hajati Nakintu; Peter Lubwaama; Sylvia Tamusuza; Members of Bazannya n'Engo Cultural Group (participants)	Kasangati, Kyaddondo

Date	Event	Performer(s)	Location
9 December, 1999	Organized performance	Wakiso Nankasa Group	Kavumba, Busiro
14 December, 1999	Training session	Hajati Nakintu; Peter Lubwaama; Sylvia Tamusuza; Members of Bazannya n'Engo Cultural Group	Kasangati, Kyaddondo
18 December, 1999	Wedding ceremony	Disco music	Makerere, Kyaddondo
25 December, 1999	Kasiki (eve of the wedding)	Agaly'awamu Cultural Group	Mpigi, Mawokota
4 January, 2000	Commission day	Ggogonnya Nuns'	Ggogonnya, Busiro
6 January, 2000	Training session	Hajati Nakintu; Peter Lubwaama; Sylvia Tamusuza; Members of Bazannya n'Engo Cultural Group	Kasangati, Kyaddondo
8 January, 2000	Commission day	Bwanda Nuns	Bwanda, Buddu
9 January, 2000	Christmas carol service	Catholic Centenary Memorial Choir	Lubaga Cathedral, Kyaddondo
11 January, 2000	Organized performance	Lwewunzika Badongo Dancers	Mpigi, Mawokota
28 January, 2000	Graduation ceremony	Ndere Troupe; Mivule Primary School	Ntinda, Kyaddondo
28 January, 2000	Graduation ceremony	Sulaiti Kalungi Badongo Group	Shelton Hotel in Kampala, Kyaddondo

Date	Event	Performer(s)	Location
30 January, 2000	Graduation ceremony	Good News Lubaga Cathedral Choir	Kikajjo, Busiro
5 February, 2000	Graduation ceremony	Disco music	Mityana, Busujju
28 February, 2000	Visited Mengo Palace	Gerhard Kubik; Sylvia Tamusuza	Mengo, Kyaddondo
26 March, 2000	Funeral rites	Kiwamirembe Catholic Choir	Katende, Mawokota
27 March, 2000	World Theater Day	Nanga Ensemble; Happy Hours Theater	Pride Theater Kampala, Kyaddondo
30 March, 2000	Rehearsal	Nandujja and the Planets	Makerere west, Kyaddondo
8 April, 2000	Inter-house music and dance competition	Mengo Senior Secondary School; Sylvia Tamusuza (Adjudicator)	Mengo, yaddondo
10 April, 2000	Rehearsals	Makerere College School	Makerere, Kyaddondo
15 April, 2000	Inter-house music and dance competition	Ndejje Senior Secondary School; Sylvia Tamusuza (Adjudicator)	Ndejje, Bulemeezi
22 April, 2000	Inter-house music and dance competition	Kawempe Muslim Senior Secondary School; Sylvia Tamusuza (Adjudicator)	Kawempe, Kyaddondo
05 May, 2000	Wedding ceremony in urban setting	Disco music	Nakulabye, Kyaddondo

Date	Event	Performer(s)	Location
06 May, 2000	Wedding cere-mony	Disco music	Ntebbe, Busiro
03 June, 2000	Uganda Catholic Martyrs' Day	Masaka Diocese Choir	Namugongo, Kyaddondo
15 June, 2000	Organized per-formance	Ssenkubuge Nankasa Group	Nabigasa, Buddu
16 June, 2000	Organized per-formance	Kirimuttu Women's Group	Kyotera, Buddu
24 June, 2000	Clan meeting	Nakinsige clan; Sylvia Tamusuza (clan member)	Mengo, Kyaddondo
26 July, 2000	Clan meeting	Nakinsige clan; Sylvia Tamusuza	Mengo, Kyaddondo
05 August, 2000	Kabaka Ronald Muwenda Mutebi II's sev-enth coronation anniversary	Tebifaanana Abi-funa Nankasa Group;Tebi-faanana Abifuna Nankasa Group;	Mpenja, Mawokota
18 July, 2002	Inter-house music and dance festival	St. Lawrence Citi-zens' High School	Nnabbingo, Kyaddondo
17 August, 2002	Makerere College School Perform-ing Art, inter-house music, dance and drama competitions	Makerere College School	Makerere, Kyaddondo
23 August, 2002	Mukono District Primary Schools' Music, Dance and Drama Competitions	Sixteen primary schools	Mukono, Kyaggwe

Appendix Five A:

Formal Interviews Conducted

Date	Name	Position	Location
16 November 1999	Sulaiti Kalungi	former court drummer, still active	Katwe, Kyaddondo
21 November 1999	Janat Nakitto	dancer	Makerere, Kyaddondo
22 November 1999	Tereza Kisolo	former court dancer, woman drummer	Kanyanya, Kyaddondo
23 November 1999	Omulangira Sama Kajjumba	drummers	Katwe, Kyaddondo
23 November 1999	Nuludini Ssekitto	drummer	Katwe, Kyaddondo
23 November 1999	Sulaimani Muk-waaya	rattle player	Katwe, Kyaddondo
23 November 1999	Omulangira Kimbuggwe	xylophone player	Katwe, Kyaddondo
24 November 1999	Idi Sserunkuuma	single-string fid-dler	Katwe, Kyaddondo
24 November 1999	Muhamood Kasujja (RIP)	former court drummer	Katwe, Kyaddondo

Date	Name	Position	Location
02 December 1999	Nnaalongo Dezi	elderly woman	Katwe, Kyaddondo
09 December 1999	Deo Musisi	drummer	Kavumba, Busiro
09 December 1999	John Baptist Kivumbi	former male dancer	Kavumba, Busiro
09 December 1999	Ssenkulu Kyaddondo	knowlegeable in Kiganda customs	Wakiso, Busiro
09 December 1999	John Bulega	drummer	Kavumba, Busiro
09 December 1999	Paulo Musoke	drummer	Kavumba, Busiro
22 December 1999	Matia Muyimbwa	single-string fiddler	Kavumba Busiro
22 December 1999	Violah Naluwooza	linguist, lecturer at Makerere University	Makerere, Kyaddondo
22 December 1999	Anatoli Kirigwajjo	linguist, lecturer at Makerere University	Makerere, Kyaddondo
23 December 1999	Peter Ggayira	former court drummer retired drum maker	Bubuule, Mawokota
23 December 1999	Paulo Kabwama	lderly man, former xylophone and lyre player	Katende, Mawokota
29 December 1999	Ssaalongo Benedicto Kansamba	drummer	Mpigi, Mawokota
07 January 2000	anonymous		Busiro
11 January 2000	Baaziriyo Nsubuga	elder, former one-string fiddle player	Mpigi, Mawokota

Date	Name	Position	Location
11 January 2000	Luyombya	singer	Mpigi, Mawokota
11 January 2000	Sarah Namutebi	dancer	Mpigi, Mawokota
11 January, 2000	Rose Namusisi	dancer	Mpigi, Mawokota
11 January 2000	Consitantino Ngobya Lwewunzika	former court dancer, retired	Mpigi, Mawokota
27 January 2000	anonymous	male dancer	Kyaddondo
07 February 2000	Nabawanda	female servant at Suuna's tombs	Wamala, Busiro
07 February 2000	Omulangira Kaggwa	elder, retired drummer	Kalagi, Kyaddondo
09 February 2000	Solome Nannyonga	female servant at Suuna's tombs	Wamala, Busiro
09 February 2000	Ezuliya Nannyonga	former dancer, female servant at Prince Walugembe's tombs	Kasengejje, Busiro
09 February 2000	Wasswa Nyanzi	male servant at Kamaanya's tombs	Kasengejje, Busiro
09 February 2000	anonymous	female servant at Prince Bamweyana's tombs	Kasengejje, Busiro
19 February 2000	anonymous	guard at Mengo Palace	Mengo, Kyaddondo
20 February 2000	Sarah Mutengomba	university graduate in music, dance ,and drama	Makerere, Kyaddondo
20 February 2000	Daudi Mukasa	elder	Kikusa, Busiro
21 February 2000	Blazio Kalyango	clan elder and attendant at Kabaka Kintu's tombs	Nnono, Busujju

Date	Name	Position	Location
25 February 2000	Ssaalongo Eriyasi	elder at Kyabaggu's tombs	Kyebando, Busiro
08 March 2000	Consitantino Lwewunzika	former male court dancer, retired	Mpigi, Mawokota
13 March 2000	Augustino Kisitu	former court drummer, retired	Kitenga, Buddu
14 March 2000	anonymous		Buddu
16 March 2000	Augustino Kisitu	former court drummer, retired	Kitenga, Buddu
16 March 2000	Richard Lubega	elder, drummer	Villa, Buddu
26 March 2000	Janet Nandujja	dancer and trainer	Makerere west, Kyaddondo
10 April 2000	Katambula Busuulwa	Kiganda music specialist, knowledgeable in Kiganda customs	Makerere, Kyaddondo
18 April, 2000	Robinah Nakiwala	music teacher	Kawempe, Kyaddondo
15 June, 2000	Harriet Nakiyiki	dancer	Kyotera, Buddu
15 June, 2000	Mathias Ssenyondo Ssenkubuge	drummer, trainer	Nabigasa, Buddu
16 June, 2000	Kirimuttu Women's Group	elderly women	Kyotera, Buddu
30 June, 2000	Ibrahim Ggayi	drummer	Makerere, Kyaddondo
30 June, 2000	Badru Ssebumpenje	drummer	Kibuye, Kyaddondo
04 July, 2000	Wasswa Steven Mpanga	male servant at Kasubi tombs	Kasubi, Kyaddondo
08 July 2000	Wasswa Steven Mpanga	male servant at Kasubi tombs	Kasubi, Kyaddondo
11 August 2000	Rehema Nnabanoba	woman drummer	Luwafu, Kyaddondo
04 November 2000	James Makubuya	music and dance trainer, specialist in Kiganda music, performer, researcher	Toronto, Canada

Date	Name	Position	Location
20 June 2002	Arthur Kayizzi	Music and dance trainer, Makerere College School	Makerere, Kyaddondo
15 July 2002	James Mugenyi	House master St. Lawrence Citizens' High School	Nnabbingo, Kyaddondo
21 July 2002	21 July 2002	Adjudicator	Makererere, Kyaddondo
25 July 2002	Shaban Kalwaza	Adjudicator	Kampala, Kyaddondo

Appendix Five B:
Personal Communications

Name	Date
Lois Anderson	October 13, 1998
Sylvia Tamale	November 12,1999
Nakayiza Sifa	December 4, 1999
Nusula Namutebi	December 15, 1999
Hajati Musisi	December 25, 1999
Gerhard Kubik	February 15, 2000
Paolo Nnyombi	February 17, 2000
Joseph Namukangula	March 13, 2000; June 2, 2000
Moses Sserwadda	April 4, 2000; December 5, 2000
Katambula Busuulwa	April 5, 11, 2000; December 10, 2000; January 5, 2001; February 8, 2001
Aurtha Kayiz1	April 17, 2000
Jean Jacque Nattiez	November 5, 2000
Jane C. Sugarman	November, 5 2000
viola Naluwooza	December 5, 13, 25, 2000; January 4, 2001
Anatoli Kiggwajjo	January 3, 2001
Kasalina Matovu	January 4, 2001
Kiggundu	January 8, 2001; February 6, 2001

Permission letter to Bazannya n'Engo Cultural Group

P.D. Box 22880
Kampala
UGANDA

15/12/99

Mukyala Madina Nakintu
Bazannya N'Engo Cultural Group
Kasangati

Nnyabo Mukyala Nakintu,

Osulayo otyanno ennaku zino era webale gy' otuusakko engalo.
Nnyabo nkuwandiikidde nga nkwalu n'obuwombefu ompexe
mukyala wange, Nnaalongo Sylvia Tuwunuze, omukisa ogw'okuyiga
amajana awamu n'ekibiina kyo Bazannya N'Engo Cultural Group.

Nnaanyuka nnyo ng'omuwadde omukisa ogwo - webale nnyo,
Omukwana akunkunnire.

Nze akunaanu ekitiibwa

Ssaalongo Justinian Tuwunuze
[signature]

271

Discography and Bibliography

SELECTED DISCOGRAPHY

Bourgine, Caroline. 1993 [1991 and 1992]. *Ouganda: aux source du Nil.* Ocora Radio France.

JVC Smithsonian Folkways. 1996. *Video Anthology of Music and Dance of Africa.* Vol.1, Egypt, Uganda, and Senegal. Tokyo: Victor Company.

Nannyonga-Tamusuza, Sylvia, Jean-Jacque Nattiez, and Justinian Tamusuza. 2002. Musique des Baganda (Music of the Baganda People). Ocora Radio France: Paris (C 560161).

Patterson, Wade and Bob Haddad. 1997. *Ngoma Music from Uganda* (CD recording). Chapel Hill, North Carolina: Music of the World.

Veuger, Joop. 1991. *Muyinda Evalisto: Traditional Music of Buganda as Formerly Played at the Court of Kabaka* (CD recording). Ethnic series, Liedn, Netherlands: Pan Record (Pan 2003 CD).

BIBLIOGRAPHY

Adair, Christy. 1992. *Women and Dance: Sylphs and Sirens.* New York: New York University Press.

Africa Report. 1993. "Museveni Restores Monarchies in Uganda." *Africa Report* 38 (5): 11.

African Weekly Review. 1995. "History Repeats Itself: Buganda Districts Allowed to Cooperate as a Unit." (August) 18: 26–27.

Agawu, V. Kofi. 1984. "The Impact of Language on Musical Composition in Ghana: An Introduction to the Musical Style of Ephraim Amu." *Ethnomusicology* 28 (1): 37–73.

———. 1995. *African Rhythm: A Northern Ewe Perspective.* Cambridge and Melbourne: Cambridge University Press.

Amadiume, Ifi. 1987. *Male Daughters, Female Husbands: Gender and Sex in an African Society.* London: Zed Books.

American Bible Society. 1992. *Good News Bible: Today's English Version.* New York: American Bible Society.

Anderson, Lois. 1968. "The Miko Modal System of Kiganda Xylophone Music." Ph.D. diss., University of California.

———— 1984. "Multi-part Relationships in Xylophone and Tuned-drum Traditions in Buganda." *Selected Reports in Ethnomusicology* 5:121–141.

Apter, David. E. 1961. *The Political Kingdom in Uganda: A Study in Bureaucratic Nationalism.* Princeton, New Jersey: Princeton University Press.

Asante, Kariamu Welsh. 1994. "Images of Women in African Dance: Sexuality and Sensuality in Dual Unity." *Sage* 8 (2): 16–19.

Ashe, R. P. 1889. *Two Kings of Uganda.* London: Cass.

Atkinson Paul, and Martyn Hammersley. 1998. "Ethnography and Participant Observation." In *Strategies of Qualitative Inquiry.* Edited by Norman K. Denzin and Yvonna S. Lincoln, 110–136. Thousand Oaks and London: Sage.

Baalbaki, Rohi. 1997. *AL-MAWRID: Modern Arabic-English Dictionary.* Beirut: Dar El-ilm Lilmalayin.

Babaraki, Carol. 1997. "What is the Difference? Reflections on Gender and Research in Village India." In *Shadows in the Field: New Perspectives for Fieldwork in Ethnomusicology.* Edited by Gregory F. Barz and Timothy J. Cooley, 121–136. New York and Oxford: Oxford University Press.

Banes, Sally. 1998. *Dancing Women: Female Bodies on Stage.* London and New York: Routledge.

Barz, Gregory and Timothy J. Cooley, ed., 1997. *Shadows in the Field: New Perspectives for Fieldwork in Ethnomusicology.* New York and Oxford: Oxford University Press.

Beaumont, W. Cryril. 1970. *A French-English Dictionary of Technical Terms Used in Classical Ballet.* London: C. W. Beaumont.

Behágue, Gerard. 1984. "Introduction." In *Performance Practice: Ethnomusicological Perspectives.* Edited by Gerard Behágue, 1–12. Westport, Connecticut and London: Greenwood Press.

Beya, Bernadette Mbuy. 1992. "Human Sexuality, Marriage, and Prostitution." In *The Will to Arise: Women, Tradition, and the Church in Africa.* Edited by Mercy Amba Oduyoye and Musimbi R. A. Kanyoro, 155–179. Maryknoll, New York: Orbis Books.

Blacking, John. 1985. "Movement, Dance, Music, and the Venda Girls' Initiation Cycle." In *Society and Dance: The Social Anthropology of Process and Performance.* Edited by Paul Spencer, 64–91. Cambridge and New York: Cambridge University Press.

————. 1995. *Music, Culture, and Experience: Selected Papers of John Blacking.* Edited by Reginald Byron. Chicago and London: University of Chicago Press.

Blakely, Pamela A. R., and Thomas D. Blakely. 1994. "Ancestors, 'Witchcraft,' and Foregrounding the Poetic: Men's Oratory and Women's Song-Dance in Hémba Funerary Performance." In *Religion in Africa: Experience and Espression.* Edited by Thomas D. Blakely, Walter E. A. Van Beek, and Dennis L. Thomson, 399–442. London: James Currey; Portsmouth, New Hamisphere: Heinemann.

Bohlman, Philip V. 1997. "Fieldwork in the Ethnomusicological Past." In *Shadows in the Field: New Perspectives for Fieldwork in Ethnomusicology.* Edited by Gregory F. Barz and Timothy J. Cooley, 139–162. New York and Oxford: Oxford University Press.

Bonvillain, Nancy. 1998 [1995]. *Women and Men: Cultural Constructs of Gender.* 2nd Edition. Upper Saddle River, New Jersey: Prentice Hall.

Brooker, Peter. 1999. *Cultural Theory: A Glossary.* London and New York: Arnold.

Brown, Winifred. 1960. "Status of Uganda Women in Relation to Marriage Laws." *African Women* 4 (1): 1–4.

Buckley, Thomas, and Alma Gottlieb. 1997 [1993]. "Critical Appraisal of Theories of Menstrual Symbolism." In *Gender in Cross-Cultural Perspective.* 2nd ed. Edited by Caroline B. Brettell and Carolyn F. Sargent, 150–160. Upper Saddle River, New Jersey: Prentice Hall.

Burnet, Alice M. 1958. "Women at Makerere." *African Women* 2 (4): 78–80.

Burnim, Mellonee. 1995. "Culture Bearer and Tradition Bearer: An Ethnomusicologist's Research on Gospel Music." *Ethnomusicology* 29 (3):432–447.

Busuulwa, Katambula. 1999. *Mujaguzo: Engoma z'Obwakabaka bwa Buganda.* Kampala: KAB Libraries.

Callaway, Barbara J. 1997 [1993]. "Hausa Socialization." In *Gender in Cross-Cultural Perspective.* 2nd ed. Edited by Caroline B. Brettell and Carolyn F. Sargent, 133–137. Upper Saddle River, New Jersey: Prentice Hall.

Chernoff, John. 1979. *African Rhythm and African Sensibility: Aesthetics and Social Action in African Musical Idioms.* Chicago and London: University of Chicago Press.

Chiener, Chou. 2002. "Experience and Fieldwork: A Native Researcher's View." In *Ethnomusicology* 46 (3):456–486.

Clifford, James. 1986. "Introduction: Partial Truth." In *Writing Culture: The Poetics and Politics of Ethnography.* Edited by James Clifford and George E. Marcus, 1–26. Berkley and Los Angeles: University of California Press.

Cooke, Peter. 1970. "Ganda Xylophone Music: Another Approach." *African Music* 4 (4): 62–80, 95.

———. 1992. "Report on Pitch Perception Experiments Carried out in Buganda and Busoga (Uganda)." *African Music* 7 (2): 119–125.

———. 1995. "Cooke." *The Golden Years: Inside the 50 years of Exciting Times of Makerere College School!* 1 (1): 23–24.

———. 1996. "Music in a Ugandan Court." *Early Music* 24 (3): 439–452.

Cooley, J. Timothy. 1997. "Casting Shadows in the Field: An Introduction." In *Shadows in the Field: New Perspectives for Fieldwork in Ethnomusicology.* Edited by Gregory F. Barz and Timothy J. Cooley, 101–120. New York and Oxford: Oxford University Press.

Cowan, Jane. 1990. *Dance and Body Politic in Northern Greece.* Princeton, New Jersey: Princeton University Press.

Cox, A. H. 1950. "The Growth and Expansion of Buganda." *Uganda Journal* 14 (2): 153–160.

Cullen, Malachy. N.d. *The Uganda Martyrs.* Jos, Nigeria: Augustinian Publications.

Cunningham, J. F. 1969 [1905]. *Uganda and its Peoples: Notes on the Protectorate of Uganda Especially the Anthropology and Ethnology of its Indigenous Races.* [1905: Hutchison]. New York: Negro Universities Press.

D'Arbela, G, Paul. 2003. "Mother Kevin's Legacy in Uganda." In *St. Francis Hospital Nsambya Celebrating A Centenary 1903–2003.* Edited by Freddie Sekitto, 19–30. Nsambya, Kampala: Nsambya Hospital.

d'Azevedo, Warren L. 1994. "Gola Womanhood and the Limits of Masculine Omnipotence." In *Religion in Africa: Experience and Expression.* Edited by Thomas D. Blakely, Walter E. A. van Beek, and Dennis L. Thomson, 343–362. London: James Currey; Portsmounth, New Hampshire: Heinemann.

Darlow, Mary. 1955. "Women's Education in East Africa." *African Women.* 1 (3): 55–60.

Doubleday, Veronica. 1999. "The Frame Drum in the Middle East: Women, Musical Instruments and Power." *Ethnomusicology* 43 (1): 101–134.

Ebel, Otto. 1902. *Women Composers: A Bibliographical Handbook of Women's Work in Music.* Brooklyn: F. H. Chandler.

Evans-Pritchard, Edward E. 1951. *Kinship and Marriage among the Nuer.* Oxford: Oxford University Press.

Fallers, Chave Margaret. 1968. [1960]. *East Central Africa Part XI: The Eastern Lacustrine Bantu (Ganda and Soga)* London: International African Institute.

Fallers, L. A. 1964. *The King's Men.* London, New York, and Nairobi: Oxford University Press.

Fanusie, Lloyda. 1992. "Sexuality and Women in African Culture." In *The Will to Arise: Women, Tradition, and the Church in Africa.* Edited by Mercy Amba Oduyoye and Musimbi R. A. Kanyoro, 135–154. Maryknoll. New York: Orbis Books.

Faupel, J. F. 1984 [1962, 1964, 1965]. *African Holocaust: The Story of the Uganda Martyrs.* N.p: St Paul Publications, Africa.

Feld, Steven. 1984. "Sound Structure As Social Structure." *Ethnomusicology* 28 (3): 383–409.

Fiedler, Anne Akia. 1999. "Women's Agenda." *African Business.* (London) 240: 21–22.

Flannery, Austin O. P. Editor. 1997 [1975]. *Vatican Council II: The Conciliar and Post-Consiliar Documents.* Bandra and Bombay: St. Pauls.

Gee, T. W. 1958. "A Century of Muhammadan Influence in Buganda, 1852–1951." *Uganda Journal* 22 (2): 139–150.

Gilman, Lisa. 2000. "Putting Colonialism into Perspective: Cultural History and the Case of Malipenga Ngoma in Malawi." Mashindano! Competitive Music

Performance in East Africa. Edited by Frank Gunderson and Gregory Barz, 407–419. Da es salaam: Mkuki na Nyota Publishers.

Goetz, Anne Marie. 1998. "Women in Politics and Gender Equity in Policy: South Africa and Uganda." *Review of African Political Economy* 25 (76): 241–263.

Gourlay, K. A. 1978. "Towards a Reassessment of the Ethnomusicologist's Role in Research." *Ethnomusicology.* 22 (1): 1–35.

Gray, Catherine. 1995. "Compositional Techniques in Roman Catholic Church Music in Uganda." *British Journal of Ethnomusicology* 4: 135–155.

Gray, John Milner. 1935. " Early History of Buganda." *Uganda Journal* 2 (4): 259–71.

———. 1947. "Ahmed bin Ibrahim: The First Arab to Reach Buganda." *Uganda Journal* 2 (2): 80–97.

———. 1950. "The Year of the Three Kings of Buganda, Mwanga—Kiwewa—Kalema, 1888–1889." *Uganda Journal* 24:15–52.

Great Britain Colonial Office. 1953. *Uganda Protectorate: Withdrawal of Recognition from Kabaka Mutesa II of Buganda.* London: Her Majesty's Stationery Office.

Grossberg, Lawrence. 1996a. "History, Politics and Postmodernism: Stuart Hall and Cultural Studies." In *Stuart Hall: Critical Dialogues in Cultural Studies.* Edited by David Morley and Kuan-Hsing Chen, 151–173. London and New York: Routledge.

———. 1996b. "On Postmodernism and Articulation: An Interview with Stuart Hall." *Stuart Hall: Critical Dialogues in Cultural Studies.* Edited by David Morley and Kuan-Hsing Chen, 131–150. London and New York: Routledge.

Håkansson, Thomas. 1988. *Bride Wealth, Women and Land: Social Change Among the Gusii of Kenya.* Stockholm: Uppsala.

Hall, Stuart. 1977. "Continuing the Discussion." In *Race and Class in Post-colonial Society: A Study of Ethnic Group Relations in English Speaking Caribbean, Bolivia, Chile and Mexico.* Paris: UNESCO.

———. 1980. "Race, Articulation and Societies Structured in Dominance." In *Sociological Theories: Race and Colonialism,* 305–345. Paris: UNESCO.

———. 1996a. "The Question of Cultural Identity." In *Modernity: An Introduction to Modern Societies.* Edited by Stuart Hall, David Held, Don Hubert, and Kenneth Thompson, 595–634. Cambridge and Oxford: Blackwell Publishers.

———. 1996b. "Introduction: Who Needs Identity?" In *Questions of Cultural Identity.* Edited by Stuart Hall and Paul Du Gay, 1–17. London and Thousand Oaks: Sage Publications.

———. 1996c. "Politics of Identity." In *Culture, Identity and Politics: Ethnic Minorities in Britain.* Edited by Terence Ranger, Yunas Samad, and Ossie Stuart, 129–135. Hong Kong and Sydney: Averbury.

Hanna, Judith Lynne. 1988. *Dance, Sex and Gender: Signs of Identity, Dominance, Defiance, and Desire.* Chicago and London: University of Chicago Press.

———. 1992. "Dance." In *Ethnomusicology: An Introduction.* Edited by Helen Myers, 315–326. London: Macmillan Press.

Hanna, Lynne Judith, and William John Hanna. 1968. "Heart Beat of Africa." *African Art* 1 (3): 42–45, 85.

Harper, Peggy. 1970. "The Role of Dance in the Gelede." *ODU.* Edited by Micheal Crowder, 4 (October): 57. Nigeria: University of Ife Press and Oxford University Press.

Hastie, Catherine. 1962. "Training Courses for Women's Club Leaders in Uganda." *African Women* 4 (4): 77–81.

Hattersley, C. W. 1968 [1908]. *The Baganda at Home.* London: Frank Cass.

Hauser-Schaublin, Brigitta. 1993. "Blood: Cultural Effectiveness of Biological Conditions." In *Sex and Gender Hierarchies.* Edited by Barbara Diane Miller, 83–107. Cambridge and New York: University of Cambridge Press.

Herdt, Gilbert H. 1997 [1993]. "Rituals of Manhood: Male Initiation in Papua New Guinea." In *Gender in Cross-Cultural Perspective.* 2nd ed. Edited by Caroline B. Brettell and Carolyn F. Sargent, 129–133. Upper Saddle River, New Jersey: Prentice Hall.

Herndon, Marcia. 1993. "Insiders, Outsiders: Knowing our Limits, Limiting Our Knowing." *World Music* 35 (1): 63–80.

Herndon, Marcia and Susanne Ziegler. 1990. *Music, Gender, and Culture.* Wilhelmshaven: Florian. Noetzel Verlag.

Hood, Mantle. 1971. *The Ethnomusicologist.* New York: McGraw-Hill.

Howel, A. E. 1948. *The Fires of Namugongo.* London: Samuel Walker.

Hunt, Nancy. 1990. "Domesticity and Colonialism in Belgian Africa: Usumbura Foyer Social, 1946–60." *Signs: Journal of Women in Culture and Society* 15 (13): 447–74.

Ingle, Dick. 1995. "The Beginning of Sixth Form Chemistry and the Music Project at Makerere College School 1962–1965." *The Golden Years: Inside the 50 years of Exciting Times of Makerere College School!* 1 (1):8–10, 12.

Irstam, Tor. 1970. *The King of Ganda: Studies in the Institutions of Sacral Kingship in Africa.* Westport, Connecticut: Negro Universities Press.

Johnston, H. H. 1902. *The Uganda Protectorate.* 2 vol., 700–705. London: Hutchinson.

Jones, L. JaFran. 1987. "A Sociohistorical Perspective on Tunisian Women as Professional Musicians." *Women and Music in Cross-Cultural Perspectives.* Edited by Ellen Koskoff, 69–83. New York and London: Greenwood Press.

Kabuga, Charles E. S. 1963. "The Genealogy of Kabaka Kintu and the Early Bakababa of Buganda." *Uganda Journal* 27 (2): 205–216.

Kaeppler, L. Adrienne. 2001. "Ethnochoreology." *The New Grove Dictionary of Music and Musicians.* 2nd ed., Vol. 8. Edited by Stanley Sadie, 361–367. London: Macmillan Publishers.

Kaggwa, Apollo. 1912a [1901]. *Ekitabo kya Basekabaka beBuganda nabeBunyoro, nabeKoki, nabeToro, nabeNkole.* London: Luzac and Co.

———. 1912b. *Ekitabo kye Bika Bya Buganda:* N.p: Columbia University Library and Makerere University.

————. 1934. *Empisa za Baganda: The Customs of the Baganda.* Translated by May Mandelbaum Edel. New York: Columbia University Press.

————.1951 [1902]. *Engero za Baganda.* London: Sheldon Press.

————. 1952 [1905, 1934]. *Ekitabo kye Mpisa za Baganda.* Kampala: Uganda Bookshop; London: Macmillan.

Kaggwa, Apollo and Henry Wright Duta. 1947. "Extracts of 'Mengo Notes'-IV: How Religion Came to Uganda." Translated by C. W. Hattersley. *Uganda Journal.* 2 (2): 110–116.

Kakoma, G. W. et al. 1964. *The First Conference on African Traditional Music.* Kampala: Makerere University College.

Kakwenzire, Joan. 1996. "Preconditions for Demarginalizing Women and Youth in Ugandan Politics." In *Law and Struggles for Democracy in East Africa.* Edited by J. Oloka-Onyango, K. Kibwama and C. Peter, 293–311. Nairobi: Claripress.

Karugire, Samwiri. 1980. *A Political History of Uganda.* Nairobi, Kenya: Heineman.

Kasirye, Joseph S. 1959 [1955]. *Abateregga ku Nnamulondo ya Buganda.* Basingstoke and London: Macmillan Education.

Kasozi, A. B. K. 1979. *The Crisis of Secondary School Education in Uganda 1960–1970.* Kampala: Longman.

Kavulu, David. 1969. *The Uganda Martyrs.* Kampala: Longmans of Uganda.

Kealiinohomoku, Joann. 1983. "An Anthropologist Looks at Ballet as a Form of Ethnic Dance" In *What is Dance: Readings in Theory and Criticism.* Edited by Roger Copeland and Marshall Cohen, 533–549. Oxford and New York: Oxford University Press.

Keil, Charles and Steven Feld. 1994. *Music Grooves.* Chicago and London: University of Chicago Press.

Kikulwe, J. M. T. 1914. "Emngule ya Basekabaka be Buganda." *Munno,* 122–124.

Kiregeya, Emmanuel. 2002. *Kisubi Seminary Celebrates 50th Anniversary.* Kisubi, Uganda: Marianum Press.

Kiwanuka, M. S. M. Semakula. 1972. *A History of Buganda: From the Foundation of the Kingdom to 1900.* New York: Africana Publishing Corporation.

Kizito, Tobi. 1915a. "Ensi Muwawa Buganda." *Munno,* 6–8.

————. 1915b. "Kintu Anonebwa e Mangira." *Munno,* 62–64.

Krige, Eileen Jensen. 1974. "Woman-marriage, with Special Reference to the Lovedu." *Africa* 44: 11–36.

Kubik, Gerhard. 1960. "The Structure of Kiganda Xylophone Music." *African Music* 2 (3): 131–65.

————. 1968. "Court Music in Uganda." *Bulletin of the International Committee on Urgent Anthropological and Ethnological Research* 10: 41–51.

————. 1969. "Compositional Techniques in Kiganda Xylophone Music—With an Introduction into Some Kiganda Musical Concepts." *African Music* 4 (3): 22–72.

Kwakwa, Abenaa Patience. 1994. "Dance and African Women." *Sage* 8 (2): 10–15.

Kyagambiddwa, Joseph. 1964. *African Oratorio of the Uganda Martyrs.* Roma: Padri Bianchi.

Langley, Esla. 1966. *Firm in their Faith: The Martyrs of Uganda.* London: Talbot Press.

Lebeuf, Annie. 1963. "The Role of Women in the Political Organization of African Societies." In *Women of Tropical Africa.* Edited by Denise Paulme, 93–119. Berkeley, California: University of California Press.

Le veux, R. P. 1994 [1882]. *Manuel de Langue Luganda.* Algiers: Maison-Caree.

Lovgren, Stefan. 1996. "Power of the Buganda: Uganda's Kings Return." *Christian Science Monitor* 88 (158): 6.

Lubowa, Angel. 2000. "Baakubye owa LC Emiggo n'Azirika: Baamulanga Kulya Bisiyaga." *Bukedde* 6 (183): 5.

Lubega, Bonnie M. 1994. *Olulimi Oluganda Amakula.* Kampala: Belinda Publishers.

Lugira, Muzzanganda A. 1970. *Ganda Art.* Kampala: Osasa Publication.

Lugumba S. M. E, and J. C. Sekamwa. 1973. *A History of Education in East Africa (1900–1973).* Kampala: Kampala Bookshop.

Lush, Allan J. 1935. "Kiganda Drums." *Uganda Journal* 3 (1): 7–24.

Magoba, Waalabyeki. N.d. "Yiga Emikolo gy'Ekiganda: Okwanjula.' Pamphlet.

Makubuya, James Kika. 1995. "Endongo: The Role and Significance of the Baganda Bowl Lyre of Uganda." Ph. D. diss., University California, Los Angeles.

Mamdani, Mahmood. 1976. *Politics and Class Formation in Uganda.* New York: Monthly Review Press.

Manyolo, E. Betty. 1960. "Clothing in Western, Buganda, and Eastern, Provinces of Uganda." BA (Fine Art) Thesis, Makerere University.

Mascarenhas-Keyes, Stella 1987. "The Native Anthropologist: Constraints and Strategies in Research." In *Anthropology at Home.* Edited by Anthony Jackson, 180–195. Londona nd New York: Tavistock Publications.

Mascia-Lees, Frances E., and Nancy Johnson Black. 2000. *Gender and Anthropology.* Prospect Heights, Illinois: Waveland Press.

Maxon, M. Robert. 1994. *East Africa: An Introductory History.* 2nd ed. Morgantown, West Virginia: West Virginia University Press.

McClary, Susan. 1991. *Feminine Endings: Music, Gender, and Sexuality.* Minnesota and Oxford: University of Minnesota Press.

McGuinness-Scott, Julia. 1983. *Movement Study and Benesh Movement Notation: An Introduction to Applications in Dance, Medicine, Anthropology, and Other Studies.* London and New York: Oxford University Press.

Merriam, Alan P. 1964. *The Anthropology of Music.* Evanston: Northwestern University Press.

Meyers, Carol. 1993. "The Drum-Dance-Song Ensemble: Women's Performance in Biblical Israel." In *Rediscovering the Muses: Women's Musical Traditions.* Edited by Kimberley Marshall, 49–67. Boston: Northwestern University Press.

Middleton, John. 1985. "The Dance Among the Lugbara of Uganda." In *Society and Dance: The Social Anthropology of Process and Performance.* Edited by Paul Spencer, 165–182. Cambridge and London: Cambridge University Press.

Middleton, Richard. 2000. "On Articulating the Popular." In *Music, Culture, and Society: A Reader.* Edited by Derek B. Scott, 137–142. Oxford: Oxford University Press.

Miller, Barbara Diane. 1993. "The Anthropology of Sex and Gender Hierarchies." In *Sex and Gender Hierarchies.* Edited by Barbara Diane Miller, 3–31. Cambridge: Cambridge University Press.

Miller, Viana. 1987. "Kin Reproduction and Elite Accumulation in Archaic States of Northwest Europe." In *Power Relations and State Formation.* Edited by Thomas. C. Patterson, and Christine W. Gailey, 81–97. Washington DC: American Anthropological Association.

Mudimbe, V. Y. 1991. *Parables and Fables.* Madison: University of Wisconsin Press.

Mugambi, Helen Nabasuta. 1994. "Intersections: Gender, Orality, Text, and Female Space in Contemporary Kiganda Radio Songs." *Research in African Literature* 25 (3): 47–70.

———. 1997. "From Story to Song: Gender, Nationhood, and the Migratory Text." In *Gendered Encounters: Challenging Cultural Boundaries and Social Hierarchies in Africa.* Edited by Maria Grosz-Ngate and Omari H. Kokole, 205–222. New York and London: Routledge.

Mukasa, Ham. 1938. *Simuda Nyuma: Ebiro bya Mutesa.* London: Society for Promoting Christian Knowledge.

———. 1946. "The Rule of the Kings of Buganda." *Uganda Journal* 10 (2):136–143.

Mulira, Enoch E. K. 1970 [1965, 1955]. *Olugero Lwa Kintu.* Vol. 2. London: Oxford University Press.

Murray, Stephen O., and Will Roscoe, 1998a. "Preface: 'All Very Confusing.'" In *Boy-Wives and Female Husbands: Studies of African Homosexualities.* Edited by Stephen O. Murray and Will Roscoe, xi-xxii. New York: St. Martin's Press.

———. 1998b. "Diversity and Identities: The Challenge of African Homosexualities." In *Boy-Wives and Female Husbands: Studies of African Homosexualities.* Edited by Stephen O. Murray and Will Roscoe, 267–278. New York: St. Martin's Press.

Musisi, Nakanyike B. 1991a. "Transformations of Baganda Women: From the Earliest Times to the Demise of the Kingdom in 1966 (Uganda)." Ph.D. diss., University of Toronto, Canada.

———. 1991b. "Women, "Elite Polygyny,' and Buganda State Formation." *Signs: Journal of Women in Culture and Society* 16 (4): 757–786.

———. 1992. "Colonial and Missionary Education: Women and Domesticity in Uganda, 1900–1945." In *African Encounters with Domesticity.* Edited by Karen Tranberg Hansen, 172–194. New Brunswick, New Jersey: Rutgers University Press.

Musisi, Meddie and Angel Lubowa. 2000. "Nabagereka Aguddewo Ofiisi mu Bulange." *Bukedde* (25 July) 6 (283): 2.

Mutibwa, Phares. 1992. *Uganda Since Independence: A Story of Unfulfilled Hopes.* London: Hurst and Company.

Muwonge, W. S. et al. 1997. *The Primary Teacher Education Self-Study Series: Cultural Studies Module CE/1: Part 2 Music Education.* Kampala: Ministry of Education, Republic of Uganda.

Nanda, Serena. 2000. *Gender Diversity: Crosscultural Variations.* Prospect Heights, Illinois: Waveland Press.

Nanono, Alexandira. 1977. "Fashions in Uganda from Pre-Independence to Military Government." BA (Fine Art) Thesis, Makerere University, Uganda.

Nanyonga [Nannyonga-Tamusuza], Sylvia. 1995. "Selected Traditional Secular and Sacred Music of the Baganda People: A Comparative Study." MA Thesis, Makerere University, Uganda.

Nannyonga-Tamusuza, Sylvia. 2000. "Baakisimba: Constructing Gender of the Baganda of Uganda through Music and Dance." *Women and Music: A Journal of Gender and Culture.* 5: 31–39.

———. 2002. "Gender, Ethnicity and Politics in Kadongo-kamu Music of Uganda: Analysing the Song Kayanda." In *Playing with Identities in Contemporary Music in Africa.* Edited by Mai Palmberg and Annemette Kirkegaard. Uppsala: Nordiska Afrikainstitutet.

Nannyonga-Tamusuza, Sylvia, Jean-Jacque Nattiez. 2003. "Rhythm, Dance and Sex: Ugandan Dance for Initiation into marriage." In *Enciclopedia della Musica, Vol. II Musiche e culture,* a cura di Jean-Jacques nattaiez, Enaduci Editore.

Nazziwa, Josephine. 1994. Distortions in African Traditional Dances: A case Study of Baakisimba. BA Thesis, Makerere University, Uganda.

Nelson, Sarah M. 1993. "Gender Hierarchy and the Queens of Silla." In *Sex and Gender Hierarchies.* Edited by Barbara Diane Miller, 297–315. Cambridge: Cambridge University Press.

Nettl, Bruno. 1964. *Theory and Method in Ethnomusicology.* New York and London: Free Press.

———. 1983. *The Study of Ethnomusicology: Twenty-Nine Issues and Concepts.* Urbana and Chicago: University of Illinois Press.

Nketia, J.H Kwabena. 1990. "The Role of the Drummer in Akan Society." In *Musical Processes, Resources, and Technologies.* Edited by Kay Kaufman Shelemay, 98–107. New York and London: Garland Publishing.

———. 1996. "Overview: The Music and Dance of Africa." In *The JVC/Smithsonian Folkways Video: Anthology of Music and Dance of Africa.* Bk. 1. Victor Company of Japan.

———. 1974. *The Music of Africa.* New York and London: W. W. Norton.

Nsimbi, M. B. 1956. "Village Life and Customs in Buganda." *Uganda Journal* 20 (1): 27–36.

———. 1964. "The Clan System in Buganda." *Uganda Journal* 28 (1): 25–30.

———. 1996 [1980]. *Amannya Amaganda n'Ennono Zaago.* [Kampala]: Uganda Bookshop.

Ntiro, Sarah. 1961. "The Busuti." *Crane,* 7–8.

Obbo, Christine. 1974. "Gender Stratification and Vulnerability in Uganda." In *Woman, Culture, and Society.* Edited by Michelle Zimbalist Rosaldo and Louise Lamphere, 182–196. Stanford, California: Stanford University Press.

———. 1976. "Dominant Male Ideology and Female Options: Three African Case Studies." *Africa* 46: 371–89.

———. 1980. *African Women: Their Struggle for Economic Independence.* London: Zed Press.

———. 1989. "Sexuality and Economic Domination in Uganda," In *Woman-Nation-State.* Edited by Nira Yuval-Davis and Floya Anthias, 79–91. New York: St Martin's Press.

———. 1990a. "Adventures with Fieldnotes." In *Fieldnotes: The Makings of Anthropology.* Edited by Roger Sanjek, 290–302. Ithaca and London: Cornell University Press.

———. 1990b. "East African Women, Work, and the Articulation of Dominance." In *Persistent Inequalities: Women and World Development.* Edited by Irene Tinker, 210–222. New York and Oxford: Oxford University Press.

Oboler, Regina Smith. 1980. "Is the Female Husband a Man?" *Ethnology* 19: 69–88.

O'Brien, Denise. 1977. "Female Husbands in Southern Bantu Societies." In *Sexual Stratification: A Cross-cultural View.* Edited by Alice Schlegel, 109–126. New York: Columbia University Press.

Ogundipe-Leslie, Molara. 1994. *Re-Creating Ourselves: African Women and Critical Transformations.* Trenton, New Jersey: African World Press.

Ortner, B. Sherry. 1974. "Is Female to Male as Nature is to Culture?" In *Woman, Culture, and Society.* Edited by Michelle Zimbalist Rosaldo and Louise Lamphere, 67–87. Stanford, California: Stanford University Press.

Osumare, Halifu. 1994. "Viewing African Women through Dance." *Sage* 8 (2): 41–45.

Owanikin, R. Modupe. 1992. "The Priesthood of Church Women in the Nigerian Context." In *The Will to Arise: Women, Tradition, and the Church in Africa.* Edited by Mercy Amba Oduyoye and Musimbi R. A. Kanyoro, 206–219. Maryknoll, New York: Orbis Books.

Pirouet, M. Louise. 1995. *Historical Dictionary of Uganda.* African Historical Dictionaries, no. 64. Metuchen, New Jersey and London: Scarecrow Press.

Ray, Benjamin C. 1991. *Myth, Ritual, and Kinship in Buganda.* New York and Oxford: Oxford University Press.

Reason, Peter. 1998. "Three Approaches to Participatory Inquiry." In *Strategies of Qualitative Inquiry.* Edited by Norman K. Denzin and Yvonna S. Lincoln, 261–292. Thousand Oaks and London: Sage Production.

Redmond, Layne. 1997. *When the Drummers were Women: A Spiritual History of Rhythm.* New York: Three Rivers Press.

Rice, Timothy. 1997. "Toward a Mediation of Field Methods and Field Experience in Ethnomusicology." In *Shadows in the Field: New Perspectives for Fieldwork in Ethnomusicology.* Edited by Gregory F. Barz and Timothy J. Cooley, 101–120. New York and Oxford: Oxford University Press.

Richards, Audrey. I. 1960. *East African Chiefs: A Study of Political Development in Some Uganda and Tanganyika Tribes*. London: Faber and Faber.

————. 1964a. "Authority Patterns in Traditional Buganda." In *The King's Men: Leadership and Status in Buganda on the Eve of Independence*. Edited by L. A. Fallers, 256–293. London, New York, and Nairobi, Kenya: Oxford University Press.

————. 1964b. "Traditional Values and Current Political Behaviour." In *The King's Men: Leadership and Status in Buganda on the Eve of Independence*. Edited by L. A. Fallers, 294–335. London, New York, and Nairobi, Kenya: Oxford University Press.

Robertson, A. B. 1939. "Girls' Education in Uganda: Encouraging Features." *Uganda Journal* 1:62–64.

Robertson, Carol E. 1987. "Power and Gender in the Musical Experience of Women." In *Women and Music in Cross-Cultural Perspective*. Edited by Ellen Koskoff, 225–244. New York and London: Greenwood Press.

Romero, Patricia W. Editor. 1988. *Life Histories of African Women*. London and Atlantic Highlands, New Jersey: Ashfield Press.

Roscoe, John. 1911. *The Baganda at Home: An Account of Their Customs and Briefs*. London: Macmillan.

Rothenberg, Paula S. 1995. "Introduction." In *Race, Class, and Gender in the United States: An Integrated Study*. 3rd ed. Edited by Paula S. Rothenberg, 1–6. New York: St Martin's Press.

Royce, Anya Peterson. 1977. *The Anthropology of Dance*. Bloomington and London: Indiana University Press.

Said, Edward. 1979 [1978]. *Orientalism*. New York: Vintage Books.

Sarkissan, Margaret. 1992. "Gender and Music." In *Ethnomusicology: An Introduction*. Edited by Helen Myers, 337–348. New York and London: Macmillan.

Sathyamurthy, T. V. 1986. *Political Developments of Uganda 1900–1986*. Aldershot, England and Brookfield, Vermont: Gower.

Schiller, Laurence. 1990. "The Royal Women of Buganda." *International Journal of African Historical Studies* 23 (3): 455–473.

Scott, James C. 1990. *Domination and the Arts of Resistance: Hidden Transcripts*. New Haven and London: Yale University Press.

Seeger, Anthony. 1987. *Why Suyá Sing: A Musical Anthropology of an Amazonian People*. Cambridge and New York: Cambridge University Press.

Seeger, Charles. 1958. "Prescriptive and Descriptive Music-Writing." *Musical Quarterly* 44 (2): 148–195.

Sempebwa, E. K. K. 1948. "Baganda Folk-Songs: A Rough Classification." *Uganda Journal* 12 (1): 16–24.

Shelemay, Kay Kaufman. 1996. "Crossing Boundaries in Music and Musical Scholarship: A Perspective from Ethnomusicology." *Music Quarterly* 80 (1): 13–30.

————. 1997. "The Ethnomusicologist, Ethnographic Method, and the Transmisson of Tradition." In *Shadows in the Field: New Perspectives for Fieldwork in*

Ethnomusicology. Edited by Gregory F. Barz and Timothy J. Cooley, 189–204. New York and Oxford: Oxford University Press.

Shorter, Aylward. 1998. *Celibacy and African Culture.* Nairobi, Kenya: Paulines Publications Africa.

Slack, Jennifer Daryl. 1996. "The Theory and Method of Articulation in Cultural Studies." In *Stuart Hall: Critical Dialogues in Cultural Studies.* Edited by David Morley and Kuan-Hsing Chen, 112–127. London and New York: Routledge.

Snoxall, R. A. 1967. *Luganda-English Dictionary.* Oxford: Claredon Press.

Sopova, Jasmina. 2000. "Moving Africa with a Dance Rhythm." *UNESCO Courier.* (October): 43–44.

Southwold, Martin. N.d. *Bureaucracy and Chiefship in Buganda: The Development of Appointive Office in the History of Buganda.* Kampala: East African Institute of Social Research.

Speke, John Hanning. 1906 [1863]. *The Discovery of the Source of the Nile.* [Reprinted 1908, 1912, 1922, 1937]. Edited by Ernest Rhys. London: J. M. Dent and Sons; New York: E. P. Dutton.

Spiro, E. Melford. 1993. "Gender Hierarchy in Burma: Cultural, Social, and Psychological Dimensions." In *Sex and Gender Hierarchies.* Edited by Barbara Miller, 316–333. Cambridge and New York: University of Cambridge Press.

Sugarman, Jane C. 1997. *Engendering Song: Singing and Subjectivity at Prespa Albanian Weddings.* Chicago and London: University of Chicago Press.

Sunket, Mark. 1995. *Mandiani Drum and Dance: Djembe Performance and Black Aesthetics from Africa to the New World.* Temple: White Cliffs Media.

Tamale, Sylvia. 1996. "Democratization in Uganda: Feminist Perspective." In *Law and the Struggle for Democracy in East Africa.* Edited by J. Oloka-Onyango, Kivutha-Kibwana, and Chris M. Peter. Nairobi: Claripress.

———. 1997. "When Hens Begin to Crow: Gender and Parliamentary Politics in Contemporary Uganda." Ph.D. diss., University of Minnesota.

———. 1999. *When Hens Begin to Crow: Gender and Parliamentary Politics in Uganda.* Boulder, Corolado and Oxford: Westview Press.

Tamusuza, Justinian. 1996. "My Compositional Style in Ekivvulu Ky'Endere: Background and Analysis." DMus diss., Northwestern University.

Taylor, John Vernon. 1979 [1958]. *The Growth of the Church in Buganda: An Attempt at an Understanding.* Westport, Connecticut: Greenwood Press.

Turino, Thomas. 1993. *Moving Away from Silence.* Chicago and London: University of Chicago Press.

Wachsmann, P. Klaus. 1953. "The Sound Instruments." In *Tribal Crafts of Uganda.* Edited by Margaret Trowel and Klaus Wachsmann, 311–415, 423. London and New York: Oxford University Press.

———. 1971. "Musical Instruments in Kiganda Tradition and Their Place in the East African Scene." In *Essays on Music and History in Africa.* Edited by Klaus Watchman, 93–134. Evanston: Northwestern University Press.

Wainwright, G. A. 1952. "The Coming of the Banana to Uganda." *Uganda Journal.* 16:145–147.

Walser, Ferdinand.1982. *Luganda Proverbs.* Berlin: Dietrich Reimer Verlag.

Wards, W. E. F and L. W. White. 1971. *East Africa: A Century of Change 1870–1970.* New York: Africana Publishing Corporation.

Warren, Lee. 1972. *The Dance of Africa: An Introduction.* New York: Prentice Hall.

Weintraub, Andrew N. 2001. "Instruments of Power: Sundanese "Multi-Laras" Gamelan in New Order Indonesia." *Ethnomusicology* 45 (2): 197–227.

Weiss, Sarah. 1993. "Gender and Gender: Gender Ideology and Female Gender Player in Central Java." In *Rediscovering the Muses: Women's Musical Traditions.* Edited by Kimberly Marshall, 21–48. Boston: Northeastern University Press.

Wheatley, Paul, and Thomas See. 1978. *From Court to Capital: A Tentative Interpretation of the Origins of the Japanese Urban Tradition.* Chicago: University of Chicago Press.

Wilson, C. T., and R. W. Felkin. 1882. *Uganda and the Egyptian Sudan.* Vol. 2. London: Sampson Low, Martson, Searle, and Rivington.

Wrigley, Christopher C. 1996. *Kingship and State: The Buganda Dynasty.* Cambridge: Cambridge University Press.

Zimbe, B. M. 1939. "Ebyafayo Bw'obwakabaka Bwe Buganda ne Kabaka" Makerere University, manuscript.

Index